Legal Aspects of Purchasing and Supply Chain Management

Third Edition

Legal Aspects of Purchasing and Supply Chain Management

Third Edition

Ian Longdin LL.M., B.A (Hons); PGCE

Cambridge
Academic

Imprints include:
Liverpool Academic Press
Liverpool Business Publishing
Tudor Educational

Third edition published by Cambridge Academic, The Studio, High Green, Gt. Shelford, Cambridge CB2 5EG.

Second edition (2007) published by Cambridge Academic, The Studio, High Green, Gt. Shelford, Cambridge CB2 5EG.

ISBN 1-903-499-51-8
978-1-903499-51-1

Printed and bound in the United Kingdom by
4edge Ltd, 7a Eldon Way Industrial Estate, Hockley, Essex, SS5 4AD.

Contents

Preface   i
Table of Cases   ii
Table of Statutes   vi
Table of Statutory Instruments   ix
Table of European Community Legislation   ix
Table of International Conventions & Treaties   x

Chapter One
Contract Formation   1

Chapter Two
Offer & Acceptance   7

Chapter Three
Practical Applications   15
    Battle of the Forms   15
    Tenders   16

Chapter Four
Consideration & Duress   21
Legality – restraint of trade clauses   23

Chapter Five
Major Vitiating Factors   29
    Mistake   29
    Misrepresentation   31

Chapter Six
Contents of Contract – Contractual Terms   37
    Express & Implied Terms   38
    Conditions & Warranties   41
    Innominate Terms   42

Chapter Seven
Remedies for Breach   47
    Liquidated Damages   47
    Unliquidated Damages   50

Chapter Eight
Exclusion Clauses   55
Force majeure clauses   62

Chapter Nine
Discharge of Contract   65

Chapter Ten
Statutory Protection – Buyers' Rights   73
     Sale of Goods   73
     Contracts for Services   83

Chapter Eleven
Transfer of Property   87

Chapter Twelve
Transfer of Title   95

Chapter Thirteen
Non-Contractual Liability   101
     Contracts (Rights of Third Parties) Act 1999   102
     Collateral Contracts   103
     Negligence Liability   104
     Civil Liability under Part One of the Consumer
     Protection Act 1987   113
     Criminal Liability under Part Two of the CPA 1987   115

Chapter Fourteen
Agency, Assignment & Bailment   117

Chapter Fifteen
Competition Law   123
     European Provisions   125
     UK Provisions   137

Chapter Sixteen
Intellectual Property Rights   153
     Patents   156
     Trade Marks   163
     Passing Off   168
     Breach of Confidentiality   174
     Design Rights   179
     Copyright   184
     Contractual Provisions   187

Chapter Seventeen
International Trade – Documentation   191

Chapter Eighteen
International Sale of Goods   205

Chapter Nineteen
Dispute Resolution   209
   Mediation & Conciliation   210
   Arbitration & Adjudication   212
   Litigation   215

Chapter Twenty
Legal Aspects of Tendering & Outsourcing   219
   Legal Analysis of Tenders   219
   E.C. Procurement Directives   222
   TUPE & Outsourcing   227
   Redundancy   231

Chapter Twenty One
The Freedom of Information Act 2000   241

Chapter Twenty Two
Insurance Law   247

Appendix One
Answering Case Studies in Law Examinations   261

Appendix Two
Legal Case Studies – How to approach their analysis   267

Appendix Three
Example of Exam Technique – Approach to Questions on
Third Party Liability   269

Appendix Four
'Landmark' Cases   273

Appendix Five
Revision Questions   277

Appendix Six
Recent Cases on Procurement Law   289

Index   **309**

Third Edition Preface

All purchasing activities take place within a context of legal regulation, a context that has been taking on increasing importance in recent years. There are a number of reasons for this development. Our involvement in the European Union has resulted in a steady flow of Regulations and Directives imposing additional rules and procedures relating to such issues as tenders, anti-competitive practices, transfer of undertakings, electronic trading and intellectual property rights. There is also a culture change within the UK that has resulted in consumers and businesses becoming increasingly aware of their legal rights and entitlements. It has therefore never been more important for purchasing practitioners to have a basic understanding of the major legal issues and principles that impact on their work. This book is an attempt to provide a clear and concise account of the underlying legal principles which affect the purchasing function.

It is also a useful revision book for candidates studying for the 'Legal Aspects for Purchasing & Supply' paper at Level Six of the Chartered Institute of Purchasing and Supply Graduate Diploma. It covers the essential legal themes in a way that focuses on common examination topics. This edition takes into account the changes to the unit specification in 2007. These include the widening of dispute resolution procedures to include mediation, conciliation and adjudication and the addition of the Freedom of Information Act 2000. Reforms in the law relating to the transfer of undertakings (TUPE) and the European public procurement rules have also been included. It also develops Competition Law and Intellectual Property Rights in more detail than is usually found in general works on commercial and business law. The book provides practical guidance on examination technique, especially relating to answering legal case studies. Advice on the approach to the study and revision of case law is also featured.

A new component of the third edition is an additional appendix which contains recent cases involving procurement law issues. These are kept separate from the main body of the book and are not essential for purposes of revising for the Legal Aspects exam. However, they do provide useful examples of how the courts have been interpreting the law in relation to a wide range of procurement activities in the recent past. These include the EU public procurement rules, contract formation, assessment of claimable damages, limitations of liability, the Transfer of Undertakings (Protection of Employment) Regulations, the Freedom of Information Act, and the Late Payment of Commercial Debts (Interest) Act.

October 2009

Table of Cases

A v National Blood Authority [2001] 3 All ER 289 113
Andrews v Singer [1934] 1KB 17..57, 279
Anglia Television v Reed [1972] 1 QB 60..53, 279
Anglo Continental Holidays Ltd v Typaldos Lines Ltd [1967] 2 Lloyd's Rep 61.......61
Annabel's (Berkely Square) v Schock [1972] RPC 838 172
Arcos Ltd v Ronaasen & Son [1933] AC 70 76
Associated Newspapers plc v Insert Media Ltd [1991] 3 All ER 535....................173
Atlas Express Ltd v Kafco Ltd [1989] QB 333..22, 273, 278
Attwood v Lamont [1920] 3KB 571...24
Avery v Bowden (1856) 5 E&B 714...53, 68, 70, 280

Baldry v Marshall [1925] 1KB 260..57, 279
Balfour Beatty Construction (Scotland) Ltd v Scottish Power [1994] UKHL 11........51
Bettini v Gye [1876] 1QBD 183..41
Birmingham Vinegar Brewery Ltd v Powell [1897] AC 710....................................170
Blackpool & Fylde Aero Club Ltd v Blackpool BC [1990] 3 All ER 25....220, 273, 283
Bollinger v Costa Bravo Wine Co Ltd [1961] 1 All ER 561 ....173, 274, 287
British Crane Hire v Ipswich Plant Hire [1975] QB 303...39
British Leyland Motor Corp Ltd v Armstrong Patents Ltd [1986] 2WLR 400..181, 275
BRS v Arthur Crutchley Ltd [1968] 1 All ER 811..17, 18, 278
British Steel Corporation v Cleveland Bridge & Engineering Co Ltd [1984] 1 All ER 504...4, 273
Brogden V Metropolitan Railway Co (1877) 2 App Cas 666.............................10, 16
Butler Machine Tool Co Ltd v Ex Cell O Ltd [1979] 1 All ER 965...............16, 17, 273

Camelot Group Plc v National Lottery Commission (2001)...........220, 221, 239, 283
Carlos Federspiel & Co v Charles Twigg & Co [1957] 1 Lloyd's Rep 240................89
Castellain v Preston (1883) 1QBD 380..256
Cehave NV v Bremer Handelsgesellschaft mbH, the Hansa Nord [1976] QB 44....78
Cellulose Acetate Silk Co v Widnes Foundry [1933] AC 20....................................48
Chandler v Webster [1904] 1 KB 493...69, 280
Chapelton v Barry UDC [1940] 1 KB 532...57
Charles Rickards v Oppenheim [1950] 1 KB 616....................................84, 274, 281
Coco v A N Clark (Engineers) Ltd [1969] RPC 41 ....177, 286
Consten & Grundig v Commission [1966] ECR 299....................................128, 274, 284
Cutter v Powell [1795] 101 ER 573...65

Dairy Crest Ltd v Wise [1994] 1QB 364..25
Darrell v Tibbits (1880) 5 QBD 560...257
Davis Contractors Ltd v Fareham UDC [1956] AC 696................................69, 280

Dawsons Ltd v Bonnin [1922] 2 AC 413...255
Donoghue v Stevenson [1932] AC 562.................104, 107, 108, 115, 263, 275, 281
Dunlop Pneumatic Tyre Co Ltd v New Garage & Motor Co Ltd [1914] AC 79.......48, 49, 273
Dunlop Pneumatic Tyre Co Ltd v Selfridge & Co Ltd [1915] AC 847............101, 274, 281

Erven Warninck v Townend & Sons (Hull) Ltd AC 731..........................173, 274, 287
Esso Petroleum Co Ltd v Harpers Garage [1968] AC 269................................26
Esso Petroleum Co Ltd v Mardon [1976] QB 801 34
Exxon Corporation v Exxon Insurance Consultants Ltd [1981] 3 All ER 241.........186

Faccenda Chicken Co Ltd v Fowler [1985] 1 All ER 724......................178, 275, 286
Farnham v Royal Insurance Co [1976] 2 Lloyd's Rep 437.............................254
Felthouse v Bindley (1862) 11 CBNS 869.............................10, 16, 273, 277
Fisher v Bell [1961] 1 QB 394..8, 277
Fraser v Thames Television Ltd [1984] 1 QB 44......................................175
Frost v Aylesbury Dairy Co [1905] 1 KB 608...78

George Mitchell v Finney Lock Seeds Ltd [1983] 1 QB 284.....................59, 275
Godley v Perry [1960] 1WLR 9...79

Hadley v Baxendale (1854) 9 Exch 341................47, 50, 51, 263, 273, 279
Hales v Reliance Fire & Accident Insurance Co Ltd [1960] 2 Lloyd's Rep 391......255
Hallelujah Trade Mark [1976] RPC 605...166
Harlingdon & Leinster Enterprises Ltd v Christopher Hull Fine Art Ltd [1990] 1 All ER 737...77
Harris v Littlewoods Organisation [1978] 2 QB 112..................................24
Harrod's Ltd v R Harrod Ltd (1924) 41 RPC 74...............................171, 287
Hartley v Ponsonby (1857) 7 E&B 872..21, 278
Hedley Byrne & Co v Heller & Partners [1964] AC 465...........33, 106, 108, 274, 281
Hochster v De La Tour (1853) 2 E&B 678.......................................53, 70
Hoenig v Isaacs [1952] 2 All ER 176..66
Hoffman La Roche v DDSA [1969] FSR 391.....................................170, 286
Hong Kong Fir Shipping Company Ltd v Kawasaki Kisen Kaisha Ltd [1962] 2 QB 26..43, 279
Hotel Services Ltd v Hilton International (UK) Ltd [2000] BLR 235................58, 296
Household Fire Insurance Co v Grant [1879] 4 Ex D 216.............................11
Hugin v Commission (Case 22/78) [1979] ECR 1869.........................134, 274, 285
Hyde v Wrench (1840) 3 Beav 334..9, 273, 277

Joscelyne v Nissen [1970] 2 QB 86...31, 278
Junior Books Ltd v Veitchi Co Ltd [1983] AC 520...............111, 112, 274, 283

King's Motors (Oxford) Ltd v Lax [1969] 3 All ER 665..5
Kores Manufacturing v Kolok Manufacturing [1959] Ch 108...................................25

Lambert v CIS Ltd [1975] 1 Lloyd's Rep 485...253
Lambert v Lewis [1981] 2 WLR 713...32, 53, 279
Leaf v International Galleries [1950] 2 KB 86......................................33, 274, 278
Lego Systems A/S v Lego M Lemelstrich Ltd [1983] FSR 155..............171, 172, 287
L'Estrange v Graucob [1934] 2 KB 394..57
Lewis v Averay [1972] 2 All ER 229..97
Lister v Romford Ice & Cold Storage Ltd [1957] AC 555....................................257
Liverpool City Council v Irwin [1977] AC 236..39
Lombard North Central plc v Butterworth [1987] QB 527....................................41
London Assurance Co v Mansel (1879) 11 Ch D 363..252

McCullogh v Lewis A May Distributors Ltd (1948) 65 RPC 58.............................170
Macaura v Northern Assurance Co Ltd [1925] 2 AC 619.....................................250
Manbre Co Ltd v Corn Products Ltd [1919] 1 KB 198................................192, 275
Maple Flock Ltd v Universal Furniture Products Ltd [1934] 1 KB 148.............83, 274
Maxim's Ltd v Dye [1977] 1 WLR 1155...170
Metropolitan Water Board v Dick, Kerr & Co [1918] AC 119..........................69, 280
Moorcock, The [1889] 14 PD 64...40
Moore & Landauer (Re) [1921] 2 KB 519..76
Munro & Co v Meyer [1930] 2 KB 312...83
Mutual Life Assurance Co (New York) v Ontario Metals Co [1925] AC 344.........252

Nordenfelt v Maxim-Nordenfelt Ltd [1894] AC 535...26
North Ocean Shipping Co v Hyundai Construction (The Atlantic Baron) [1979] QB
705..22, 278

Olley v Marlborough Court Hotel [1949] 1 KB 532...56, 279
Orwoola [1910] 1 Ch 130...166

Parker Knoll v Knoll International [1962] RPC 265..172
Parsons (Livestock) Ltd v Uttley Ingham & Co [1978] QB 791.......................52, 279
Payzu Ltd v Saunders [1919] 2 KB 581..53
Phillip Head & Sons v Showfronts [1970] 1 Lloyd's Rep 140..............................90
Phoenix Assurance Co v Spooner [1905] 2 KB 753..258
Planche v Colburn [1831] 131 ER 305...67
Portakabin v Portablast [1990] RPC 471...167
Poussard v Spiers [1876] 1QBD 410...40
Provincial Insurance Co v Morgan [1933] AC 240..256

Raffles v Wichelhaus (1864) 2 H&C 906...30

Reckitt & Colman v Borden [1990] RPC 341..169
Robinson v Davison [1871] LR 6 Exch 269..68
Rowland v Divall [1923] 2 KB 500..75

St Albans City & District Council v ICL [1995] FSR 686...............................60, 280
Saltman Engineering Ltd v Campbell Engineering Ltd [1963] 3 All ER 413.........174,
175, 188, 274, 286
Saunders v Anglia Building Society [1971] AC 1004..30
Schering Chemicals v Falman [1981] 2 All ER 321...176
Scott v Coulson [1903] 2 Ch 249..30, 273
Seager v Copydex Ltd [1969] RPC 250...177, 275, 286
Shanklin Pier v Detel Products Ltd [1951] 2 KB 854..................104, 270, 274, 281
Simaan General Contracting Ltd v Pilkington Glass Ltd [1988] QB 758.......111, 112,
274, 282
Spartan Steel & Alloys Ltd v Martin & Co [1973] QB 27......................................111
Stilk v Myrick (1809) 2 Camp 317...21, 278
Sumptor v Hedges [1898] 1QB 673..66

Taylor v Caldwell (1863) 3 B&S 826...................................67, 68, 98, 263, 274, 280
Tetra Pak v Commission (Case T83/91) [1994] ECR II- 755.................135, 274, 284
Thomas Marshall (Exports) v Guinle [1976] FSR 345...............................174, 176
Trollope & Colls v Atomic Energy Constructions Ltd [1962] 3 All ER 1035...............4

United Brands v Commission (Case 22/76) [1978] ECR 207...............132, 134, 274

Victoria Laundry v Newman Industries [1949] 1 All ER 997.........................51, 279
Volk v Vervaeke (Case 5/69) [1969] ECR 295..128
Volkswagen Financial Services (UK) Ltd v George Ramage (Cambridge) [2007].......295

Wagamama Ltd v City Centre Restaurants [1995] FSR 713...............................167
Watford Electronics Ltd v Sanderson CFL Ltd [2001] 1 All ER 696................60, 274
West of England Fire Insurance Co v Isaacs [1897] 1 QB 226............................257
Williams & Co v Roffey Bros [1991] 1QB 1.....................................22, 273, 278
Wilson v Rickett, Cockerell & Co [1954] 1QB 598...77
Windsurfing International v Tabur Marine GB [1985] RPC 59...............................160
Wombles Ltd v Wombles Skips Ltd [1977] RPC 99.....................................171, 286

Yianni v Edwin Evans & Sons [1982] QB 438...107

Table of Statutes

Arbitration Act 1996   212

Carriage of Goods by Sea Act 1992   196

Competition Act 1998   137

        Chapter One prohibition   137
        Chapter Two prohibition   137
        s.26   139
        s.27   140
        s.28   140

Consumer Credit Act 1974   3

Consumer Protection Act 1987   112
        s.2(1)   113
        s.3   113
        s.4   114
        s.5   114
        Part Two   115

Contracts (Applicable Law) Act 1990   207

Contracts (Rights of Third Parties) Act 1999   102

Copyright, Designs & Patents Act 1988   182
        s.3   185, 186
        s.12   185
        s.16   186
        s.29   187
        s.30   187
        s.213(2)   183
        s.213(3)   183

Enterprise Act 2002   145
        Part Four   147
        Part Five   146

Factors Act 1889   96
        s.2   96

Fair Trading Act 1973   124, 137, 140, 145, 146,
                                                        147, 149

Freedom of Information Act 2000   241
    s.1   242
    s.19   241
    s.41   243
    s.43   243

Hire Purchase Act 1957 (Part Three)   99

Law of Property Act 1925   119
    s.136   119

Law Reform (Frustrated Contracts) Act 1943   70

Marine Insurance Act 1906   247

Misrepresentation Act 1967   33
    s.2(1)   33
    s.2(2)   33

Patents Act 1977   159
    s.1(1)   159, 162
    s.1(2)   161
    s.1(3)   161
    s.2(1)   160
    S.2(2)   160
    s.3   160
    s.7   163
    s.39   163
    s.40   163
    s.60   162

Registered Designs Act 1949   180
    s.1(1)   180

Sale of Goods Act 1979   29, 41, 42, 43-44, 61, 73
    s.11(4)   44
    s.12   41, 74, 75, 95
    s.13   41, 74, 75, 77, 82
    s.14(2)   41, 74, 77, 79
    s.14(3)   41, 74, 78, 294
    s.15   41, 74, 78
    s.16   88
    s.17   88
    s.18   88
    s.20   87
    s.21(1)   95, 96

Sale of Goods Act 1979 (continued)
    s.23   97
    s.24   98
    s.25   98
    s.30   66
    s.35   44
    s.35(2)   44

Sale and Supply of Goods Act 1994   79

Supply of Goods and Services Act 1982   83
    s.2   83
    s.3   83
    s.4(1)   83
    s.4(2)   83
    s.5   83
    s.13   84
    s.14   84
    s.15   85

Trade Marks Act 1994   164
    s.1(1)   164
    s.3   165
    s.4   166
    s.5   166
    s.5(3)   168
    s.9   167
    s.10(1)   167
    s.10(2)   167
    s.10(3)   167

Unfair Contract Terms Act 1977   56, 81
    s.2   58
    s.3   58
    s.6   61
    s.7   82
    Schedule 2   59

Uniform Laws on International Sales Act 1967   205

Table of Statutory Instruments

Commercial Agents (Council Directive) Regulations 1993   118

Competition Act (Land & Vertical Agreements Exclusion) Order 2000   138

General Product Safety Regulations 1994   115

Public Contracts Regulations 2006   222, 302

Transfer of Undertakings (Protection of Employment) Regulations 2006   227

Unfair Terms in Consumer Contracts Regulations 1999   56

Table of European Community Legislation

Acquired Rights Directive 2001/23   227

Block Exemption Regulations:

Exclusive distribution Regulation 1983/83 OJ 1983 L 173/1   133
Exclusive purchasing Regulation 1984/83 OJ 1983 L 173/5   133
Research & Development Regulation 418/85 OJ 1985 L 53/5   131
Franchising Regulation 4087/85 OJ 1988 L 359/46   131
Technology Transfer Regulation 240/96 OJ 1996 L 31/2   131
Motor Vehicle Distribution and Servicing Regulation 123/85 OJ
1985 L 15/16   131

European Treaty (Treaty of Rome) 1957
Article 81   135
Article 82   135

Merger Regulation (Regulation 4064/89)   136

Public Procurement Directive 2004/18/EC   222

Treaty of Amsterdam 1997   134

Unfair Contract Terms Directive   56

International Conventions and Treaties

Hague Convention on International Sale of Goods 1964   205

Paris Convention for Industrial Property 1883   182

Rome Convention on the Law Applicable to
Contractual Obligations 1980   207

Vienna Convention on International Sale of Goods 1980   206

Chapter One
Contract Formation

The purpose of this opening chapter is to provide you with a basic understanding of the requirements of a valid contract. It contains a description of the following issues:

- Definition of contract.
- Distinctions between deeds and simple contracts.
- Essentials of a simple contract.
- Distinctions between void, voidable & unenforceable contracts.
- Issues relating to letters of intent and comfort.

Contracts form a major part of any organisation's business activities. They will have to be negotiated on a wide range of matters including:
- initial purchase of premises (or lease).
- purchase of raw materials, plant and machinery.
- purchase of stock prior to resale.
- employment of labour.
- sale of goods or services involved.

> **A contract is defined as a legally binding agreement (enforceable in a court of law).**

Form

Contracts are classified into two categories:
- **Deeds**
- **Simple Contracts**

The former are exceptional but are required in certain situations e.g. transferring ownership of a house. Sometimes they are used in order to give an agreement a degree of gravity and respectability which can impress on the parties the significance of the situation. (e.g. a partnership agreement; high value contracts between commercial undertakings). They must state on the face of the document that they are deeds and be signed and witnessed to be effective. Another situation where a deed is required is when a gift is being made the subject of a binding and enforceable agreement. Traditionally, local authorities entered into contracts by deed. Although this is no longer required in most cases, the practice does continue but to a far smaller extent. One benefit of entering into a contract by deed is the ability to sue for breach lasts for 12 years, unlike simple contracts where the limitation period lasts for only six years.

Simple contracts constitute by far the most important category of contract. Almost all commercial and consumer transactions are made in this form. The word "simple" denotes the ease by which such contracts can be made e.g. in written form, by word of mouth, by a combination of the two, or by implication (the conduct of the parties implying a contract has been made). There are a few exceptions where the law insists on the contract being made in written form e.g. consumer credit transactions, contracts for the sale or other disposition of land, contracts of marine insurance.

Essentials of a Simple Contract

Such contracts must satisfy the following requirements in order to be valid:
- The unconditional acceptance of an offer.
- The presence of "consideration" (a bargain; both parties gaining and losing from the transaction.
- An intention to enter into serious legal relations.
- Contractual capacity ('persons' with limited capacity include registered companies, minors and those registered as of unsound mind).
- Legality of objects (illegal contracts such as cartels in restraint of trade are not enforceable in a court).
- The absence of any "vitiating factors" (See below).

Defective Contracts

If any of the above requirements are not satisfied, the contract will be defective. There are three varieties of defective contract:

Void Contracts

These are destitute of all legal effect, and cannot be enforced under any circumstances. The parties must be returned to the original position as if no contract had been made at all. Goods must be returned as well as any money already handed over.

The following "vitiating factors" will cause a contract to be declared void:
- illegality.

- fundamental mistake.
- absence of consideration.

Voidable Contracts

These are defective but give the "innocent party" an option either to put an end to the contract (to rescind it) or continue and enforce rights under it if necessary. However, until the contract is rescinded, the contract is treated as valid and rights can pass. For example, if goods sold under a voidable contract are subsequently resold to an innocent second buyer, he will obtain good title if he receives them before the original contract is rescinded.

The following "vitiating factors" cause a contract to be declared voidable:

- duress.
- undue influence.
- misrepresentation.

Unenforceable Contracts

These are valid contracts but ones which cannot be enforced because of some technical defect. An example would be the absence of a signed agreement containing specific information as required by the Consumer Credit Act 1974 where a regulated credit agreement is involved. There are not many such examples today.

Letters of Intent and Comfort

Letters of intent often lack the essential of serious legal intent. Examples are letters from a prospective purchaser to a prospective contractor indicating that it is his intention to place a contract with him in the near future. On strict legal analysis, it will be difficult to use a letter of intent as a basis of complaint in court. It will depend critically on the wording found in the letter. If it simply states "We are pleased to inform you that we intend placing an order with you in the near future", the letter will lack serious legal intent. If its wording amounts to a clear acceptance, the fact that it is headed 'Letter of Intent' will not prevent it becoming a binding contract.

The most difficult scenario involves a letter expressing an intention to contract coupled with a requirement that the contractor begins to purchase materials or commence work. Here, it can be argued that we are looking at an 'instruction to proceed' – a document authorising the undertaking of expenditure. If, however, this document does not specifically refer to reimbursement, there could still be significant difficulties in claiming the return of monies spent or payment for work carried out.

British Steel Corporation v Cleveland Bridge & Engineering Co Ltd. is an authority illustrating the problems of claiming under a letter of intent.

British Steel Corporation v Cleveland Bridge & Engineering Co Ltd

BSC were negotiating a contract for the sale of steel nodes to be used by CBE on a construction project. CBE had failed to agree on a range of terms and conditions including the price to be paid. However, a letter of intent was received by BSC asking it to commence work on the manufacture of the nodes. This was done and delivery of all the nodes eventually took place whilst the two undertakings continued to negotiate. When BSC brought an action for non-payment it was held that no contract existed and it was not entitled to sue for breach, despite the letter of intent. It was decided, however, that a claim for *quantum meruit* (as much as is deserved) was available. This entitles a business to claim a reasonable amount for work carried out in circumstances where it was reasonable to expect payment.

Where a contract has been subsequently agreed, there is authority to say that payment for work done prior to agreement will be on the basis of what was agreed in the contract i.e. it will operate retrospectively and cover the earlier period of work undertaken as a result of a letter of intent. This prevents the contractor from bringing a *quantum meruit* claim which might result in a higher payment figure in some cases **(Trollope & Colls Ltd v Atomic Energy Constructions Ltd)**.

Similarly, **letters of comfort** lack legal enforceability. These represent assurances from a holding company within a corporate group that contracts being negotiated by one of its subsidiaries (often relating to the seeking of loans) will be honoured and performed satisfactorily. Again, although poor practice, the holding company could not be taken to court if the contract was broken by the subsidiary and it refused to honour the agreement.

Vagueness

It is common to find negotiators unwilling to commit themselves to complete and precise expression of the resulting contractual obligations. This could be caution based on a desire to keep one's options open – avoiding firm commitments which take away flexibility. It could be simply an assumption that where the two businesses have been in regular dealings with each other, there is no need to dot the 'i's and cross the 't's with every new transaction.

There is however a danger that if the agreement lacks sufficient coherence it will be regarded as lacking certainty and declared void. Although the courts will look to previous courses of dealing and widely known national conditions of contract (found in some standard forms of contract), there is a limit to such a willingness to find the missing elements. The courts will not construct a contract on behalf of the parties.

King's Motors (Oxford) Ltd v LAX

A lease contained an option for a further period of years 'at such rental as may be agreed upon between the parties'. When the tenant attempted to exercise this option the landlord gave notice of termination, claiming the option lacked certainty and was therefore void.
Held: In the absence of an arbitration clause allowing for a procedure to quantify the new rental, it was void through lack of certainty.

In conclusion:

- A contract is a legally binding agreement, enforceable in a court of law.

- The great majority of contracts are classified as 'simple', meaning there is a flexibility as to how they can be created – they do not have to be in writing.

- Unlike deeds, simple contracts require the presence of 'consideration', and have a limitation period of 6 years instead of 12 years.

- If any of the essentials of a simple contract are missing, the contract is defective.

- Void contracts are so fundamentally flawed that the court will never permit rights or duties to be enforceable – they are a nullity – of no legal effect whatsoever.

- Voidable contracts, although defective, can be enforced by the innocent party if it opts to do so. Alternatively, it can opt to rescind (cancel) the contract.

- Letters of intent and letters of comfort often lack the essential of intention to enter into legal relations. However, it is vital to examine the precise wording before a conclusion can be drawn.

- Agreements can be declared invalid for a lack of clarity where aspects of the agreement are considered too vague (the rules of offer and acceptance having been improperly observed).

Chapter Two

Offer and Acceptance

We now need to examine the technical rules of offer and acceptance. This provides a background in order to study such practical issues as the Battle of the Forms and the tender process. The chapter contains a discussion of the following legal principles:

- Definition of offer.
- Distinction between offer and invitation to treat.
- Termination of offer.
- Requirements for a valid acceptance.
- Communication of acceptance.

All agreements must contain an offer by one person which has been accepted by another (or group of persons). A body of legal rules has been drawn up over the last century which is intended to make sure that all contracts contain clear, definite commitments and have been specifically agreed beyond doubt.

Business negotiators prefer to deal with each other on a more flexible basis often making much looser arrangements which can be modified or added to at a later stage. This approach can backfire if the agreement becomes the subject of a legal action in court and is declared of no legal effect giving no legal rights to either party.

Offer and Acceptance - Basic Legal Requirements

Offer

An **offer** is a clear, specific commitment to be legally bound to a proposal simply by its acceptance.

[The word 'offer' will often not be used in practice – alternatives such as proposal, bid and tender will be far more common]

An offer must be distinguished from other statements made during contractual preliminaries **(invitations to treat).** The latter do not normally produce legal commitments or obligations – they are merely concerned with information requesting or providing. Only a firm offer, clearly indicating that the offeror intends to be bound without further negotiations, is capable of acceptance so that a binding contract is achieved.

The following situations have been held to be invitations to treat, not offers. In each case the reason is practical rather than strictly arrived at by logic.

Displays of goods for sale
These are considered to be invitations for offers to be made by the customer. This protects the shop if a wrong price has been placed on the item involved.

Fisher v Bell

A shopkeeper was prosecuted for 'offering' offensive weapons for sale, by having flick-knives on display in his window.

Held: Technically, he was not offering the goods for sale – he was inviting offers from customers. He had to be acquitted. *[The legislation was amended to make 'displaying goods for purposes of sale' also an offence].*

Advertisements, circulars, price lists and catalogues
These are usually held to be invitations for offers to be made by the potential buyers. Sometimes the reason is "best price" opportunity (adverts); sometimes it is to prevent difficulties relating to shortage of stock (catalogues, circulars)

Auctions
The auctioneer is said to be inviting offers from members in the audience. This enables him to accept the highest offer.

N.B. Tenders submitted by outside contractors are regarded as offers. The original proposal requesting for tenders to be submitted is an invitation for offers to be made (enabling the firm receiving the tenders to pick the best bid).

Offers must be **clear and specific**, not vague.

Offers can be accepted at any time until they terminate.

Termination of offer can occur by:
•   Revocation (withdrawal)

- Rejection (including counter offer) -
  By its rejection, the offer automatically ceases to exist. The same result occurs when a counter offer is made – it is as if the person making the counter offer had rejected the first offer, even if he uses words suggesting acceptance ("Your offer is accepted (if) …").

- Lapse of time -
  An offer will lapse either at the end of a specified time if one was attached to the offer (7 days, 28 days) or a reasonable period of time where none is specified. What is reasonable depends on the circumstances of each case – the nature of the goods, the context in which the offer was sent etc.

- Failure of a condition precedent -
  An example would be an offer to sell goods, subject to obtaining the necessary export licence. If the licence is not granted, the offer would terminate.

- Death of the offeror.

Acceptance

Acceptance of an offer must be **unqualified**.
The only legitimate way to accept an offer is to do so unconditionally, without provisos, or amendments or additions. Where the latter are involved it is considered, in law, to be a **rejection** of the original offer (although in business practice it is seen more in terms of feeling one's way to an eventual agreement).

Such conditional acceptances are regarded in law to be counter offers still requiring acceptance by the other party.

Hyde v Wrench

The defendant offered his farm to the plaintiff for £1000. The plaintiff replied offering £950. The defendant subsequently rejected this, so the plaintiff purported to accept the original £1000 offer. It was held that there was no contract since the original offer had been extinguished by the counter offer. Although expressed as an acceptance, it was in fact a fresh offer.

One example of this principle is seen in the clause "subject to contract". Although most frequently seen in connection with house sales it can apply to any business contract. Its effect is to ensure that the parties are not bound until a formal contract is drawn up and signed. This provides a breathing space in which to check on certain matters in the meantime e.g. finance, surveys etc. The reason why the agreement is not yet binding is because the offer was accepted with conditions - "subject to contract" and was not therefore a proper acceptance. *[Requests for clarification and further information do not amount to counter offer though.]*

Acceptance must be **communicated** to the offeror (by words or conduct). Silence cannot be taken to mean acceptance e.g. "If I don't hear from you in the next week, I'll take it that you've accepted my offer".

Felthouse v Bindley

An uncle wrote to his nephew offering to buy the nephew's horse for £30. 15s. and stating "If I don't hear any more about him I shall consider the horse mine at that price". The nephew gave instructions to the defendant, an auctioneer, not to sell the horse as he intended it for his uncle. The defendant inadvertently sold the horse, and the uncle sued him in the tort of conversion.
Held: The horse had not become the uncle's property – no contract had been concluded.

Acceptance can be **implied by conduct**.

Brogden v Metropolitan Railway Co.

The railway company had been supplied with coal from Brogden for many years. The company was keen to have a formal agreement. It drew up a draft agreement, which was sent to Brogden, and was returned by him to the company marked "approved", although he had inserted a new term to the draft. For the next two years coal was supplied and paid for between the parties in accordance with the draft agreement, although the company never gave notification that they had accepted it. In fact over the two years it lay in a desk drawer. Then a dispute arose between the parties. Brogden alleged that there was no contract binding them. The House of Lords disagreed, taking the view that there was a contract, based on conduct. This occurred when the order was placed for the coal on the terms of the draft agreement, although it had never been formally accepted.

When is acceptance effective?

Normally acceptance is effective from the moment when the communication is received by the offeree. This applies to instantaneous methods of communication, which includes acceptances by fax. Failure in the transmission of a fax containing an acceptance therefore means no contract has been concluded – even though it was sent, it was not received. The position regarding e-mails is less clear cut, partly because it is unclear whether it amounts to instantaneous communication or delayed communication. It is also affected by whether a common server is used by both organisations or separate servers(!).

Acceptance communicated through the post is an exception.

The Postal Rule

1.   Where the post is the recognised medium of communication the **acceptance** is complete **as soon as it is properly put in the post**.

Household Fire Insurance Co. v Grant

Grant had applied for some shares in the claimant company. The company wrote a letter of acceptance which was duly posted, but subsequently lost before arriving at Grant's address. When the company went into liquidation shortly afterwards, the liquidator insisted that Grant pay for the shares.
Held: The contract had been concluded when the letter of acceptance had been posted and he was therefore obliged to pay for the shares.

2.   The rules as to postal communications apply similarly to telegrams.

In other words, one set of rules apply to instant delivery methods of communication e.g. phone, telex, face to face; another set of rules apply to delayed communications e.g. post, telegrams. The postal rule of acceptance can be overridden if the offer specifically states that acceptance will not be effective until received e.g. upon notification of acceptance.

In conclusion:

*   An offer is a clear, specific commitment to be bound by a proposal – all that is required is an acceptance for it to be transformed into a binding contract.

*   Words used in lieu of 'offer' include bid, proposal, price and tender.

*   An invitation to treat is a preliminary stage prior to an offer being made – where a party is encouraging an offer from the other party.

*   Classic examples of invitation to treat are circulars, price lists, most advertisements, requests for tenders, auctions and goods on display in shops.

*   Offers terminate in a number of ways, including revocation (withdrawal), rejection (including counter offer) and lapse of time.

- Acceptance must be unqualified, otherwise it is a rejection (by counter offer).
- Acceptance must be positively communicated – silence is not enough

- Acceptance is effective only when received if an instantaneous method of communication is used

- Acceptance is effective as soon as it is sent (posted) if a delayed method of communication is used

Chapter Three
Practical Applications

The Battle of the Forms

The next chapter concentrates on the issues relating to whose set of terms will govern the contract – those of the buyer or supplier. This topic involves a direct application of the rules of offer and acceptance discussed in Chapter Two. It will therefore be important to have read and understood the earlier material. This chapter includes discussion of the following principles and issues:

- Meaning and significance of standard form contracts.
- Why important to win the battle of the forms.
- Legal analysis of documentation stage.
- Landmark cases.

It is normal business practice at the negotiation stage for both the buyer and the seller to utilise pre-printed contractual documentation – their standard terms of purchase or supply. Agreements reached on the basis of these documents are known as standard form contracts. It saves time in concluding contracts and allows central management to control the specific terms and conditions being agreed by their staff at different locations.

It is obvious that these standard terms will be drafted in ways that are favourable to the purchaser or seller in question. Examples of how the pre-printed terms can vary include:

- Termination and cancellation rights of the buyer for late delivery
- Price (whether fixed or variable)
- Risk liability (for accidental loss or damage)
- Passing of ownership (whether on delivery or retained until payment)
- Exclusion of liability

For these reasons (and others) it is important for the buyer to successfully impose its terms over those of the seller – to win the battle of the forms. Let us take a typical sequence of events leading up to the conclusion of a contract:

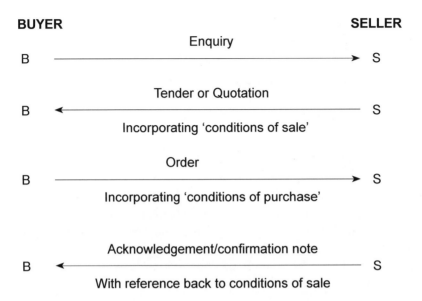

BUYER   **SELLER**

Enquiry

B ————————————————————————————→ S

Tender or Quotation

B ←———————————————————————————— S

Incorporating 'conditions of sale'

Order

B ————————————————————————————→ S

Incorporating 'conditions of purchase'

Acknowledgement/confirmation note

B ←———————————————————————————— S

With reference back to conditions of sale

What do each of these stages represent in the language of offer and acceptance?

Stage One   **Invitation to treat**
Stage Two   **Offer (in most cases)**
Stage Three   **Counter offer (changing the terms which apply)**
Stage Four   **Counter offer (again, changing the terms)**

This could be the conclusion of any correspondence between the parties. The fact that the buyer does not reply to the acknowledgement note cannot be taken to be acceptance of this last counter-offer - silence is not sufficient **(Felthouse v Bindley)**.

In practice, delivery is often the next event. If the buyer receives delivery of the relevant goods, his conduct (in allowing the delivery to take place) will be taken to be implied acceptance of the counter-offer **(Brogden v Metropolitan Rly Co.)**. This may be further reinforced by signing the seller's delivery documentation which could refer to conditions of sale again. In such a case, the seller's terms will govern the contract. In the words of Lord Denning, the battle of the forms is won by the party who 'fires the last shot.' This normally favours the seller whose acknowledgement note is often the last document to be sent.

What then can the buyer do? Initial correspondence (such as general enquiries) should refer to conditions of purchase governing the contract, as should the order form when submitted (it is usual to include a term insisting that 'our terms shall prevail' over any others which may be subsequently introduced. The case of **Butler Machine Tool Co. Ltd v Ex Cell O Ltd.** makes clear that such assertions do not bring victory as they are contained on documents which cease to be effective once rejected by a counter offer.) The buyer should include a tear-off slip to be returned with acceptance of the order – the slip confirming that the contract is to be concluded on the buyer's terms. If the seller fails to return the slip (and returns an acknowledgement note referring to seller's terms) the buyer should reply and require acceptance on buyer's terms only. At this juncture, market forces (or a combination of ignorance and/or inertia) will decide who is successful.

The two leading cases which illustrate the battle of the forms are **Butler Machine Tool Co. Ltd v Ex Cell O Ltd. and BRS Ltd v Arthur Crutchley Ltd.**

Butler Machine Tool v E-CELL-O Corporation (1979)

Negotiations took place for the purchase of some heavy machinery. A quotation was sent which included a delivery date and price - £75,500). On the back of the quote it stated:

"All orders accepted only upon and subject to the terms set out in our quotation and the following conditions. These terms shall prevail over any terms in the buyer's order."

The terms included a price variation clause.

The buyer submitted an order for the purchase of the machinery which included the following wording :

"Please supply on terms and conditions as below and overleaf".

These terms stipulated a fixed price. The order had a tear off slip (acknowledgement) to be returned stating :

"We accept your order on the terms and conditions stated thereon".

The acknowledgement slip was duly signed but a covering letter was also sent stating :

"This is being entered in accordance with our revised quotation of the 23 May".

A dispute then arose concerning the price to be paid. Whose terms govern the contract?

Held: The buyer's terms governed the contract. The return of the buyer's acknowledgement slip was the critical issue. The accompanying letter was not worded in strong enough language to suggest a re-imposition of the seller's terms.

It simply confirmed the original details relating to price and identity of the machine. (The position would not have been clear if such strong language had been used in the covering letter – or a copy of the seller's acknowledgement note referring to the seller's conditions had been included with the buyer's acknowledgement slip).

It can be argued that such a reply causes so much uncertainty that no agreement has been made and that it does not even amount to a counter-offer. Remember, offers must consist of clear, specific commitments. There is no authority for this particular scenario and it is possible that a court could rule the buyer's slip to be effective and not negated by the accompanying material.

BRS v Arthur Crutchley Ltd.

A road haulage company "agreed" a contract to deliver a consignment of whisky to a wholesaler (Crutchley Ltd.). During the negotiations various documents (conditions of carriage; conditions of supply) had been referred to but never confirmed. The driver for the haulage company arrived at the gates of the wholesale company and handed the warehouse manager a delivery note (incorporating their conditions of carriage). The note was stamped by the manager "received under Crutchley's conditions". The whisky was taken off the lorry and stored in the warehouse. A dispute subsequently occurred and it was necessary to know whose conditions governed the contract.
Held: By stamping the note, Crutchley's manager had made a counter offer which was accepted by implication – the conduct of the driver (acting as agent for BRS), in allowing the goods to be taken off his lorry, amounting to an acceptance of this counter offer. Consequently, Crutchley's terms governed the contract.

In conclusion

• Standard form contracts (pre-printed, containing identical terms for all customers/suppliers) comprise the basis of most business transactions.

• Each party's terms are drafted in ways favourable to its own position – hence the need to win the battle of the forms.

• Each attempt to change the basis of the contract from one set of terms to another set is technically a counter offer and therefore a rejection of the previous offer.

• The battle is usually won by 'he who fires the last shot' – the party who submits the final document stating that its terms will govern the contract.

• The contract may not strictly be agreed until delivery, when receiving the goods may be treated as implied acceptance of the terms submitted in the supplier's acknowledgement note.

Chapter Four

Consideration and Duress

This chapter focuses on some of the more practical issues relating to two of the essentials of a simple contract outlined in Chapter One – the need for consideration and consent to be present in the transaction. It covers the following legal principles:

- Consideration – basic definition.
- Adequacy of consideration.
- Consideration must be new and additional.
- Duress – basic definitions (including economic duress).
- Landmark cases.

Consideration

All simple contracts require consideration. This means the presence of a bargain. Both parties must be seen to sacrifice something in return for the benefit obtained. There must be a give and take - an exchange. It need not be adequate. The courts will not come to the rescue of a person who has made a bad bargain - unless there is some further element of undue pressure or misrepresentation involved. The sacrifice must be something new and additional to any existing commitments or obligations though. Merely promising again to perform an existing obligation is not valid consideration. This is particularly relevant where existing contracts are subject to some amendment or revision during their lifetime.

Compare: **Stilk v Myrick**
              Hartley v Ponsonby

In the former case, a ship's crew was promised an extra £10 each if they agreed to sail the ship home light-handed (two of the crew had deserted). When they were not paid at the end of the voyage they sued for breach of contract. The court held that in effect they were doing nothing more in substance than they were already obliged to do under their existing contract. They lost their claim.

In the Hartley case, a similar promise was made but in a situation where half the crew had deserted. In this case the claims were successful. The court decided

21

that the new arrangement was substantially different to the initial agreement and involved serious safety hazards. New consideration had therefore been provided.

A more recent case of importance is **Atlas Express Ltd. v Kafco Ltd**. Kafco were heavily dependent on a contract to supply basketware to Woolworths. Atlas were aware of this. A contract price for delivering the goods to Woolworths had been agreed by Atlas, who were road hauliers. It had been made on the assumption that the lorries would be fully loaded which in practice turned out not to be the case - they were often half empty. Subsequently, Atlas insisted on an increase in their charges at short notice and in a way which clearly jeopardised Kafco's future relations with Woolworths. Reluctantly, Kafco agreed but later refused to pay the increase. The court held that the claim for breach of contract had to fail for two reasons:

1. there had been **no consideration** by Atlas - they were doing nothing more than they were already obliged to do under the existing contract
2. their threat (not to deliver the goods) amounted to **economic duress** (see below.) *promise to pay more = invalid*

A very controversial case in this area is **Williams & Co v Roffey Bros**.
Roffey had contracted to refurbish a block of flats. They had subcontracted the joinery work to Williams for a price of £20,000. Roffey became aware of financial problems that Williams were getting into and the fact that they would not complete the joinery work on schedule. This would result in Roffey being hit by substantial liquidated damages for late completion of the refurbishment. Roffey therefore offered to pay Williams an additional sum for each flat completed. At the end of the work they refused to pay this extra money and were sued for breach of contract.

The court held that:
1. Consideration had been provided by Williams in that the new arrangement had enabled Roffey to avoid paying the liquidated damages which would otherwise have been payable.
2. There had been no economic duress involved - Roffey had been the party to suggest making the payment and therefore there had been no coercion.

Accordingly, Williams' claim for breach of contract was successful and they were entitled to the extra payments. There is clearly a very fine line to be drawn between the normal cut and thrust of commercial bargaining and unfairly forcing a party to agree to terms without the necessary element of consent. Each case will have to be considered on its own merits and the ability to predict court decisions will be inevitably extremely difficult.

Duress

A contract will be voidable if one of the parties was coerced into making the agreement. This can be either the result of physical threats (presumably not too

Threat of unlawful action

Classic duress - Threat of physical harm. *Economic duress" common", most us.*

Agreeing to contract variat-ion or breech of contract

common in business circles) or threats affecting the economic position of the business. The latter form involves the unfair manipulation of a party by <u>unlawful means.</u> Usually, it will occur when one party is aware of the <u>other party's economic</u> <u>or financial</u> vulnerability and it decides to take <u>advantage</u> of this knowledge in order to coerce the other <u>side</u> into agreeing to a contract or contract variation.

A clear example of the latter is the case discussed above - **Atlas Express Ltd. v Kafco Ltd.** *- know!*

Another case illustrating the principle is **North Ocean Shipping Co. v Hyundai Construction (The Atlantic Baron)**. A contract had been agreed for the building of a ship. Whilst the ship was being built, the builders insisted on an additional 10% on the price. Without the ship, the buyers would have lost a profitable contract for the charter of the vessel. The buyers paid the additional money and then sued for its recovery, arguing economic duress. The court decided that the actions of the builders constituted economic duress but, because the buyers had delayed bringing their claim, they had affirmed the new arrangement and were obliged to pay the extra money.

Restraint of Trade

One of the essentials of a simple contract is that of legality of objects – the purpose of the contract must be lawful. There is a connection between this requirement and agreements made in restraint of trade. As a generalisation, agreements which restrict a person's future freedom of movement are initially considered to be illegal. They are said to be prima facie (at first evidence), void. It is against public policy to permit such restrictions. However, as always in law, there are some exceptions to this general position and we shall consider them now.

Restraint of trade agreements operate in three main areas:

- Contracts of employment.
- Sale of a business.
- Solus agreements.

Contracts of employment

It is not uncommon for employers to want to restrict the future employment options of their employees. Can they do this within the law? It is argued that employment restrictions are void, unless reasonable:

- in the parties' interests.

23

- in the public interest.

The Parties' Interest

The starting point is to state that an employer cannot simply restrict competition. An employee will inevitably acquire a range of generic skills and knowledge whilst working for an employer. These assets cannot be controlled by an employer if the employee decides to use them elsewhere later.

Attwood v Lamont

A tailor's assistant was held not bound by a restraint agreement affecting his freedom of movement after leaving his employer. In the course of the judgement it was declared that an employer cannot restrict an employee's future employment if there was no special interest to protect. He cannot simply restrict competition for its own sake.

The position changes where the employer is trying to protect what is sometimes called a 'genuine proprietary interest'. This includes trade secrets and confidential information but also extends to influence over clients (called 'trade connection'). The use of this information or influence could be seriously damaging to the commercial interests of the employer and the courts have been more sympathetic to allowing restrictions.

Harris v Littlewoods Organisation

Harris had been employed as a director in the mail order division of the defendant's business. He had signed a restraint agreement by which he would not work for any rival business for at least 12 months after leaving the defendant. Despite this restriction, he started working for Great Universal Stores Ltd (GUS), a direct rival of Littlewoods.
Held: In his position as a director, he would have had access to commercially sensitive information which could have been extremely damaging to his previous employer if used in competition. The defendant successfully applied for an injunction to prevent him from continuing to work for GUS.

However, even where there is a genuine proprietary interest, the courts do not give carte blanche to the employer to restrict the employee's future career. The restraint involved must be reasonable:
- in time.
- in geographical area.

What is reasonable will clearly depend on individual circumstances, including the extent of the employer's trading area. It could be limited to a single town or village (e.g. a hairdressing assistant) or be as extensive as to include an entire region within the world (e.g. a senior marketing manager responsible for trade across several countries). Some of the earlier cases relating to time are now somewhat dated and more recent case law is requiring employers to impose shorter time limits – information becomes stale more quickly in modern trading conditions). Restrictions of six months to one year seem to be about as long as will normally be permitted today.

One issue that can affect the validity of a restraint agreement is where the employer is in breach of the contract of employment with the employee. This can release the employer from the obligation imposed by the restraint.

Dairy Crest Ltd v Wise

A milk roundsman had signed a restraint agreement stating that he would not set up a rival delivery service if and when he left his present employer. During the final months of his employment with his employer, there had been a re-organisation and he had felt aggrieved about his treatment. He resigned and then set up a rival business. He was taken to court for an alleged infringement of the restraint. Held: the duty to observe a restraint agreement no longer applies if, before the employee leaves the employment, an employer can be seen to be in breach of contract. In this case, the court found that the employer had broken an implied duty to maintain the trust and confidence of the employee. Consequently, the employee was no longer bound by the restriction.

The Public Interest

In some exceptional cases, the legal position can be affected by wider considerations where the public interest has to be taken into account. The courts have sometimes referred to this requirement (e.g. **Kores Manufacturing V Kolok Manufacturing**, where two rival manufacturers agreed between themselves not to engage any employee who had worked for the other firm during the previous 5 years; it was thought that such an agreement could be against public interest). However, it remains somewhat unclear when and how this issue can affect the validity of a restraint clause.

Sale of a Business

A significant element of the purchase price of an existing business is the payment for goodwill – the fact that there are existing customers with a degree of loyalty to purchasing goods or services from a known supplier. Having paid for this goodwill, the purchaser will obviously not want the seller to set up a rival business (or work for a competitor) and take away this custom.

It can therefore be argued that he has a genuine proprietary interest in seeking to restrict the future activities of the seller. Once again, the test of reasonableness is central to success – is the extent of the restraint reasonable in the specific circumstances involved? The most famous case illustrating this concept is, on its facts, quite exceptional:

Nordenfelt v Maxim-Nordenfelt Ltd

Nordenfelt was a world famous inventor and manufacturer of guns and ammunition. When he sold his business, he agreed not to set up a rival business anywhere in the world for 25 years. When he attempted to do this he was taken to court for breach of contract.
Held: Despite the exceptionally wide limits of this restraint, it was reasonable and enforceable. He was so well-known that, if he had set up a rival business, it would have had a devastating effect on the business position of the existing one.

Solus agreements

Sometimes, a company agrees to provide initial capital to help set up an individual in business in exchange for restricting his/her freedom of choice when selling products subsequently. Classic examples are garages (supported by petroleum companies), pubs (supported by breweries) and a variety of other franchises. Given this financial backing, the courts have again been more sympathetic in allowing such restrictions. However, once again, the restraint must be reasonable and not too extensive.

ESSO Petroleum Ltd v Harpers Garage

In this case there were two solus agreements. One was to last for four and a half years; the other was to last for 21 years. It was held that the shorter one was valid, since it was reasonable in the interests of the petrol company being able to maintain a stable system of distribution. However, the 21- year restraint was too long – it was simply preventing competition.

N.B. There is a close link between restraint of trade agreements and the legal doctrine of confidentiality. Confidentiality is considered in detail later in this book under the general theme of intellectual property rights.

•   Consideration is the presence of a sacrifice in exchange for a benefit from both parties.

- Consideration does not have to be adequate (unless misrepresentation or duress is involved).

- Consideration must involve the sacrifice of something new and additional – using existing obligations is not a valid basis for obtaining new benefits.
- Duress involves coercion – the forcing of a person into a contract against his will.

- Economic duress operates where knowledge of an organisation's economic needs is used to its detriment in an unfair manner by insisting that it enters into an unfavourable contract.

- Although restraint of trade agreements are, at first evidence, illegal, they can be enforceable if there is a genuine proprietary interest being protected and the extent of the restriction is reasonable in geographical area and time.

Chapter Five

Major Vitiating Factors

- **Mistake**
- **Misrepresentation**

We are still examining the essentials of a valid contract. In the last chapter, we saw that the required consent (genuine agreement) was lacking if the agreement was made under duress. In this chapter, it will become apparent that certain types of mistake can invalidate agreements.

Additionally, where a party has been misled in a way which amounts to misrepresentation, the resulting agreement can be declared invalid. Damages may also be available. In both these cases, the defect relates to the lack of genuine consent obtained. This chapter covers the following legal principles:

- Mistake – normal position (*Caveat Emptor*).
- Exceptions – types of fundamental (or operative mistake).
- Misrepresentation – definition.
- Distinction from traders' puff and contractual terms.
- Remedies for misrepresentation.

Mistake

The usual approach of the courts where one or both parties have made a mistake is to insist that the contract must stand. The courts will not come to the protection of parties who have made a bad bargain (*Caveat Emptor* - Let the Buyer Beware). This maxim applies in fact to both parties - the seller as well as the buyer. However, in a few exceptional situations the courts will declare a contract to be void for **"operative"** or **"fundamental"** mistake:

Common Mistake as to the Existence of the Subject-Matter e.g. agreeing to buy/sell specific goods which have already been destroyed at the time of the agreement. (The **Sale of Goods Act 1979** recognises this exception in section 7).

29

Scott v Coulson

G. agreed to assign to H an assurance policy on the life of L. L. had died before the agreement was made.

Held: There was no contract.

Mutual Mistake - where the two parties have been completely at cross purposes from the very start and have never been agreeing to the same deal at all.

Raffles v Wichelhaus

An agreement was made by which a quantity of cotton was to arrive "ex-Peerless from Bombay". There were two SS Peerless vessels sailing from Bombay – the defendant intended the one arriving in October; the claimant intended the one arriving in December.

Held: The court was unable to decide which party had formed the correct interpretation. The contract was therefore declared void.

Mistake as to the Identity of the Other party (Unilateral Mistake) - this exception normally involves one party attempting to commit fraud on the other by pretending to be some other person or firm. It will not usually apply where the two parties are dealing with each other face to face - it is argued that misrepresentation is the appropriate vitiating factor in this situation.

Non Est Factum ("It is not my deed") - i.e. the person who signed the contract did not realise the very nature (or type) of contract being entered into. It is extremely difficult to use this defence successfully because you have to prove that:

- you mistook the type of agreement involved (not just its contents or detail), and
- you were not negligent in doing so.
- something which in practice may be quite difficult to prove.

Saunders v Anglia Building Society

Mrs. Gallie, a 78 year-old widow, signed a document without reading it – her glasses were broken at the time. She had been assured by a friend of her nephew that it was a deed of gift to her nephew. In fact it was a deed of gift to the friend. Soon after he mortgaged the property to the building society. Mrs. Gallie argued that the contract was void through *non est factum*.

Held: Her action failed because, although it was accepted that she had not been careless, the document was not fundamentally different to the one she intended to sign.

Occasionally, the courts will operate the remedy of rectification where a document has been completed in error and does not represent the true wishes of the parties. Rather than declaring the entire agreement to be void, the court amends the document to bring it into line with the original wishes of the two parties e.g. where a typographical error has been made and not discovered on proofreading.

Joscelyne v Nissen

The plaintiff agreed to transfer his car-hire business to his daughter in return for her agreeing to pay a number of household expenses. When a written contract was subsequently drawn up it did not mention payment of these expenses.
Held: The agreement should be rectified to include this commitment.

Mistake

General position → **Mistake is no excuse**

→ **Contract must stand**

→ **Caveat Emptor [Let the Buyer Beware]**

Exceptions (Operative Mistake)

1.   **Common Mistake as to the Existence of the Subject Matter.**

2.   **Mutual Mistake.**

3.   **Mistake as to the Identity of the Other Party.**

4.   ***Non Est Factum*** **(It is not my deed).**

Misrepresentation

If a person has been misled during the preliminary stages leading to a contract, s/he will want to know what rights, if any, s/he possesses. These depend on the nature of the false statement and how it can be classified legally. There are three main types of false statement:
*   Traders' Puff.
*   Misrepresentation.
*   Contractual Term.

Traders' Puff

Certain statements made by a trader are regarded as mere "puffs" not intended to have any legal consequences. In **Lambert v Lewis** the manufacturers of a towing hitch claimed in promotional literature that it was "foolproof" and "required no maintenance". One hitch which was sold with a defect caused a serious accident. The Court of Appeal held that the promotional claims were not intended to be serious promises which gave rise to any contractual rights in themselves.

Misrepresentation

A misrepresentation may be defined as a false statement of fact which induces the other party to enter into a contract. It must be a statement of fact, not future intention (unless it can be proved that at the time of the false statement, the person making it must not have believed in its accuracy). It must also induce (or at least partly induce) the other party to enter into the contract. If s/he knew it was untrue or did not believe in its truth and yet went ahead with the deal it did not act as an inducement.

[Misrepresentations differ from contractual terms in that they remain outside the contract once it has been agreed. In other words, they influence a party to enter into the agreement but, in the circumstances, are not seen to be a part of the actual contract. Remedies for misrepresentation are therefore not strictly contractual – they arise through a combination of statutory rights and use of the law of tort].

Remedies for Misrepresentation

This will depend on the type of misrepresentation. There are three categories:
* Fraudulent.
* Negligent.
* Wholly Innocent.

Fraudulent
A misstatement is made fraudulently if it is made knowingly, or without belief in its truth, or recklessly, careless whether it be true of false. Fraud is very difficult to prove in practice. The innocent party can claim:
* **Rescission of the contract** (but see below - loss of right to rescind).
* **Damages for the tort of deceit.**

Negligent
A false statement of fact will be deemed to have been made negligently unless the party making the statement "proves that he had reasonable ground to believe and

did believe up to the time the contract was made that the facts were true [Section 2(1) Misrepresentation Act 1967]. The burden of proof is on the trader to disprove negligence. The innocent party can claim :
- **Rescission of the contract (unless the judge uses his discretion to award damages in lieu) [Section 2(1)].**
- **Damages.**

N.B. It will not be possible under Section 2(1) of the Misrepresentation Act 1967 to claim rights if you did not enter into a contract with the maker of the false statement, but have nevertheless suffered financial loss as a result e.g. a house purchaser who relies on the report of a valuer acting for the building society. It may be possible to bring a claim for negligence (a tort action) using the precedent of **Hedley Byrne & Co v Heller & Partners (1964).**

If a special relationship exists between the maker of a false statement and another (usually where the former is in a professional position and whose judgement will be relied upon to a high degree) s/he owes the latter a duty of care and can be liable for damage (including economic loss) caused by a breach of duty.

Wholly Innocent
Section 2(2) Misrepresentation Act 1967 entitles to innocent party to:
- **Rescission of the contract (unless the judge uses discretion to award damages in lieu)**

Loss of Right to Rescind
- where the innocent party has already affirmed the contract.
- where the judge uses discretion and awards damages in lieu.
- if an innocent third party has acquired rights to the goods already.
- if it has become impossible to restore the original position e.g. the goods have been altered in their appearance.
- lapse of time (after reasonable length of time) – at some point the other party should be entitled to feel secure that the contract must stand.

Leaf v International Galleries

The claimant bought a painting in 1944, relying on a statement by the defendant that it was painted by Constable. In 1949 he discovered it was an imitation and worth much less. He brought an action for rescission of the contract and the return of his purchase price.
Held: It was too late for such a claim – a reasonable period of time had already elapsed and he had now accepted the painting.

There is a degree of overlap between pre-contractual statements that constitute misrepresentations and those amounting to contractual terms. Sometimes, the court has elevated a misrepresentation to the status of a contractual term:

Esso Petroleum Co. Ltd v Mardon

An over-optimistic sales forecast made by a senior sales executive of Esso (that the throughput of a filling station would amount to 200,000 gallons per year) was held to constitute a breach of contract – the statement amounting to a warranty. This was the case even though it had not been included in the specific terms written into the contract.

Misrepresentation

Fraudulent ⟶ **made knowingly, or recklessly**

Negligent ⟶ **honest belief, but with no reasonable grounds**

Innocent ⟶ **honest belief, and with reasonable grounds**

Remedies

	Rescission	Damages
Fraudulent	Yes	Yes – tort claim for deceit
Negligent	Yes	Yes, either: a) statutory claim under s.2.1 Misrepresentation Act 1967,or b) tort claim in negligence (Hedley Byrne v Heller & Pns)
Innocent	Yes	No, unless judge uses discretion to award damages in lieu (s.2.2)

In conclusion:

- Mistakes do not usually affect the validity of a contract (*Caveat Emptor* – Let the buyer beware).

- Operative mistakes are the exceptions – ones which are so fundamental that it is as if no agreement has been made at all.

- The main examples of operative mistake are common mistake as to the existence of the subject-matter, mutual mistake, mistake as to the identity of the other party and *non est factum* ('it is not my deed').

- The court may rectify (correct) a document where its wording, by oversight, does not reflect the true intentions of the parties.

- Misrepresentation is a false statement of fact which induces the other party to enter into a contract.

- Remedies for misrepresentation are not contractual – by definition, the misrepresentation has not been incorporated as a term in the contract.

- Rescission (avoidance) of the contract is nearly always available.

- The availability of damages as a remedy depends on whether the misrepresentation was committed fraudulently, negligently or innocently.

Chapter Six

The Contents of a Contract: Contractual Terms

So far we have been examining issues connected with formation of contract and whether contracts will be invalid for one reason or another. The next chapter focuses on the substance of a contract – what it actually contains. Its terms can be classified in a number of ways and the following material introduces you to the topic. Breach of contract and available remedies play a central part in this discussion. The chapter covers the following issues:

- Terms – classification according to manner of creation.
- Terms – classification according to importance (conditions, warranties, innominate).
- Remedies for breach.
- Acceptance of goods – effect on right of buyer to repudiate.

Most business transactions contain a combination of basic obligations and ones that are less significant. The make of a washing machine, for instance, as well as its colour, price, and date of delivery are all detailed provisions of how the contract is to be performed. These details are known as the **terms of the contract**. All contracts contain such terms. *They comprise the more specific detailed undertakings of how the basic obligations are to be performed.*

In a contract for the construction of a new factory building, the start and completion dates, the design of the building, the materials to be used, the extent to which work can be subcontracted etc are all integral parts of the contract and are all equally enforceable.

Terms can be classified in two different ways:

- According to their manner of creation.

- According to their importance to the contract.

Classification of Terms (1)

Manner of Creation

- **Express Terms** - *These are the details of the contract that have been specifically and mutually agreed upon before or at the time the contract is made.*

They are intended by the parties to form part of the contract. They can be made orally, or they can be reduced to writing.

The problem here is that not everything said in the negotiations to an agreement forms an integral part of it. Express terms must be distinguished from mere representations (statements made prior to the agreement, at the negotiation stage, which induce one party to enter into the contract but do not form part of it).

If the statement made turns out to be false, even if made innocently or negligently, then this will amount to misrepresentation and damages can now be paid under the Misrepresentation Act 1967. (This payment can be, however, at the discretion of the courts).

- **Implied Terms** - *Terms will sometimes be attached to contracts by operation of law. This enables terms to be added which the law either thinks fitting and appropriate to include in the agreement or need to be added in order to give the contract the business effect intended by the parties.*

Attachment can be by:

1. Commercial Custom.
2. Previous dealing.
3. Common Law.
4. Act of Parliament.

1.   Commercial Custom

In a variety of industries and trades, there have grown up a number of well-known ('notorious') practices which have established themselves as legal rights and duties – simply because they have become so well-established by the traders involved. The courts have considered it appropriate to give legal recognition to these practices. They may relate to such issues as credit periods and delivery arrangements etc. This approach has been adopted where a transaction has been entered into which is covered by a widely-known and recognised standard set of terms applied in the industry to such agreements. It will be implied that those standard terms apply to the transaction.

British Crane Hire v Ipswich Plant Hire

The owner of a crane hired it to a contractor who was engaged in the same industry. It was held that the owner's terms (the model terms used in the construction industry for hiring cranes, and which were therefore standard in the industry), were binding on the hirer even though they had not actually been communicated at the time of hiring.

2.   *Previous Dealing*
Where two traders have had a regular course of dealing with each over a period of time and on the same terms and conditions, the courts have felt able to imply the same set of terms even where there was no reference to express terms in their latest transaction.

3.   *Common Law*
Judges, over the years, have devised a number of tests that enable them to imply terms into contracts which seem to possess gaps that would create unfortunate results. The following tests are two of the more well-known ones:

> **a)   The Business Efficacy test**
> Here is a quote where the above test was explained and justified:
> 'an unexpressed term can be implied if, and only if, the court finds that the parties must have intended that term to form part of their contract; it is not enough for the court to find that such a term would have been adopted by the parties as reasonable men if it had been suggested to them; it must have been a term that went without saying, a term necessary to give business efficacy to the contract, a term which, although tacit, formed part of the contract which the parties made for themselves.'

Liverpool City Council v Irwin

It was held that there was an implied term of a lease of a flat in a council block that the landlord should take reasonable care to keep the public areas (stairwells and lifts etc) in a reasonable state of repair (there was no express provision requiring such a commitment).

> **b)   The Officious Bystander test**
> Here is another quote again explaining when this test can be applied:
> '... something so obvious that it goes without saying; so that, if while one of the parties were making their bargain, an officious bystander were to

suggest some express provision for it in the agreement, they would testily suppress him with a common: "oh, of course".'

The Moorcock

A ship had been moored in a wharf. When the tide went out, the water level in the wharf fell and the ship was damaged by a rock embedded in the bottom of the wharf. It was held that there was an implied term in the contract that the wharf would be safe for the use of ships – one that clearly had been broken on the facts. Damages were awarded.

Classification of Terms (2)

Importance to the Contract

Condition - A major term of the contract; one that is so vital that, if it is broken, it renders performance of the contract fundamentally different from that which had originally been envisaged, e.g. if you had continuously stressed the importance of a particular completion date to a supplier and it fails to deliver or complete on time, it is highly probable that the courts would interpret this as a breach of a condition.

Warranty - A minor term of the contract; one that is not so vital that breach of it results in a totally different contract. It is a subsidiary term which merely adds the details to other more important terms. The importance of the distinction between a condition and a warranty will become obvious when it is related to the area of remedies for breach of contract. If a condition of the contract is broken, then fairly serious and drastic remedies will be available against the party in breach. *The injured party can repudiate the contract (regard it as over) and claim damages, or he may continue with the contract and claim damages.*

Poussard v Spiers

A famous opera singer was engaged to perform in a lead role for a production to last for three months. She missed the first week of performances due to illness. When she found her contract had been terminated, she sued the opera company for breach of contract.
Held: She had broken a condition of the contract by missing a vital week affecting the future success of the production. The opera company were therefore within its rights to terminate her contract.

If a warranty of the contract is broken, however, then the remedies available will not be so far-reaching; *the injured party must continue with the contract, and only claim damages.*

Bettini v Gye

A lead singer in a musical was under contract for six months. One of the terms of the contract was to attend rehearsals for seven days prior to first performance. He missed the first three days of rehearsals due to illness. He arrived on the morning of the fourth day of rehearsals to be informed that his contract had been terminated for breach. He sued the theatrical company.

Held: The singer had only broken a warranty of the contract, given that he had not missed any actual performances and would have been able to attend the rest of the rehearsals week. Therefore, his claim for breach was successful and he was awarded damages.

You might well be a little confused by the choice of wording used here. Written contracts often contain the heading "Terms and Conditions." This is mere terminology as they will contain both conditions and warranties as defined above. Equally, the expression "warranty" is often used to mean a form of guarantee when purchasing goods. This is simply another use of the word and is not relevant to the classification of terms in a contract.

How to determine whether condition or warranty?

1.   It may be self evident in the situation e.g. completion of construction work to meet a known deadline (the Millennium Dome, facilities for the next Olympics).

2.   It may be specified by law, either in legislation e.g. the implied duties relating to goods found ss 12-15 **Sale of Goods Act 1979** are stipulated to be conditions by the Act itself), or common law e.g. an 'expedited readiness to load' clause in a charterparty (contract for carriage of goods by sea) is presumed to be a condition.

3.   Self-Description in the contract – although not conclusive, it will be taken into account by the court and influence its decision. In **Lombard North Central plc v Butterworth**, a contract for the lease of a computer involved instalment payments. The contract specified that prompt payments were of the essence. When payment was late the court held that this entitled the supplier to terminate the contract – a condition having been broken. [there is a presumption in sale of goods contracts that time for payment is not a condition – in the absence of other factors].

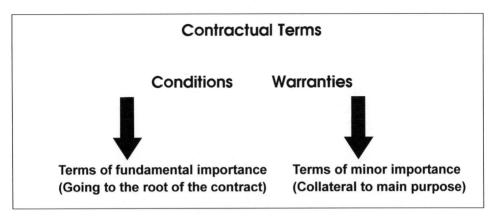

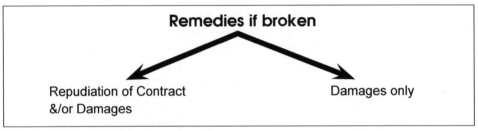

• **But check if buyer has "accepted" the goods – see later**

"Innominate Terms"

Traditionally, terms have been divided into two types - conditions and warranties. A condition is a term of major importance; if it is broken, the other party is entitled to treat the contract as at an end as well as claiming damages. A warranty is a less important term; for breach of a warranty the other party may recover damages only, but may not treat the contract as terminated. In other words, if someone has failed to perform a condition in the contract, he has effectively repudiated the contract with the result that the other party is released from his contractual obligations and need not perform either. Sometimes it is clear whether a term is a condition or a warranty, eg. when the matter is covered by legislation.

The **Sale of Goods Act 1979** identifies implied conditions relating to the quality and fitness of goods sold for example. Where a seller breaks such a provision a buyer is entitled to reject the goods, claim a full refund of any money paid, and in addition recover damages, eg. where the goods are defective and the market price of similar goods is higher than the agreed contract price. However, where the provision is an express one, the task is more difficult. Nor is the matter of interpretation of the provisions made easier by the fact that the agreement uses words like "condition" or "warranty", for it may well be that the parties, who are commercial people, not lawyers, have not used the words in a legalistic sense but are using them as synonyms for "provision" or "term". The question to be decided usually is whether the parties intended the term to be an important or fundamental term going to the root of the contract (a condition) or thought it less significant (a warranty).

However, that straightforward division of terms into 2 types was disturbed by the sensible and vitally important decision in 1962 - the **Hong Kong Fir Shipping** case. This case introduced the concept of the innominate term (or intermediate term). This is a term which, when the contract is first made, cannot be put into one of the two traditional pigeon holes as it covers a multitude of possible breaches of small or large significance. So the remedy of the innocent party will depend on the nature, consequences, and effect of the breach ie. whether the term is broken seriously or not.

The Hong Kong Fir case is a clear illustration. That case was concerned with an obligation of seaworthiness of a ship. The Court of Appeal pointed out that the breaches which might occur were various. They might be extremely trivial - the omission of a nail; they might be extremely grave - a serious defect in the hull or in the machinery. So the Court decided that it was impossible to identify the seaworthiness obligation as a condition; the parties would have to wait to see how, if at all, the term was broken.

These innominate terms (called 'innominate' because you cannot easily categorise or nominate then into either condition or warranty at the time of drafting) are therefore sometimes called 'wait and see' terms i.e. you have to wait until the breach occurs during performance of the contract and see how big an impact it is having on performance of the contract. If it is having a fundamental impact, it will allow for termination of the contract. If it is having a minor effect, there will be no right to terminate (only damages will be claimable).

Breach of Contract - Loss of Right to Repudiate

Where a condition or major term of a contract is broken by the seller, the buyer's primary remedy, apart from compensation for loss, is the right of rejection - the right to refuse to take delivery or, if the goods have already been delivered, to make the seller collect them, and in addition, to have any advance payment returned by the seller. This right is lost however where the buyer has "accepted" the goods e.g. made up the raw materials or fitted components into his end product; or kept the goods for an unreasonably long time without rejecting rather than contacting his supplier promptly he finds something wrong. The relevant provisions are found in the Sale of Goods Act 1979:

Sale of Goods Act 1979

SECTION 11 (4)
"WHERE A CONTRACT OF SALE IS NOT SEVERABLE AND THE BUYER HAS ACCEPTED THE GOODS OR PART OF THEM...THE BREACH OF A CONDITION TO BE FULFILLED BY THE SELLER CAN ONLY BE TREATED AS A BREACH OF WARRANTY, AND NOT AS A GROUND FOR REJECTING THE GOODS AND TREATING THE CONTRACT AS REPUDIATED, UNLESS THERE IS AN EXPRESS OR IMPLIED TERM OF THE CONTRACT TO THAT EFFECT."

SECTION 35(2)
WHERE GOODS ARE DELIVERED TO THE BUYER, AND HE HAS NOT PREVIOUSLY EXAMINED THEM, HE IS NOT DEEMED TO HAVE ACCEPTED THEM...UNTIL HE HAS HAD A REASONABLE OPPORTUNITY OF EXAMINING THEM FOR THE PURPOSE –
OF ASCERTAINING WHETHER THEY ARE IN CONFORMITY WITH THE CONTRACT

SECTION 35
(1) "THE BUYER IS DEEMED TO HAVE ACCEPTED THE GOODS :
  (a)   WHEN HE INTIMATES TO THE SELLER THAT HE HAS ACCEPTED THEM,
        OR,
  (b)   WHEN THE GOODS HAVE BEEN DELIVERED TO HIM AND HE DOES ANY ACT IN RELATION TO THEM WHICH IS INCONSISTENT WITH THE OWNERSHIP OF THE SELLER,
        OR,
(4) WHEN AFTER THE LAPSE OF A REASONABLE TIME, HE RETAINS THE GOODS WITHOUT INTIMATING TO THE SELLER THAT HE HAS REJECTED THEM."

In conclusion:

• Contractual terms can be classified according to how they were created (express; implied), or according to their importance to the contract (conditions; warranties).

• Express terms are agreed between the parties; implied terms are automatically incorporated by operation of law (chiefly by statute or common law).

- Conditions are terms of fundamental importance, breach of which entitles the injured party to repudiate (terminate) the contract and/or claim damages.

- Warranties are terms of relatively minor importance, breach of which entitles the injured party to claim damages – it cannot repudiate the contract.

- Sometimes, it is impossible to determine whether breach of a term entitles the injured party to repudiate the contract until after the breach has taken place and its consequences on the entire contract assessed – these are called innominate terms.

- A buyer loses the right to repudiate a contract for breach of a condition once the goods in question have been accepted.

Chapter Seven

Remedies for Breach

- **Liquidated Damages and Penalties**
- **Unliquidated Damages (Damages at Large)**

Damages are always available for breach of contract. Sometimes the claimable amount will have been specified in the contract. Sometimes, it will have to be assessed by the court. The following chapter examines the legal principles relevant to the awarding of compensation. It covers the following principles:

- Liquidated damages – definition.
- Distinction from penalties.
- Advantages of LDs.
- Unliquidated damages – underlying purpose.
- The market rule.
- The rule in Hadley v Baxendale.
- Claimable loss.
- Proximity of loss to breach.
- Mitigation of loss.
- Anticipatory breach.

Liquidated Damages

Many contracts include a term providing that specified damages shall be payable in the event of a particular type of breach. There are clear advantages in such a procedure, particularly in avoiding uncertainty and in setting a known limit on the liabilities of the parties. However, a distinction has been made by the courts between liquidated damages clauses and penalty clauses. The significance of this distinction is that the former are enforceable, while the latter are not. This principle is founded on the idea that damages are compensation for loss; a threat designed to compel performance does not qualify as "damages".

The leading case in this area is **Dunlop Pneumatic Tyre Co. Ltd v New Garage & Motor Co. Ltd (1915)**. The following principles were laid down in this case.

- The terminology used by the parties is not conclusive. It is a matter of construction for the courts to decide whether a clause is for liquidated damages or a penalty; regardless of how it is described in the contract itself.

- A liquidated damages clause must be a genuine **pre-estimate** of the actual loss that will be suffered in the event of a breach. The nature of a penalty clause in quite different; it is intended to coerce performance from one of the parties, and a sign of this would be if the amount stipulated is excessive ("**extravagant and unconscionable** in amount in comparison with the greatest loss that could conceivably be proved to have followed from the breach." - *per Lord Dunedin.*

- The burden of proof is on the party alleging that the clause is a penalty clause.

Apart from the criterion already mentioned ("extravagant & unconscionable in amount") another indication that a clause is a penalty is when a single sum is fixed in relation to any possible breach, even though some breaches would clearly cause more loss than others.

If a clause is construed as liquidated damages, then the amount specified in the clause is what the injured party can recover, regardless of the amount of actual loss:

Cellulose Acetate Silk Co. v Widnes Foundry

The defendants had agreed to erect a plant by a specified date. The contract contained a clause requiring them to pay 'by way of penalty' a sum of £20 per week for each week of delay. They were 30 weeks late. The plaintiff claimed their actual losses amounting to £5,850. The defendants relied on the contract provision requiring them to pay only £600.
Held: Although called a penalty, the clause was in fact a reasonable attempt to anticipate likely losses and was therefore a liquidated damages clause and effective. The plaintiff was only entitled to £600.

An LD clause should always contain a ceiling or maximum on claimable compensation (e.g. up to a maximum of 5% of the contract price). It is argued that the injured party should have made suitable re-arrangements after a reasonable length of time, after which no further losses should be sustained.

If the clause is construed as a penalty, then it will not be enforceable and the injured party will have to claim for unliquidated damages (assessed by the court).

The obvious advantages of a liquidated damages clause are:

- The fixing of a set amount in advance of any breach, providing both parties with a clearer picture of the financial consequences and thus making it easier to negotiate a price, which will include suitable insurance costs to cover any claims.

- The ability of the buyer to deduct any liquidated damages from the payment of the purchase price before sending on the balance (a right of 'set-off'). This avoids the need to go to court and run into the inevitable problems of cost and delay.

These benefits have to be offset against the risks that the buyer's clause may entitle him to less compensation than the actual loss sustained, and the possibility that it may be challenged as a penalty clause.

Liquidated Damages and Penalties

- **LD are enforceable; Penalties are void**

- **LD are genuine pre-estimates of losses for breach of contract**

- **Penalties are attempts to coerce performance**

- **Terminology in contract is not conclusive**

- **Excessive amounts = penalty ("unfair, extravagant & unconscionable" – Dunlop Co. Ltd v New Garage Ltd)**

- **Single sum claimable for all/any type of breach?**

- **Should have some maximum limit for compensation**

- **Should not be a compromise figure**

- **LD fixes claimable sum even if inaccurate!**

Unliquidated Damages

In the absence of a contractual provision covering damages (or if there is one but it is held to be a penalty clause) it will be necessary to resort to the courts in order to claim compensation for a breach of contract.

Judges attempt to give business effect to the contract – **to put the parties in the same financial position they would have been in if the contract had been properly performed.**

[Unlike the U.S, punitive damages - acting as a deterrent to future breaches of contract - are not awarded].

Where there is an available market in which the goods can be purchased or sold elsewhere, the difference between the original contract price and the price paid/ obtained subsequently will determine available damages **(The Market Rule)**.

e.g.   Seller fails to deliver goods to buyer (original contract price - £12,000)
Buyer now has to obtain goods from a different seller and pays £13500
Court will award £1500 to buyer in order to achieve the above objective.

Where there is no such market, loss of profit is the measure of damages.

There is an important restriction on the ability of the injured party to recover for loss suffered from a breach of contract. Claimable loss must have been reasonably foreseeable at the time of the contract as likely to arise from breach of the contract. This is known as the **Rule in Hadley v Baxendale**. It has the following consequences:

*   **Natural loss which is the direct consequence of the breach is claimable** e.g. predictable costs incurred by the injured party including replacement purchases, loss of normal profits from lost orders dependent on the original goods arriving on time;

*   **Unusual loss is not claimable unless the other party was informed of it at the time the contract was agreed.**

Cases putting Rule into Practice

Hadley v Baxendale

A mill belonging to X had a broken shaft. It made a contract with a firm of hauliers to take the shaft to a manufacturer for it to be copied and a new one made. The hauliers were in breach of contract by delaying delivery beyond a reasonable length of time. In the meantime, the mill had been at a standstill. A claim for this lost production was brought against the hauliers.

Held: The mill was unusual in not possessing a reserve mill shaft. The hauliers had not been informed about this state of affairs and would not have foreseen its occurrence. The claim for lost production was not allowed.

Victoria Laundry v Newman Industries

V bought from N a boiler for use in his laundry. Delivery was to be made on 5th June but was not made until November. V claimed:

1)   loss of the profits the laundry would have made had the boiler been delivered in time;
2)   loss of profit from some highly profitable dyeing contracts.

Held:
1)   the laundry profits lost were recoverable, as N must have contemplated their loss if there was delay;
2)   the loss on the dyeing contracts, which could not have been contemplated, could not be recovered.

Balfour Beatty Construction v Scottish Power

Balfour Beatty (BB) engaged Scottish Power (SP) to supply electricity for use in the construction of an aqueduct. The work required continuous pour of new concrete. SP was in breach of contract – the electricity supply was cut because of a rupture of fuses. The concrete hardened before it could be added to the existing structure. BB could not simply cut a line through the work & re-start – the aqueduct had to be water-proof. BB had to demolish the existing half-built aqueduct and start again. It claimed full compensation for the consequent losses.

Held: SP had not been made aware of the need for continuous pour or of the impact it would have if the flow was interrupted. Loss was therefore not reasonably foreseeable. The claim for full losses failed.

A party may be liable for consequences which, although within the reasonable contemplation of the parties, are significantly more serious than would have been expected:

Parsons (Livestock) Ltd v Uttley Ingham & Co.

The claimants, who bred pigs, purchased a food hopper from the defendants. The latter were negligent in their erection of the hopper in that they failed to unseal a ventilator at the top of the hopper. This caused the pig food which was subsequently stored in the hopper to become mouldy. When fed to the pigs they contracted a rare intestinal disease from which they all died.

Held: The defendants were liable for the loss. It was predictable that food stored in the hopper would become unfit for consumption if not properly ventilated. Once this was established, all the consequent losses were recoverable, even though the seriousness of the illness was not predictable.

What 'damage' can be claimed for breach of contract?
1) Physical injury resulting.

2) Damage to property.

3) Economic loss.

Economic loss includes consequential losses such as lost profits and liability for breach of contract to customers resulting from the initial breach.

The breach must cause the damage.
Sometimes, although a contract has been broken and damage sustained, it can be argued that the cause of the injury was some other, supervening event. There is a break in the chain of causation between the breach and the damage. The claim would be defeated on this argument.

Lambert v Lewis

A farmer had been held primarily liable for a motoring accident resulting in the death of 2 people. He had been negligent in failing to remedy a defective towing hitch which had resulted in a trailer becoming detached and crashing into a saloon car. He sought to claim damages for breach of contract against the dealer from whom he had bought the hitch (on the grounds of lack of fitness for purpose – there was already a design weakness inherent in the part).

Held: The cause of the farmer's loss was his own negligence in failing to repair the hitch when the defect had become known to him. Therefore, the breach by the dealer had not caused his loss. His action failed. Sometimes the basis of the claim will be lost expenditure, rather than lost revenue. This could be the case where it is virtually impossible to quantify potential revenue losses:

Anglia T.V. v Reed

The claimants incurred considerable expenditure preparing for a television play. A contract had been agreed with the actor Oliver Reed who was to play the lead role. He broke the contract by refusing to perform the part. Despite making reasonable efforts to find a replacement, no-one was found and the production was cancelled. Anglia claimed for the lost expenditure, partly because of the difficulties of predicting the future success of the play (lost revenue).
Held: They were entitled to claim on the basis of wasted expenditure.

Mitigation of Loss

The injured party is under a duty to take reasonable steps to minimise the loss suffered as a consequence of the breach of contract. Thus, replacement goods of a similar specification and quality should be purchased and not more expensive, upmarket ones. The court would not allow such unnecessary expenditure to be compensated for in the award.

Payzu Ltd v Saunders

A contract had been agreed for the sale of fabric, delivery and payment to be made by instalment. When the buyer was late in making the first payment, the supplier refused to make any further deliveries unless they were paid for in cash. The buyer refused to accept this change and sued for breach of contract.
Held: The supplier had no right to repudiate the contract for the late payment and was therefore in breach. However, the buyer should have mitigated his losses by accepting the offer of cash on delivery terms. The damages award was restricted to what he would have lost under those terms, namely, interest over the repayment period.

(**Hochster v De La Tour**). It does not have to wait until the breach actually takes place. This is called anticipatory breach of contract. Of course, the injured party may wish to delay such action in the hope that the other party can be persuaded to carry out its obligations. The only risk in doing so arises if a frustrating event occurs in the meantime. The contract would then become void, disallowing any claim for breach (**Avery v Bowden**).

In conclusion:

- Damages can be either stipulated in the contract (liquidated damages) or assessed by the court (unliquidated damages).

- Liquidated damages clauses (LDs) are a genuine pre-estimate of the likely loss to be suffered from a breach of the contract and are enforceable.

- Penalty clauses are punitive attempts to coerce performance and are void.

- LDs are binding even if inaccurate – any shortfall cannot then be recovered.

- Unliquidated damages attempt to place the injured party in the same position as if the contract had been properly performed.

- It is possible to claim for personal injury, damage to property and economic loss caused by a breach of contract.

- The market rule helps ascertain resulting losses caused by a breach.

- The rules in **Hadley v Baxendale** limit damages to those which are reasonably foreseeable at the time of the contract.

- The breach must cause the damage.

- The injured party must mitigate his losses – take reasonable steps to minimise the losses.

Chapter Eight
Exclusion Clauses

Clearly it is in the supplier's interests to limit or completely exclude responsibility for damage or loss sustained as a result of breach of contract or negligence on its part. The following chapter examines how the law has changed in recent years and how it is becoming increasingly difficult for suppliers to attach enforceable exclusions to contracts. The chapter concentrates on the following issues:

* Exclusion – definition, justification and dangers
* Common law restrictions – reasonable notification
* Common law restrictions – *contra proferentem*
* Unfair Contract Terms Act 1977 – main provisions
* Test of reasonableness
* Cases illustrating the test

Background Issues

An exclusion (or exemption) clause is a term in a contract which seeks to exempt one of the parties from liability in certain events. These include non-performance of contract, defective performance, misrepresentation and negligence.

Between parties of equal bargaining strength such clauses may be legitimate and can serve useful purposes. They can operate as a form of pricing policy by which firms can reduce their prices in exchange for lowering their obligations. It also enables firms to avoid the use of lawyers and the courts, against which they have a traditional distrust.

Problems arise however where there is an inequality of bargaining strength. Potential abuses can be the result of consumer ignorance of their existence in the contract, inability to understand their meaning or inability to resist their inclusion.

The law has a dilemma if it attempts to intervene where abuses are happening. Contract law is built on the doctrine of *laissez faire* which requires the state to leave the parties alone to make their own arrangements. It is for the parties to make sure that they make a sound deal and must live with the consequences without the "luxury" of being rescued by the courts subsequently.

This harsh position has been modified as the problems of abuse and the growing number of consumer transactions has compelled a change of approach. Initially, the common law introduced a number of restrictions on exclusion clauses (see later) but these were always piece-meal and very limited in operation. Eventually, Parliament passed legislation which provided more significant barriers or restrictions to the use of these clauses.

The most important Act in this area is the **UNFAIR CONTRACT TERMS ACT 1977**, whose provisions will need to be studied closely. More recently, the European Union has required member countries to satisfy the requirements of the **UNFAIR CONTRACT TERMS DIRECTIVE**. The UK has issued regulations in 1994 to meet this requirement. These regulations have recently been revised in the light of experience and are now entitled the **Unfair Terms in Consumer Contracts Regulations 1999**. Clearly these regulations do not apply to contracts made between businesses.

Exclusion Clauses - Common Law Restrictions

The common law established two barriers to the abuse of exemption clauses.

Test 1: Was the clause a term of the contract at all?

There is a general principle of contract which states that no term will be effective and binding unless the other party was given reasonable notice of its existence by the time the contract is completed. Examples of unreasonable notice include:

a) After the contract has already been made

Olley v Marlborough Court Hotel

Husband and wife booked into an hotel; their bedroom had a notice limiting liability for lost or stolen articles unless handed to the manageress for safe keeping. Furs belonging to the wife were stolen, partly because of the negligence of the hotel. **Held:** The notice was ineffective because it was not brought to their attention until after the contract had been made at the reception desk on the ground floor.

b) Illegible writing

c) Where the exclusion is contained on a piece of paper which the other party is unlikely to consider to be part of the contract:

e.g. on notices which are not obvious to the other party at the time of the contract; or,

e.g. on a receipt provided as proof of payment. (Whether tickets are contractual documents or mere receipts depends on the circumstances).

Chapelton v Barry UDC

Notice board on promenade stated "Deckchairs for Hire - 2d per session of 3 hours. Take one from the stand". When payment was collected later, a ticket was issued which contained an exclusion clause.

Held: Unreasonable to communicate conditions by a mere receipt when there was a notice board nearby.

Where the exclusion is contained in the contract and the other party has signed the agreement the general principle is that reasonable notice must be given. It will be no defence to argue that you did not realise what you were signing.

L'Estrange v Graucob

Plaintiff bought a cigarette vending machine and signed a sales agreement which excluded "any express or implied condition, warranty, statutory or otherwise".

Held: The clause was binding on her even though she had not read the agreement.

Test 2: Did the exemption clause cover the loss or damage when properly construed?

The courts construe such clauses *"contra proferentem"* (against the person wishing to rely on the exclusion) so that any ambiguity or doubt will cause it to fail.

Baldry v Marshall

Plaintiff asked for a car "suitable for touring purposes". Defendant suggested a Bugatti and excluded liability for "any other guarantee, or warranty, statutory or otherwise".

Held: The purpose for which the car was required was a condition, not a warranty. The exemption was ineffective.

Andrews v Singer

Andrews agreed to buy some new Singer cars from Singer. Singer excluded "all conditions, warranties and liabilities implied by statute, common law or otherwise".

One of the cars supplied was a used car.
Held: Exclusion did not cover express terms. Singer were liable for damages.

Hotel Services LTD v Hilton International

A contract had been agreed for the supply of minibars to some of the hotels within the Hilton Hotel group. Some of the minibars were faulty and were leaking gas in the bedrooms. Hilton argued breach of contract (goods not fit for purpose, not of satisfactory quality) and claimed damages for (amongst other things) loss of profits from the minibars not being in the bedrooms. Hotel Services defence was that the contract contained an exclusion clause - they would not be liable 'for indirect or consequential loss…'.
Held: Costs and loss of profits were direct loss, not indirect or consequential loss. The exclusion clause therefore did not relate to the type of loss claimed. Damages were claimable.

Various other legal concepts were used by the courts to resist unfair exclusion attempts. These included <u>the doctrine of fundamental breach, the presence of misrepresentation and the collateral contract</u>. Ultimately it was recognised that a more comprehensive regulation of exclusion clauses was needed. This led to the passing of UCTA 1977. Two of its main provisions are found on the following pages:

The Unfair Contract Terms Act 1977

Section 2 (Negligence Liability)

Any attempt to exclude liability for death or personal injury caused by negligence is void

Section 2(1)

Any attempt to exclude liability for damage to property or financial loss caused by negligence is void, unless proved to be fair & reasonable in the circumstances

Section 2(2)

Section 3 (Breach of Contract Liability)

Applies to all contracts involving a consumer and to contracts between businesses where standard form documentation is used

Any attempt to exclude liability for breach of contract is void, unless proved to be fair & reasonable in the circumstances.

Factors used to decide Fairness

- Relative bargaining strength.

- Presence of any inducements.

- Availability of alternative suppliers.

- Obviousness of the exclusion to the other party.

- Whether goods were manufactured or adapted to the order of the customer.

- Presence of known trade customs or previous dealings.

(Schedule 2)

Cases Applying the Reasonableness Test

George Mitchell v Finney Lock Seeds Ltd (1983)

Finney Lock were a firm of seed merchants. They contracted to sell to Mitchell 30lbs of Dutch winter cabbage seed for £201.60. M. planted 63 acres with the seeds. The resultant crop was worthless, partly because the seed which had been delivered was autumn seed not winter seed and partly because, in any case, the seed was of low quality. M sued for damages of £361,000 for loss of profit. F relied on a standard clause in their conditions of sale which limited their liability to replacing the defective seeds or refunding payment.
Held: F's limitation clause was unreasonable and therefore F were liable to compensate M for loss of profits. The main factor which swayed the House of Lords was that F gave evidence that they attempted to negotiate settlements above the price of the seeds in cases where they considered the customer's complaint to be "genuine" and "justified" – a tacit admission that their limitation clause was unreasonable.

Two further factors were in favour of M:1) F had been negligent in that, irrespective of its quality, the variety of seed supplied to M could not be grown commercially in the area where M's farm was situated; 2) Farmers could not be expected to insure against losses of this kind but F could insure against happenings such as occurred in this case without needing to increase their prices significantly[1].

---

1. Although not in the non-exhaustive list of relevant factors found in Schedule 2 of UCTA, the relative ease and cost of obtaining insurance to deal with risks instead of relying on disclaimers/ limitation clauses is a significant issue in many cases.

St. Albans City & District Council V International Computers Limited (1995)

The council entered into a contract with ICL for a computer system which it required to determine a new community charge. The software was defective and as a result the charge was set at too low a level. The council brought an action for breach of contract and negligent misrepresentation. ICL relied on their limitation clause which limited its liability to £100,000. The council had objected to this limit during negotiations but did not pursue the issue because of time pressures.
Held: ICL was fully liable for the loss. The contract had been entered into on the written standard terms of business of ICL within section 3 of UCTA. In deciding that the limitation was unreasonable the following factors were taken into account:

*   ICL was a large company in a strong bargaining position and in a better position to bear losses than St Albans, which would have to meet losses out of an increased community charge or reduced services.

*   The limitation of £100,000 bore no relation to ICL's insurance cover of £50m.

St Albans had not been offered any inducement, such as a reduction in price, to accept the limitation and they had no opportunity of getting better terms elsewhere because other suppliers were offering similar terms. However, it is important to realise that since around the year 2000, there has been a series of decisions where the courts have tended to be less supportive of business purchasers. The new approach has been to emphasize that, if an exclusion clause was clearly written into the contract and the commercial buyer was aware of its existence and meaning, then he should not be able to claim unreasonableness after signing up to the deal. In other words, people who are in business buying goods and services should be sufficiently sophisticated to know what they are doing. The Act should not be available to them as some sort of escape route after the event. A case illustrating this tougher line is:

Watford Electronics Ltd v Sanderson CFL Ltd

An item of software had been supplied by the defendant which was defective and a claim for over £5m damages was brought by the claimant. The contract had been agreed on the supplier's standard terms of supply which contained a clause limiting its liability to the purchase price of the software - just over £100,000.
The Court of Appeal decided that the limitation was reasonable because the contract had been negotiated between experienced businessmen of equal bargaining power and skill.

N.B. Section 3 covers substantially different performance of a contract as well as breach of contract i.e. where, although there is technically no breach of contract, the manner of performance has become significantly different to the one originally proposed. A pre UCTA case which illustrates this situation is:

Anglo Continental Holidays Ltd v Typaldos Lines Ltd

The claimant had booked Mediterranean holiday cruises on behalf of clients with the defendant. Typaldos substituted an older, inferior ship and a less interesting schedule of events less than a fortnight before the scheduled sailing date. The defendant argued it was not in breach of contract, relying on the following exclusion clause:

"Steamers, sailing dates, rates and itineraries are subject to change without prior notice."

Held: [Pre UCTA], the court decided that such a radical departure from the original contract arrangement could not be covered legitimately by an exclusion.

[Post UCTA, the court would rely on the test of reasonableness as the basis for declaring this clause void.]

N.B. Section 6 UCTA regulates attempts by a seller to disclaim responsibility for breaking the implied duties (relating to the goods) found in the Sale of Goods Act 1979. We shall examine its content after we have looked at the implied duties (see Chapter 10).

Exclusion v Insurance

One of the factors used by the courts to decide the reasonableness of an exclusion or limitation clause is the issue of insurance. Selling defective goods or providing substandard services is clearly a risk of business. As such, two alternatives measures can be taken:

- Obtaining insurance cover and using the policy to pay compensation.
- Using exclusion/limitation clauses in contracts with customers.

The courts will want to establish how costly and difficult it was for the supplier to obtain insurance in the circumstances to help decide whether it was appropriate to opt for disclaimers. If it was not expensive or impracticable to obtain insurance, the court may well conclude that their exclusion clause is void through unreasonableness. Hence it is important for organisations to carefully consider the possibilities of insurance when deciding how to protect themselves against breach of contract and negligence liability.

Force Majeure Clauses – an example of exclusion of liability

The doctrine of frustration of contract is sometimes available to sellers who find that performance of the contract has become either impossible or a commercial nonsense. The doctrine operates where intervening events have taken place which are outside their control. There are however serious risks in relying on the doctrine if problems in performance arise. The courts interpret the doctrine narrowly and strictly and they frequently refuse to accept its use (see later).

It is often considered wiser to introduce into contracts a clause defining in advance the rights and duties of the parties if certain events beyond their control occur, whether or not such events would result, in legal terms, in frustration of the contract. Such a clause is known as a force majeure clause.

Force majeure events are events which are beyond the control of the parties and the expression has been judicially defined in one case to cover "all circumstances beyond the will of man, and which it is not in his power to control, and such force majeure is sufficient to justify the non-execution of a contract." Thus, war, fire, flood, other natural disasters and epidemics can constitute force majeure events as well as the strikes of workmen. However, it is important to realise that, in English law, there is no official definition of the concept and it will be a matter for each individual contract to provide its own definition of what represents force majeure. Sellers' terms and conditions will often include an extensive list of events. Buyers' terms will be narrower and often specifically exclude events such as unofficial strike action.

The effect of the force majeure event is to bring the clause into operation and, in accordance with its terms, the contract is either suspended or discharged by agreement. This prevents claims for breach of contract being brought by the other party.

Although the wording of these clauses varies according to the nature of the contract, most sale of goods agreements contain wording similar to the following:

Strikes, lockouts, labour disturbances, anomalous working conditions, accident to machinery, delays en route, policies or restrictions of governments, including restrictions of export and other licences, or any other contingency whatsoever beyond seller's control, including war, to be sufficient excuse for any delay or non-fulfilment traceable to any of these causes."

In other words, a list of possible force majeure events capable of impeding or preventing performance are provided, together with a 'sweeping-up' phrase designed to ensure that there are no gaps in the formula.

The clause will then provide for the parties to suspend or cancel the contract depending on the circumstances. The parties are usually under a duty to keep each other notified regarding their respective positions.

Benefits of Force Majeure Clauses

- Wider range of events can be included to escape performance than is possible using the doctrine of frustration.
- No need to resort to litigation as would be likely if frustration of contract was being argued.
- More flexible options are possible – suspension of the contract instead of contract always becoming void under the doctrine of frustration.

Force majeure clauses are a variety of exclusion clause and therefore subject to the legal restrictions imposed on such clauses. The most important control is found in section 3 of the Unfair Contract Terms Act 1977 and subjects the clause to the test of reasonableness in the circumstances. As a general rule, most standard force majeure clauses are seen to satisfy this test, the event or events causing the delay or non-performance being outside the control of the seller.

- Exclusion clauses attempt to deny (or limit) liability for such events as breach of contract, negligence and misrepresentation.

- Although freedom of contract *(laissez faire)* restricted legal intervention where abuses occurred, there have always been some curbs on their effectiveness.

- Common law restrictions included the requirement of reasonable notification and the *contra proferentem* rule of interpretation in cases of ambiguity.
- The Unfair Contract Terms Act (UCTA) 1977 introduced far more extensive restrictions.

- Some exclusions are banned by UCTA e.g. death or injury caused by negligence.

- The test of reasonableness has become the basis of regulation in most situations, with a presumption against validity.

- A non-exhaustive list of criteria to help decide reasonableness is contained in UCTA.

- Force majeure clauses strengthen the position of the supplier (and occasionally the buyer) in providing a longer list of events entitling suspension and/or cancellation of the contract.

- Force majeure clauses are a variety of exclusion and therefore subject to the test of reasonableness set out in UCTA 1977 (section 3).

Chapter Nine
Discharge of Contract

Contracts can be discharged in one of four ways:
1. Performance
2. Agreement
3. Frustration
4. Breach

1. Performance

The traditional common law approach was to demand exact and total compliance with what had been promised before payment could be claimed. This was certainly the case with what are called 'entire' agreements.

Cutter v Powell

Cutter, a seaman, signed on to crew a ship from Jamaica to Liverpool at a wage of £31 10s. After almost two months as a member of the crew and 19 days before the ship reached Liverpool, Cutter died. His widow claimed a proportion of his wages as a *quantum meruit*.
Held: The contract was entire and, as Cutter had only partially performed his obligation, he (and, therefore, his widow) was entitled to nothing.

The position is different with 'divisible' contracts, such as ones where stage payments are an entitlement at the completion of each identified stage of the work. Building contracts are usually based on such arrangements.

Exceptions to the entire contracts rule:
1. Substantial performance
2. Acceptance of partial performance
3. Prevention of performance by the other party

• **The doctrine of substantial performance**

Where an entire contract has been substantially performed, the·claimant may claim the agreed price for the work, less an amount which represents the incomplete or defective part.

Hoenig v Isaacs

The defendant engaged the claimant as an interior decorator. The work involved the decoration of a flat combined with provision of suitable furniture, the price being £750. Some payments were made as work progressed, but when asked to pay the remaining balance of £450, he paid only £150. He argued that the work had been performed incompetently. The work was independently assessed and it was found that there were defects to a wardrobe and a bookcase which would require about £55 to put right.

Held: the contract had been substantially performed and the decorator was therefore awarded the balance of the price, less the amount needed to put the defects right.

- **Acceptance of partial performance**

If one party shows he is willing to accept partial performance, the other party can claim for the appropriate proportion of the contract price. Under the Sale of Goods Act 1979, a buyer can accept a short delivery of goods if he chooses. He is then required to pay on a pro rata basis for what has been delivered (section 30).

If, however, the innocent party had no choice but to accept partial performance, this principle does not apply:

Sumptor v Hedges *Exception of an exception*

A building contractor agreed to do work on the defendant's land for a lump sum of £565. Before the work was finished, the contractor told the defendant that he had run out of funds and could not, therefore, complete the work. The defendant completed the work using materials which the contractor had left on site. The claimant now sued for payment in respect of the work he had done and the materials which he had supplied.

Held: The contractor was not entitled to payment for the work done, because the defendant had not accepted partial performance: since the building was on his land, he had no choice in the matter. However, the contractor was entitled to payment for the materials which he had supplied.

- **Prevention of performance by the other party**

When performance is prevented by the wrongful act of the other party, the innocent party is entitled to payment for what he has done under the contract.

Planche v Colburn

The claimant agreed to write a book (one of a series of books) for the defendant for £100. Planche started work but Colburn decided not to go ahead with the series. He also refused to pay him for the work already done, arguing that he had not completed the work.
Held: The claimant was entitled to £50 in damages since it was the default of the defendant which had caused Planche to give up the work.

2. Agreement of Breach

The parties are able to terminate a contract by mutual agreement. This can be achieved by express provision within the original contract terms. This could allow for termination by notice at any time. It could specify termination at the end of a specified period. In the absence of such contractual provision, the common law allows the two parties to discharge themselves from the contract by mutual agreement. The complication with such an arrangement is that the rules of consideration require that both parties are seen to provide some new consideration in order to achieve this result.

In many cases this is seen to be satisfied by the two parties releasing themselves from any further obligations under the contract – each providing the other with a new benefit. This is not so easy where one of the parties has already performed all his obligations and the other party has remaining commitments. There are technical ways around this problem involving such concepts as promissory estoppel and the doctrine of waiver.

3. Frustration of Contract

Until the last century, the obligation to perform contract was absolute. If it became physically impossible for a party to perform his side of the bargain, he nevertheless had to pay damages for breach, and if external events took away the whole purpose of the contract without the fault of either party, the parties still had to continue with the agreement.

Starting with the case of Taylor v Caldwell (1863) the courts have developed the doctrine of frustration of contract. If some event occurs, for which neither party is responsible and which makes total nonsense of the original agreement, then the contract will be discharged by frustration. A radical change in circumstances can sometimes, therefore, be pleaded by a party as a valid excuse for not performing his side of the bargain. This doctrine must be approached with caution, however, because the courts have understandably been reluctant to accept anything but the most fundamental events. The following are the main examples:

- **Subsequent physical impossibility**

This will occur where, after the contract was made, it becomes physically impossible or impracticable to perform it.

Taylor v Caldwell

A music hall hired for a series of concerts was burnt down before the date for the first performance. This was held to frustrate the contract, because there was no longer any hall to hire. The hirer, therefore, no longer had to pay.
[If it were already impossible when the contract was made (because the subject matter had already been destroyed), the agreement would be void through fundamental mistake from the outset.]
[However, a contract will not be frustrated if the goods that have been destroyed can be obtained by the seller from other sources in time for them to be delivered to the buyer.]

Robinson v Davison

A pianist, who was engaged to give a concert on a specified, became ill and was incapable of appearing. It was held that this frustrated the contract – the personal nature of this agreement was key to this decision. Engaging another pianist would not have been an appropriate solution.

- **Subsequent illegality**

This will occur where, after the contract was made, a change in the law or in the circumstances renders it illegal to perform the agreement.

Avery v Bowden

The contract to load a cargo at Odessa was eventually discharged by the outbreak of the Crimean War, which made it illegal to trade with the enemy.

- **Basis of the contract removed**

The contract may be frustrated where both parties made it on the basis of a future event that does not take place.

Chandler v Webster

The contract was for the hire of a room in Pall Mall for the day of Edward VII's coronation procession. The rent was over £140, because the procession would pass directly beneath the window. Unfortunately the coronation was postponed when the King became ill. This was held to frustrate the contract. The entire basis of the contract had been removed.

- **Frustration of the commercial purpose of the contract**

A change may occur which makes a total nonsense of what was originally agreed, so that what the parties would have to perform bears no relation to what was originally intended. This change must be radical; an event that merely makes it more difficult or expensive for a party to perform the contract will be no excuse. It is rare for a contract to be frustrated on this ground.

Metropolitan Water Board v Dick, Kerr & Co.

A firm of contractors agreed in 1914 to build a reservoir. In 1916, under wartime emergency powers, the government requisitioned the plant for the war effort. This was held to frustrate the contract. Although it might eventually be possible to start work again after the war, the enforced hold-up for an indefinite period made nonsense of the contract.

c.f. Davis Contractors v Fareham U.D.C.

Builders contracted with Fareham Council to build 78 houses for a fixed sum within a period of eight months. Owing to lack of adequate supplies of labour it took the builders 22 months to complete the work. The costs of building having risen, the builders claimed that their contract with the council was frustrated and that they were entitled to a higher sum than the contract price (based on a claim for *quantum meruit* – as much as is deserved).
Held: What had taken place was an unexpected turn of events that made the contract more onerous than had been contemplated, but this did not operate to frustrate the contract. If a seller wishes to protect himself against liability to the buyer for delays due to such matters as strikes or non-delivery of raw materials, he should make special provision for this in the contract (See *Force Majeure* Clauses.)

Frustrated Contracts – Consequences

Frustration automatically brings the contract to an end and renders it void. As a general rule, all sums paid by either party in pursuance of the contract before it was discharged are recoverable, and all sums not yet paid cease to be due. However, the **Law Reform (Frustrated Contracts) Act 1943** modifies this in the following ways: If one party has, before the time of discharge, incurred expenses in performing it, the court may in its discretion, allow him to keep or recover all or part of sums already paid or due under the contract.

4.   Breach of Contract

As we have already seen, breach of a condition of the contract entitles the injured party to repudiate the contract. This does not automatically happen – it requires the injured party to notify the other party of his intention to terminate the contract (to accept the other party's repudiation) and to exercise his right to be discharged from the contract.

• **N.B. Anticipatory Breach**

Sometimes, a party is given advance warning of a future breach of contract. The defaulting party indicates his intention to default e.g. fail to deliver the goods, do the work or pay for the goods/services supplied. In this situation, the injured party is entitled to bring a legal claim as soon as they are informed. It does not have to wait until the breach actually takes place.

Hochster v De La Tour

Hochster entered into a contract with the defendant on 12th April under which he would act as a tour guide beginning on 1st June. On 11th May, the defendant informed Hochster that he had changed his mind and the tour was cancelled. On 22nd May, the claimant issued a writ claiming damages for breach of contract. **Held:** The claimant did not have to wait until the actual breach occurred in June. He was entitled to pursue a claim for breach as soon as he became aware that a breach was clearly going to take place.
This is called anticipatory breach of contract. Of course, the injured party may wish to delay such action in the hope that the other party can be persuaded to carry out its obligations. The only risk in doing so arises if a frustrating event occurs in the meantime. The contract would then become void, disallowing any claim for breach.

Avery v Bowden

Avery chartered a ship to Bowden under which the defendant agreed to load the vessel with cargo at Odessa within 45 days. At Odessa, Bowden told the ship's captain that he had no cargo for the ship and advised the ship to depart. The ship

nevertheless remained. Before the 45 days had expired, the Crimean War broke out, frustrating the contract.
Held: The contract was void through frustration. No claim for breach of contract was now possible.

In conclusion:

- Contracts can be discharged by performance, agreement, frustration or acceptance of breach.

- There are a number of exceptions to the general principle that payment can only be claimed for complete performance of the obligations agreed to in the contract.

- The most important exceptions are substantial performance, acceptance of partial performance and prevention of performance by the other party.

- Contracts can be discharged by mutual agreement, provided the requirements of consideration are satisfied.

- The doctrine of frustration of contract excuses performance where subsequent events outside the parties control render it impossible, illegal or a commercial nonsense to expect performance to take place.

- The doctrine is strictly and narrowly interpreted and operates in only a small number of extreme situations.

- These exceptions are subsequent physical impossibility, subsequent illegality, basis of contract removed and frustration of the commercial purpose of the contract.

- Frustrated contracts become void and a number of rules aimed at restoring the original position are set out in the Law Reform (Frustrated Contracts) Act 1943,

- Acceptance of breach enables the injured party to treat the contract as discharged provided it is a breach of condition.

- An injured party can bring an immediate claim where he is given advance notification of a future breach of contract (anticipatory breach).

Chapter Ten

Statutory Protection – Buyers' Rights

- ## Sale of Goods
- ## Supply of Services

Contracts have been increasingly regulated by legislation during the C20 especially in the context of consumer agreements. We now need to examine the rights which have been extended to buyers (commercial as well as consumer) through the incorporation of implied terms into sale of goods contracts and contracts for services (whether for work and materials or for pure services).

The chapter covers the following legal principles and issues:

- Background to Sale of Goods Act 1979 (SOGA) – a *laissez faire* Act.
- Implied duties of a seller under SOGA.
- Cases illustrating infringements of implied duties.
- Changes introduced in 1994.
- Exclusion of implied terms.
- Specific rules relating to delivery to delivery of wrong quantity.
- Instalment deliveries and defective performance.
- Implied duties of a supplier in contracts for services under **Supply of Goods & Services Act 1982**.

Sale of Goods

The most important type of contract (in terms of volume and value) is sale of goods. The law regulating sale of goods is predominantly statutory with the **Sale of Goods Act 1979** forming its core. The 1979 Act has been amended several times to reflect changing commercial practice, most significantly in 1994. This Act is an example of *laissez faire* legislation, which (apart from a few exceptions) does not impose its provisions on the parties to the contract. They are left free to draft their rights and duties and depart from those specified in the Act. The Act can be seen as a "fall-back" code of principles, which applies where the parties have not agreed their position. That is why many of the sections in the Act begin with the expression "Unless otherwise agreed..."

Some of its most important provisions from the point of view of buyers' rights are found in ss. 12-15. These provide a series of obligations imposed on the seller relating to his rights to sell, and the description, quality and fitness of the goods in question. The ability of the seller to exclude liability for infringing these implied duties has been severely constrained since the passing of the **Unfair Contract Terms Act 1979**, in particular, section 6 (see later). As such they represent something of an exception to the liberal, *laissez faire* approach indicated above. The following page contains the main provisions:

Sale of Goods Act 1979

SECTION 12
THE SELLER MUST HAVE THE RIGHT TO SELL (GOOD TITLE)

SECTION 13
WHERE THERE IS A CONTRACT TO SELL GOODS BY DESCRIPTION, THE GOODS MUST CORRESPOND WITH THE DESCRIPTION

SECTION 14(2)
WHERE THE SELLER SELLS GOODS IN THE COURSE OF A BUSINESS, THE GOODS MUST BE OF SATISFACTORY QUALITY

Goods will be of satisfactory quality if they meet the standard that a reasonable person would regard as satisfactory, taking account of any description of the goods, the price if relevant, and all other relevant circumstances.

The quality of goods includes their state and condition, which can include the following:
a) fitness for all the purposes for which goods of the kind in question are commonly supplied;

b) appearance and finish;

c) freedom from minor defects;

d) safety; and

e) durability

SECTION 14(3)
WHERE THE SELLER SELLS IN THE COURSE OF A BUSINESS AND THE
BUYER MAKES KNOWN TO THE SELLER ANY PARTICULAR PURPOSE
FOR WHICH THE GOODS ARE BEING BOUGHT, THE GOODS SUPPLIED
MUST BE REASONABLY FIT FOR THAT PURPOSE

SECTION 15
WHERE GOODS ARE SOLD BY SAMPLE, THE BULK MUST
CORRESPOND

Breach of Contract – Strict Liability

It is important to realise that breach of contract is based on the concept of strict liability. In other words, the injured party does not have to prove that the defendant was to blame or was at fault in order to succeed. It is regarded as a risk of business that firms who break contracts are liable even if they are not responsible for the failure. However, where a firm has been made liable for supplying faulty goods, they in turn can bring a claim against their suppliers for breach of contract

The Implied Conditions – Detail and Cases

Section 12 (Title)

This has been described as the most important obligation of all those imposed on the seller. The entire basis of the contract (and the consideration for the price) is the passing on of ownership to the buyer.

Rowland v Divall

The plaintiff dealer bought a car from the defendant in May. He sold it in July, but in September the police took possession of the vehicle on the ground that it was a stolen car and that the person who had sold it to the defendant had no title to sell it. The plaintiff sued to recover the price that he had paid the defendant for the car. **Held:** He was entitled to succeed as the defendant had been in breach of Section 12.

There are two implied warranties also found in Section 12 relating to the buyer receiving goods without encumbrances and having quiet possession of the goods. This covers such issues as goods being subject to patents and liens.

Section 13 (Description)

"Description" applies to such matters as specification of goods, weight, ingredients and composition). The description has to be in the contract itself, although previous adverts have been held to be relevant in descriptions of the goods. The rule is a strict one and minor discrepancies have given buyers the right to cancel the contract.

Arcos Ltd v Ronaasen & Son

Suppliers agreed to deliver half inch wooden staves for use in building work (there was no margin of tolerance indicated in the agreement). When they arrived, the purchaser claimed to reject them on the ground that they did not correspond with the description in that some were slightly above and some were slightly below the required width.

Held: They were entitled to reject (even though all would have been usable by the purchaser without any disadvantage).

Re Moore & Landauer

A contract was agreed for the sale of canned fruit to be packed in cases, each case to contain 30 tins. On delivery about half of the cases contained 24 tins. The total delivered was however correct.

Held: The buyer was able to reject the entire consignment (again, even though no commercial disadvantage had been sustained by the purchaser).

More recently a less rigorous approach has been evident where minor infringements have been seen as entitling the buyer only to claim damages (as if a warranty had been broken instead). Since 1994, Section 15(A) of the Act now requires trade buyers to treat minor breaches of any of the implied conditions as breach of warranties. The standard is what a reasonable person would judge to be minor. Consumers can still reject for minor infringements.

The section only applies if the sale involved is "by description". This applies to almost all sales e.g. all orders for unascertained or future goods, and even sales of identified goods selected by customers in shops. Possible the only situation where it dies not apply is where the seller shows the buyer the goods in question and immediately states that they are to be sold "just as they are, with no guarantees attached". This may then disconnect the goods from any "description" that would otherwise attach to them. The buyer must have relied on the description before the section applies.

Harlingdon & Leinster Enterprises Ltd v Christopher Hull Fine Art Ltd

The defendant art dealer had been asked to sell two paintings which had been described in an auction catalogue as being painted by Gabrielle Munter, an important German Expressionist. The dealer was not an expert in this school of painting. He contacted the plaintiffs who were specialists in this field. Having looked at the painting they decided to buy one of the paintings for £6000. This decision was taken despite the defendant having made clear that he did not know much about the paintings and that he was not an expert in that field. The painting was in fact a forgery and the plaintiff claimed breach of Section 13 to obtain repayment of the purchase price.

Held: Their action must fail. There had not been a sale by description. The buyers were basing their decision on their own inspection of the painting and not on any statements as to origin by the dealer.

Section 14 (2) (Satisfactory Quality)

The sale must be in the course of a business. This is not limited to dealers in the goods in question but extends to any organisation which finds itself selling some goods in the course of its operations e.g. car rental firm selling its existing stock to buy new; professional firms selling office equipment to buy new. Public sector organisations such as local councils can therefore also sell in the course of a business in this situation.

What is "satisfactory quality"? The standard is what a reasonable person would regard as satisfactory in the circumstances. [Section 14(2)(A)] This should take into account such issues as the price paid, whether the goods are new or second hand, and any description applied to them. The new consumer focus has introduced new criteria in deciding what is satisfactory - fitness for purpose (a previous one); appearance, freedom from minor defects, safety and durability [Section 14(2) (B)].

The section does not apply to defects which have been specifically brought to the buyer's attention before the contract is concluded. It also does not apply to obvious defects which should have been detected by the buyer if he has had the opportunity to examine the goods prior to sale.

Wilson v Rickett, Cockerell & Co.

The plaintiff and her husband sued the defendant coal merchants for damage to their dining room caused by an explosion in the firegrate. This was caused by a detonator having been admixed in the coalite purchased.

Held: This was a breach of satisfactory quality.

The standard need not be significantly demanding, particularly in the context of second hand goods, and to a smaller extent, commercial (as against consumer) contracts.

Cehave NV v Bremer Handelsgesellschaft mbH (The Hansa Nord Case)

A cargo of citrus pulp pellets which had been damaged through overheating whilst in transit was held to be of "merchantable quality" (the pre-1994 equivalent of satisfactory quality). The court accepted that the goods were far from perfect. However, they had remained saleable for the purpose for which they could normally be bought. The pellets were bought to be fed to cattle and were still capable of fulfilling this purpose. It would seem the Court took the view that the reasonable commercial buyer would have considered obtaining a discount as a more appropriate approach rather than rejecting the consignment.

Section 14 (3) (Fitness for Purpose)

As with the previous condition, this only applies if the sale is in the course of a business. In addition it will only apply if the buyer has made known to the seller the particular purpose for which the goods are to be used. This can be done expressly (through discussion etc.) or by implication (where the goods have only one normal use - food, clothing, cars, washing machines etc.). It becomes important to inform the seller of special uses and seek reliance on his judgement where the goods can be used in a range of situations. (e.g. needing a car which will be capable of being used on a hill farm in muddy conditions).

Frost v Aylesbury Dairy Co.

The defendant milk dealers supplied the plaintiff with milk for himself and his family. On one occasion, the milk contained typhoid bacteria from which his wife contracted typhoid and died. The husband brought a claim for breach of Section 14(3).
Held: The claim was successful. It was irrelevant that the defendants had not been negligent. Breach of contract is based on strict liability.

Section 15 (Sample)

This is less extensive in application. It only applies when it is customary for a sample to be shown prior to a contract being agreed. Examples in consumer sales include contracts for the sale of carpets, furnishings (curtains etc.) and in some situations, sale of paint. In the trade context, sale of bulk chemicals will often be preceded by a sample. Compliance with the sample is strict. However, remember that since 1994, trade buyers may have to treat minor infringements as a breach of warranty only, depriving them of any right to refuse delivery and cancel the contract.

Godley v Perry

The owner of a toy shop sold a plastic toy catapult to a six year-old boy. The catapult broke during normal use and injured the boy in the eye. After paying damages to the boy (breach of satisfactory quality and fitness for purpose) the shop owner brought a claim for breach of contract against his supplier. Prior to purchasing the catapults the shop owner had been shown a sample.
Held: In addition to breach of quality and fitness, Section 15 had also been infringed – the bulk not corresponding to the sample in terms of quality.

Sale and Supply of Goods Act 1994

This Act made significant modifications to the 1979 Act, the main examples of which are outlined below. It is important to understand that the 1994 Act did not in any way 'replace' the earlier one. It simply altered its provisions so that new copies of the 1979 Act contain amended sections. It is still the 1979 Act that forms the basis of sale of goods law in the UK.

Replacement of "Merchantable Quality"

One of the recommendations of the Law Commission was that there should be changes to section 14(2) of the **Sale of Goods Act 1979 (SOGA)** which states that where the seller sells goods in the course of a business there is an implied term that the goods supplied shall be of merchantable quality. This has now been replaced by an expanded text which sets a rather higher standard by the substitution of the phrase "satisfactory quality". The new Act prescribes that the quality of goods shall include their state and condition and the following other matters where appropriate:

a)   Fitness for all the purposes for which goods of the kind in question are commonly supplied.
b)   Appearance and finish.
c)   Freedom from minor defects.
d)   Safety.
e)   Durability.

The 1994 Act also makes some minor amendments as compared with the former definition of merchantable quality. It prescribes that goods are of satisfactory quality if they meet the standard that a reasonable person would regard as satisfactory, taking account of any description of the goods, the price if relevant and all other relevant circumstances. It retains the present exclusions in respect of matters making the quality of goods unsatisfactory which are drawn to the buyer's attention before the contract is made or which ought to have been revealed by a buyer's examination of the goods or a sample of them.

Virtually the same definition of "satisfactory quality" is imported into the implied terms where goods are supplied on hire or hire purchase or the other circumstances mentioned earlier.

Acceptance and Rejection

Another area of the law that has given rise to problems is the question whether a buyer of goods which turn out to be unsatisfactory has a right to reject them. The Act makes two main changes here.

Where goods are delivered to the buyer and he has not previously examined them, he will in future not be deemed to have accepted them until he has a reasonable opportunity of examining them to ascertain whether they are in conformity with the contract and, where appropriate, with any sample. Furthermore, where the buyer deals as consumer, he will not lose his right to examine the goods by agreement, waiver or otherwise.

The Sale of Goods Act 1979 provides that the buyer is deemed to have accepted goods when after the lapse of reasonable time he retains the goods without intimating that he has rejected them. This provision is retained but in addition the buyer is not deemed to have accepted the goods merely because he asks for or agrees to their repair by or under an arrangement with the seller or he delivers the goods to another under a sub-sale. In part this reflects case law since 1979.

Right of Partial Rejection

The Act inserts a new section in the SOGA 1979 (but not in the other Acts modified) giving the buyer a right to reject some of the goods where these are defective and accept the rest.

Trivial Breaches - Commercial Buyer

The Act provides that where a buyer would have the right to reject goods because of a breach of the implied terms as to description, quality or fitness but the breach is so slight that it would be unreasonable for the buyer to reject the goods, then if the buyer does not "deal as consumer" the breach shall not be treated as a breach of

condition (giving a right to reject) but may be treated as a breach of warranty (giving rise to a claim for damages). A similar provision applies to hire purchase.
A further clause provides that where a seller delivers a quantity of goods either slightly larger of slightly less than the quantity contracted for, a commercial buyer shall not have the right to reject the whole quantity although he could reject any minor excess. There are no similar clauses in respect of hire purchase, hire or other supplies of goods.

Exclusion of implied conditions

Can the seller deny liability for breaking any of the obligations contained in sections 12-15? The **Unfair Contract Terms Act 1977** deals with this issue in section 6:

Section 6 (Liability for breach of ss 12-15 Sale of Goods Act 1979)

S. 12	(Title)	Can never be excluded (void)
Ss 13-15	(Description Satisfactory Quality Fitness for Purpose Sample)	Depends type of sale

Consumer Sales

Where the seller is selling goods in the course of a business (and the goods are of a type normally sold in this situation) and the buyer is purchasing the goods for personal and private use.

None of the above implied conditions can be excluded in consumer sales (void).

Non-Consumer Sales

Basically contracts made between two businesses. Both seller and buyer are making the contract in the course of their businesses.

Ss. 13 - 15 cannot be excluded by the seller unless proved to be fair and reasonable in the circumstances.

[See earlier factors for deciding fairness and reasonableness]

Notices in shops suggesting that customers have no rights to complain constitute a criminal offence apart from being void.

> e.g.   "No refunds or exchanges allowed".

Section 7 of the Unfair Contract Terms Act 1977 contains a similar provision relating to the implied terms in the Supply of Goods & Services Act 1982. Sections 2-5 contain identical obligations on the supplier (right to sell, description, satisfactory quality, fitness for purpose, sample). The same approach as seen in Section 6 is followed in Section 7. (For details of Sections 2-5, see next page.)

Sale of Goods - Delivery of Wrong Quantity

Where the wrong quantity is delivered, there is a breach of Section 13 SOGA 1979 – there is a discrepancy between the description of the goods (which includes the quantity involved) and the actual goods supplied. The rights of the buyer are then found in s.30 as amended. The following rules apply:

- If less than contract quantity – buyer can reject or accept and pay at contract rate.

- If more than contract quantity – buyer can accept the whole (and pay for surplus at contract rate) or reject the surplus and accept the proper quantity.

- If in addition to contract goods, goods of a different description are delivered – buyer can reject all the consignment or just the non-contract ones.

- The buyer cannot accept goods of a type not contracted for except under a new contract.

Instalment Deliveries and Defective Performance

Whilst on the theme of delivery and breach it may be useful to consider the position of instalment deliveries. Where a contract consists of a series of instalment deliveries the question can arise whether the buyer can terminate the remainder of the contract when a breach of contract has occurred e.g. sub-standard goods have been delivered, or non-delivery of a consignment.

In the case of substandard goods or goods which are not of correct specification it is clearly within the rights of the buyer to reject that particular delivery. But can he cancel the remaining deliveries? According to tests laid down in the **Maple Flock case** (see below), two questions are central to this issue:

1. **How serious is the breach in comparison to the contract as a whole?**
2. **How likely is it that the breach is likely to be repeated in the future?**

Munro & Co. v Meyer

The first half of a series of instalments were discovered to be of substandard quality.   *✱ contaminated goods - all turned out to*
Held: The buyer was entitled to repudiate the contract.   *be contaminated*

Maple Flock Ltd. v Universal Furniture Products Ltd.

A single instalment (the sixteenth out of a total of 75) consisted of substandard goods. The buyer repudiated the contract.   *over the top - was a*
Held: Breach of contract by the buyer.   *one-off breech.*

A buyer cannot be compelled to take delivery by instalments unless this was agreed in the contract.

Contracts for Services

These contracts (and contracts for personal services) are governed by the **Supply of Goods and Services Act 1982.**

Part 1 of the Supply of Goods and Services Act relates to "contracts for the transfer of property in goods" i.e. contracts for work and materials. The supply of goods is governed by Part 1 of the 1982 Act and the services supplied (or the work element) are governed by Part II of the Act.

Contracts of exchange or barter, hire, rental or leasing are governed by Part 1, while contracts for services only, are governed by Part II.

In Part 1 of the Act, Sections 2-5 provide for statutory implied terms on the part of the seller similar to those in S.12-15 of the Sale of Goods Act 1979. In other words:

-      The supplier must have the right to sell   s.2
-      The goods must correspond with description   s.3
-      The goods must be of satisfactory quality   s.4(1)
-      The goods must be fit for the purpose intended   s.4(2)
-      The goods must correspond with sample   s.5

The Supply of Goods and Services Act 1982 includes a number of implied terms relating specifically to services.

Section 13

There is an implied term that where the supplier is acting in the course of a business, the service will be carried out with reasonable care and skill. This requires the contractor to perform the work to a level that is the average, normal level for the type of contractor involved – the market norm if you like. The expected level of skill will therefore vary depending on the type of contractor involved. Mistakes can be made without necessarily infringing this implied duty, provided they are of a sort that would be made by most competent contractors engaged in the work involved. However, when the seriousness of the defective performance is of a higher order, or the frequency of mistakes is greater than the norm, we could well be looking at a breach of s.13. Evidence of the industry norm would need to be provided to the court to support the claim or defence in the case.

Section 14

There is an implied term that where the supplier is acting in the course of a business and the time for the service to be carried out is not fixed by the contract or determined by the course of dealings between the parties, the supplier shall carry out the contract within a *reasonable time*.

Usually, the contract will have dealt with time for performance (delivery, payment etc.). If time has been made of the essence, it is treated as a condition of the contract and entitles the injured party to cancel the contract e.g. for late delivery. Where it has not been made clear, it will depend on the individual circumstances whether it will be a condition, although the courts will often find that it is so. There is a presumption that time for payment is not a condition though. It is possible to make time for delivery of the essence even where it was not made explicit at the time when the contract was first agreed. This is done by giving notice to the supplier that time is now to be regarded as of the essence. Subject to the period of time for delivery being reasonable, it will now be treated as a condition of the contract.

Rickards (Charles) v Oppenheim

C agreed to sell to O a Rolls Royce chassis with a body built on it, delivery to be made by March 20. It was not delivered then. O pressed for delivery and finally said in June that he would not accept delivery after July 25. Delivery was not made then and O bought another car. Delivery was offered in October but O refused it. C sued for the price.

Held: The action failed. O had waived the original time for delivery but was entitled, on giving reasonable notice, to make time of the essence of the contract.

Section 15

There is an implied term that where the consideration is not determined by a contract or by the course of dealings between the parties, the party contracting with the supplier shall pay a *reasonable price*. There is a general presumption that estimates are not legally binding whereas quotations are legally binding. However, the court would always look at the individual circumstances of each case and not rely on the heading used.

In conclusion:

- Two Acts imply terms into contracts for sale of goods and provision of services – the **Sale of Goods Act (SOGA) 1979** and the **Supply of Goods & Services Act (SGSA) 1982**.

- SOGA 1979 is an example of *laissez faire* legislation – most of its 'rules' can be modified by contractual provision ("unless otherwise agreed").

- SOGA 1979 creates 5 important implied duties on the seller relating to the goods – the right to sell (title), correspondence with description, satisfactory quality, fitness for purpose and correspondence with sample.

- SOGA 1979 has been amended on several occasions (especially in 1994).

- Exclusion of the implied duties is impossible in consumer sales, but still possible in non-consumer sales where it is subject to the test of reasonableness as set out in UCTA 1979 (title can never be excluded though).

- SGSA 1982 (Part One) contains a similar set of implied duties relating to materials supplied under a contract for work and materials or hire; Part Two contains a number of implied duties relating to competency, time and price.

- Delivery of the wrong quantity is a breach of section 13 SOGA 1979 (description) and subject to various rights made available to the buyer in Section 30.

- The ability of the injured party to terminate the rest of an instalment delivery contract for breach of a single instalment (or several) depends on the relative seriousness of the breach compared with the entire contract and the likelihood of repetition.

Chapter Eleven

Transfer of Property

The **Sale of Goods Act 1979** uses the expression 'property' to denote ownership of the goods – the seller "agreeing to transfer the property in goods to the buyer in return for a money consideration called the price." The concept of ownership is expressed as 'title' in other parts of the Act. 'Title' tends to be used more when the central issue is the validity of ownership – whether good title or defective title has passed to the buyer.

The SOGA 1979 provides a set of rules relating to when ownership passes from seller to buyer. Once again, the laissez faire approach of the Act is evident by allowing the parties to make their own arrangements, the statutory rules being a fall-back position if it is not possible to establish the parties' intentions.

The chapter covers the following principles and rules:

- Reasons why important to know when property passes from seller to buyer.
- Classification of goods – specific and unascertained.
- Rules deciding when property passes.
- Cases illustrating rules in operation.

The essence of a sale of goods is the passing of ownership from the seller to the buyer. It is important to know not only whether ownership ('property') has transferred but also when it has passed for a number of reasons:

1) It affects the question of **risk** (who bears the loss for accidents?)
Under s.20 (1) SGA 1979, risk passes with ownership (unless otherwise agreed). This has important implications for insurance purposes. Both parties will wish to minimise the costs of insurance policies and will therefore only insure for the time they are at risk i.e. hold ownership of the goods. This transition of ownership and risk at the same time can be modified by agreement however ('Unless otherwise agreed') e.g. by having a retention of title clause delaying transfer of ownership until payment has been made. The seller will often insist that risk passes upon delivery.

N.B. The party in possession is liable for damage caused by his own negligence – even if ownership belongs to the other party. The goods are being held in a bailee capacity, and as bailee, a duty to take reasonable care of the goods exists.

2)   It affects the **rights of the liquidator** in insolvency proceedings – he cannot sell goods which are not owned by the insolvent company.

When does ownership transfer?

This depends on which category of goods is involved. Are they specific, ascertained goods or unascertained goods?

Specific Goods
Goods which have been identified and agreed upon at the time of the sale. Examples include buying second-hand vehicles and purchasing food, clothes etc in high street shops and supermarkets.

Unascertained Goods
Goods described but not yet identified at the time of sale. Examples include ordering goods by invoice (quantity and specification indicated), purchase of new vehicles and ordering goods by mail order.

Relevant Sections

S.16 states that property in unascertained goods cannot pass until goods of the correct description are ascertained (see s.18 rule 5 below).

S.17 states that property in specific, ascertained goods passes according to the intentions of the parties – judged by the wording of the contract and the circumstances of the case.

The contract may remain silent on the matter though. Then a series of rules found in s.18 decide the outcome.

Section 18

Rule 1 (Specific, ascertained goods in a deliverable state)

In an unconditional contract for the sale of specific goods, in a deliverable state, property passes when the contract is made (even if the time for payment and/or delivery is postponed).

The goods must be 'in a deliverable state'. This is defined in s.62 as "when they are in such a state that the buyer would under the contract be bound to take delivery of them."

Rule 2 (Specific, ascertained goods not in a deliverable state)

If the seller is bound to do something to put the specific goods into a deliverable state, property passes when the action is taken and the buyer notified.

Rule 3 (specific, ascertained goods in a deliverable state but which need to be weighed, measured or tested by the seller to establish the price.)

Property will pass when the seller has weighed, measured etc. the goods and notified the buyer.

Rule 4 (specific, ascertained goods sent on approval or sale or return)

Here, property passes:

a)   when the buyer approves the transaction either by telling the seller, or doing any other act which adopts the transaction, or,

b)   when the buyer, without giving notice of rejection, retains the goods for the agreed time, or if no time has been agreed, for a reasonable time.

Rule 5 (unascertained or future goods)

In a contract for the sale of unascertained or future goods identifiable by description, property passes when goods of the correct description in a deliverable state are unconditionally appropriated to the contract by one party with the consent of the other party. Such consent may be express or implied, and may be given either before or after the appropriation is made. On a self-service garage forecourt petrol is pumped by the customer (the buyer) with the consent of the seller. Where the forecourt is attended the seller will make the unconditional appropriation with the consent of the buyer.

The goods must be unconditionally appropriated to the contract. This means irrevocably attached to that contract so that they cannot be use for any other transaction.

Federspiel (Carlos) v Charles Twigg & Co.

F., a Costa Rican company, bought from T., an English company, 85 bicycles under a contract providing that T. should ship them in June. F. paid the purchase price in advance. In July a receiver was appointed for T. and all the assets, including the bicycles, were to be sold in the liquidation. F. alleged that as the bicycles had been duly packed into cases, marked with their name, were registered for consignment, and shipping space was reserved for them in a named ship, this setting aside of the goods amounted to an unconditional appropriation and that property had therefore passed to them.

Held: The intention of the parties was that the property should pass on shipment. There had not yet been an unconditional appropriation. The bicycles could still be unpacked and used in other contracts.

The unconditional appropriation normally takes place on delivery. It could take place earlier though e.g. if the goods have been handed over to an independent carrier without reserving the right of disposal.

The goods must already be in a deliverable state:

Phillip Head & Sons v Showfronts

A buyer ordered carpeting which was to be laid by the house furnishers selling it. The carpets were delivered but were stolen before they could be laid.

Held: The house furnishers must bear the loss because property had not passed to the buyer. The carpeting was not in a 'deliverable state' until it had been laid and so goods in a deliverable state had not been unconditionally appropriated to the contract.

Retention of Title Clauses (RoT)

During periods when market conditions are difficult and insolvencies more common place, contractors will seek to put themselves in a stronger position than they might otherwise enjoy in reliance upon the Sale of Goods Act 1979. The most common method of achieving this stronger protection is through the use of clauses which allow the contractor to deliver goods but which seek to delay the passing of title from the date of delivery to the date upon which payment for the goods is received by the contractor. Some will go further, reserving title not only until the specific goods have been paid for, but until goods delivered under other contracts have also been paid for. Essentially, such clauses are referred to as **"reservation of title"** clauses or **"Romalpa"** clauses after the original case in which they were considered in the UK.

The main advantage or retaining title is to create greater security in the event of a purchaser going insolvent between receipt of the goods but prior to paying for them. Although a RoT clause can, in some circumstances, significantly assist a supplier, the degree of protection they afford is frequently misunderstood, with unfortunate consequences for the supplier.

The advantage of an RoT clause is best illustrated by the important decision in:

Aluminium Industrie Vaassen BV v Romalpa Aluminium Ltd ("Romalpa")

AIV sold aluminium to Romalpa, the conditions of sale containing a RoT clause, reserving title until the aluminium had been paid for. Romalpa sold the aluminium but, before it could pay AIV, a Receiver was appointed. AIV claimed that as the aluminium belonged to them and as the proceeds of the sale from the aluminium were identifiable, they could trace their interest into the proceeds of sale and were entitled to these proceeds. The Court of Appeal upheld AIV's claim.

It was largely as a result of this case and the resulting publicity it received that the use of RoT clauses increased dramatically, as suppliers saw them as a panacea to deal with the problems otherwise caused by the purchaser's insolvency. However, RoT clauses have been considered on a number of occasions by the courts and the protection they afford is not necessarily as broad as might at first appear to be the case.

Firstly, the goods which are the subject of the RoT clause must be tangible. The clause will no longer bite if the goods have ceased to exist as a separate and distinct item. A good example is the case of:

Borden (UK) Ltd v Scottish Timber Products Ltd

Scottish Timber supplied resin which was used by Borden to manufacture chipboard, which was then sold. The resin was supplied on a RoT clause and Borden went into liquidation before Scottish Timber had been paid for the resin. Scottish Timber claimed that their interest in the resin could be traced into the chipboard and then into the proceeds of sale of the chipboard.

The Court of Appeal held that Scottish Timber were not entitled to trace their interest into the proceeds of sale. The resin ceased to have any separated identity once incorporated into the chipboard and the reservation of title clause could not be effective.

Similarly, if the goods are of the 'stand alone' type, a RoT clause may not be fully effective if quantities of goods have been supplied, some of which have been paid for, whilst others have not, and the supplier is unable to demonstrate which particular ones are subject to the RoT clause e.g. by reference to batch numbers, serial numbers or the like on invoices and which have not been paid for.

How effective can RoT clauses be in recovering the proceeds of sale of the goods in question? Where such clauses are used, a Liquidator or Receiver will seek to argue that the RoT clause operates as a floating charge over the assets of the purchaser and is therefore void unless it is registered at Companies House in accordance with the requirements of s. 396 of the Companies Act 1985. This section requires mortgages, floating charges and charges on any goods or of any interest in the goods to be registered. If the RoT clause seeks to give the supplier an entitlement in the proceeds of the sale of the goods, the clause may be void through lack of registration, unless it succeeds in creating a legal right to trace the interest in the goods into the proceeds of sale.

To achieve this, it would be necessary to require the purchaser to hold the goods in a fiduciary capacity, the proceeds of sale would need to be kept in a distinct and separate account and there might need to be an entitlement to payment on delivery, with the supplier having a discretion not to enforce payment. RoT clauses should be seen as an addition to well defined payment terms supported by strong credit control measures and appropriate action to recover outstanding monies where necessary.

Transfer of Property (Ownership)

Section 18 Rules

Rule I
Where there is an unconditional contract for the sale of specific goods, in a deliverable state, the property in the goods passes to the buyer when the contract is made, and it is immaterial whether the time for payment or the time of delivery, or both, is postponed.

Rule 2
Where there is a contract for the sale of specific goods and the seller is bound to do something to the goods, for the purpose of putting them into a deliverable state, the property does not pass until such thing is done, and the buyer has notice thereof.

Rule 3
Where there is a contract for the sale of specific goods in a deliverable state, but the seller is bound to weigh, measure, test, or do some other act to the goods to establish the price, the property does not pass until such act is done and the buyer has notice thereof.

Rule 4

When goods are delivered to the buyer on approval or "on sale or return" or other similar terms the property therein passes to the buyer:

(a)   when he signifies his approval or acceptance to the seller or does some other act adopting the transaction:

(b)   if he retains the goods without giving notice of rejection, then, if a time has been fixed for the return of the goods, on the expiration of such time, and, if no time has been fixed, on the expiration of a reasonable time.

Transfer of Property

Section 18 Rules (Continued)

Rule 5

Where there is a contract for the sale of unascertained or future goods by description, and goods of that description and in a deliverable state are unconditionally appropriated to the contract, either by the seller with the assent of the buyer, or by the buyer with the assent of the seller, the property in the goods thereupon passes to the buyer.

In conclusion:

•   Transfer of property means transfer of ownership.

•   It is important to know when ownership passes for reasons of risk (who bears the loss of accidental damage?) and liquidator's rights in the event of insolvency.

•   It is necessary to know which category of goods is involved to establish the relevant rules governing transfer of ownership – are they specific goods or unascertained goods?

•   Specific goods are ones which have been identified and agreed upon at the time of contract –it is known precisely which goods are to be used for that contract; unascertained goods are described (specification, quantity etc.) but not yet identified.

•   If the contract is silent on the matter, property in specific goods passes according to Rules 1- 4 in section 18 SOGA 1979.

•   Property in unascertained goods passes according to section 18 Rule 5.

Chapter Twelve

Transfer of Title

The SOGA 1979 provides a set of rules governing situations where the seller did not have the right to sell the goods. Normally the original owner is protected by the so-called *Nemo Dat* Doctrine which basically states that you cannot pass on a better title than the one you possess yourself. However, in order to encourage commerce, the Act has created a number of exceptions where protection is given to the innocent buyer who will be able to keep the goods and resist claims for repossession by the original owner.

The chapter covers:

*   The basic position – *Nemo Dat* Doctrine.
*   Exceptions.
*   Cases illustrating exceptions.

Problems may arise where the seller did not have the right to sell the goods that have been purchased in good faith by an innocent buyer. Examples include stolen goods, goods obtained by deception and goods in the possession of someone who has no authority to sell. One of two innocent parties will have to lose out – either the original owner or the innocent third party purchaser.

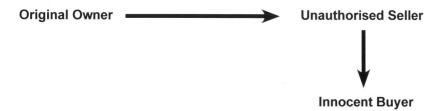

Original Owner ──────────────▶ **Unauthorised Seller**

Innocent Buyer

The general rule is that property rights will be protected and therefore the original owner will be able to recover the goods from the third party purchaser. The doctrine known as *'Nemo Dat Quod Non Habet'* is applied ('No-one can give a better title than the one they themselves possess').

This is stated in s.21 (1) SGA 1979 All that the buyer can do here is to bring an action for breach of contract against the seller (breach of s.12 Sale of Goods Act 1979 – seller must have the right to sell). The classic example of nemo dat in operation is where stolen goods are subsequently sold to an innocent buyer. The latter receives no protection and the goods can be repossessed by the original owner. However, this doctrine has been the subject of a large number of exceptions intended to protect buyers and encourage commerce. The following are the most important examples:

- Estoppel.
- Sale by a mercantile agent.
- Sale under a voidable title.
- Sale by a seller in possession.
- Sale by a buyer in possession.
- Sale of a motor vehicle on hire purchase.

Estoppel (s.21(1))

If the seller or buyer, by his conduct, makes the other party believe that a certain fact is true, and the other party alters his position, then he will later be denied (estopped) from saying that the fact is untrue. For example, this has arisen where a party has, for complicated reasons involving refinancing deals, signed a statement that their own property belongs to someone else and then ends up 'buying back' their own property. They may be estopped from denying the statement they made falsely about the ownership of the property **(Eastern Distributors Ltd v Goldring).**

The doctrine essentially deprives a person of their normal legal rights because of their irresponsible behaviour. They have allowed a false impression to be gained by another person who will suffer as a result if the doctrine were not applied. An early example **(Pickard v Sears)** involved a farmer who allowed a neighbour to borrow some of his equipment. The neighbour proceeded to enter negotiations with a third party for its sale. Despite discovering these negotiations, the farmer made no attempt to intervene. It was only after the third party had bought the equipment that the farmer insisted on its return. The court held that the farmer would be estopped from claiming his normal rights (repossession as the true owner) because of his irresponsible behaviour.

To be claimed successfully, estoppel can only be raised against a person who had actual knowledge of the facts and actually agreed to them knowing that a third party may rely on the 'apparent authority'. Clearly, misrepresentation is always involved with the doctrine.

Sale by a mercantile agent (s.2 Factors Act 1889)

A mercantile agent is one 'having in the customary course of business as such agent, authority either to sell goods or to consign goods for the purposes of sale or to buy goods, or to raise money on the security of goods (s.1 Factors Act 1889). So, for example, where the third party as a consumer buys a car from an agent who is in the car trade, this provision may apply.

The Factors Act 1889 states that the owner is bound by the actions of a mercantile agent in the following circumstances:

If the agent has possession of the goods or the documents of title, with the owner's consent and makes any sale, pledge or other disposition of them in the ordinary course of business, whether or not the owner authorised it. In **Folkes v King**, a car was sold by a dealer at below a stipulated minimum price. It was held that the sale was valid, that the buyer was therefore entitled to claim ownership, and that the only claim available to the seller was against the dealer for breach of warranty of authority.

The buyer must however be innocent of the lack of authority of the agent at the time of sale. In **Pearson v Rose & Young,** the owner of a car took it to the dealer and asked him to obtain offers. The owner did not intend to hand over the registration book, but left it with the dealer by mistake. The dealer sold the car with the book to an innocent buyer. The question of the true ownership of the car was raised. It was held that the dealer had obtained the car 'with the consent of the owner' but this consent did not extend to the registration book, hence the sale must be treated as a sale without registration book and the buyer could not get good title to the car.

The agent must have received possession of the goods in their capacity as agents for sale – not in some other capacity such as for repair. In the latter situation, any sale of the goods would not be valid and the goods could be repossessed by the original owner.

Sale under a voidable title (s.23)

If the seller has a voidable title to goods and his title has not been avoided at the time of sale, the buyer acquires a good title to the goods, provided he did not know of the seller's defect of title.

Lewis v Averay

L. sold a car to a rogue, who resold it to A. L had been persuaded to accept a cheque from the rogue by his pretence to be Richard Greene, the well-known film actor. This was a misrepresentation and made the contract voidable. If L had taken steps to cancel the contract with the rogue before the car had been resold to A, he would have been able to repossess it. However, as the resale had already taken place, A was protected under s.23 and could keep the vehicle.

Because of difficulties of locating rogues in order to cancel the original contract it has been held, in the case of cars, that notifying the police amounts to avoidance of the contract **(Car & Universal Finance v Caldwell).**

Sale by a seller in possession (s.24)

A contract of sale can be complete and valid even where the goods are still in the possession of the seller (s.24), e.g. awaiting delivery. If in this situation, the seller sells the goods to a second buyer, the second buyer will obtain a good title to those goods if delivery of them is taken. However, the goods must be taken in good faith and without notice of the original sale. This leaves the first buyer in the position of having to sue the seller for breach of contract.

In **Pacific Motor Auctions Ltd v Motor Credits (Hire Finance) Ltd,** a car dealer sold a number of vehicles to the claimant under a 'display agreement'. This allowed the seller to retain possession of the cars for display in their showroom. He was paid 90% of the purchase price and was authorised to sell the cars as agents for the claimant. The seller got into financial difficulties and the claimant revoked its authority to sell the cars. However, the dealer sold a number of them to the defendant who took them in good faith and without notice of the previous sale. Whilst the defendant knew about the display agreement it was presumed that the dealer had the authority to sell the cars.

As a result it was held that s.24 applied and that as the defendant had obtained a good title to the cars, the claimant would fail in their claim for the return of the vehicles.

Sale by a buyer in possession (s.25)

Disposition by a buyer in possession is a corresponding situation, where the buyer possesses the goods but the seller has retained property in them. Then, if the buyer has the goods and any necessary documents of title with the consent of the seller, and transfers these to an innocent second buyer, the latter will obtain a good title to the goods. Again, this is subject to the proviso that the second buyer takes the goods in good faith and without notice of any claims on the goods by the original seller (s.25). In **Cahn v Pockett's Bristol Channel Co.** it was held that possession of a bill of lading with the owner's consent, was sufficient to pass good title to a third party under s.25.

This provision is obviously significant where a reservation of title clause was part of the original contract of sale. A subsequent resale of the goods to an innocent second buyer may well be valid under s.25, although the position can be complicated and will vary from case to case.

In **Worcester Works Finance Ltd v Cooden Engineering Ltd**, a finance company sold a car to a buyer (Griffiths) who paid for it by cheque. Griffiths then resold the car to another finance company under a hire purchase agreement. He remained in possession of the car. His original cheque bounced and the original owner cancelled the contract and repossessed the car. The second finance company brought an action against them, claiming that they owned the car and had a right to repossess.

Held: They could not recover the car - S.25 applied as the buyer was clearly a buyer in possession.

Sale of a motor vehicle on hire purchase (Part 3 Hire Purchase Act 1957)

There is a special protection afforded innocent private purchasers of cars sold when under hire purchase agreements. The innocent private buyer is able to claim ownership and can resist any claim by the finance company to repossess the vehicle. This protection does not apply to any other goods on hire purchase.

In conclusion:

- Transfer of title is concerned with whether (rather than when) ownership has passed – whether good title or a defective title has been transferred.

- Problems can arise where a person without authority to sell proceeds to 'sell' goods to an innocent buyer.

- Normally the original owner is protected under the *Nemo Dat* Doctrine (You cannot give a better title than the one you yourself possess) and will be able to insist on their return.

- In order to encourage commerce, a number of exceptions to the doctrine have been created – in each case the innocent third party buyer is protected and will be able to keep the goods.

- The main exceptions are **estoppel, sale by a mercantile agent, sale under a voidable title, sale by a seller in possession, sale by a buyer in possession and sale of a motor vehicle under hire purchase.**

Chapter Thirteen
Non-Contractual Liability

In the absence of a contract on which to base a claim, it may be necessary to resort to alternative legal actions found either in the law of tort (in particular, negligence) or in statute (especially the Consumer Protection Act – Part One). These claims tend to be more difficult to bring successfully for a number of reasons, some of which are identified below.

The chapter covers

*   Doctrine of privity of contract.
*   Contracts (Rights of Third Parties) Act 1999.
*   Collateral contracts.
*   Negligence liability.
*   Civil liability under Part One of Consumer Protection Act 1987 (CPA).
*   Criminal liability under Part Two of the CPA 1987.

The most straightforward claim available to an injured party will usually be one for breach of contract. If he/she had purchased the faulty goods or substandard services directly, an action based on contract imposes strict liability on the supplier. There are, however, circumstances where the injured party has not entered into a contract with the organisation that caused the problem. Examples include purchasers of construction work where subcontractors have performed work incompetently, and passengers in a car which has been manufactured with design weaknesses and has crashed.

Claims against the subcontractor or car manufacturer cannot be based on a normal contract action – the victim has not entered into a contract with them. The doctrine known as **'privity of contract'** operates – only the parties to a contract can claim rights based on the contract. The leading case illustrating this doctrine is:

Dunlop Tyre Ltd v Selfridge & Co.

Dunlop sold tyres to a distributor on condition that they would not be resold at any subsequent stage of the supply chain at below the list price (this case was decided long before competition legislation banned such resale price maintenance). The distributor sold them to Selfridge who offered to sell them to the public at below the list price.

Held: Dunlop were not a party to the contract between the distributor and Selfridge and therefore had no rights to claim for an infringement of one of its terms.

The doctrine of privity of contract has led to considerable hardship or commercial inconvenience where, for example, exclusions from liability or indemnities in favour of third parties could not be enforced directly by the third parties involved. However, the doctrine has been modified by the passing of the **Contracts (Rights of Third Parties) Act 1999** which came into force on 11th May 2000. It also brings English law more into line with other systems of contract law. The Act defines a third party as a person who is not a party to a contract. It gives a third party a right to enforce a contractual term in two situations:

1. **Where the contract expressly provides that he may;**

2. **Where the term 'purports' to confer a benefit on him, unless on a true construction of the wording, it appears that the parties did not intend such a right of enforcement.**

It is perfectly legitimate for the contract to contain a clause excluding the right of third parties to enforce its terms. The 1999 Act does not compel the contracting parties to grant enforceable rights to third parties. The Unfair Contract Terms Act cannot therefore be used to attack such an exclusion.

The third party must be expressly identified in the contract, although it is sufficient to fall within an identified class, or within the terms of a particular description. The Act gives the third party the same rights to obtain damages, an injunction, or order for specific performance as if it had been a party to the contract. It is possible to assign (transfer) the right to another organisation.

Specific Examples

1) In construction or building projects, the original parties (developer, contractors, consultants) may wish to encourage subsequent buyers or tenants by providing them with independently enforceable rights to complain about construction or design defects. It also permits contracts between a main contractor and sub-contractors to contain clauses enabling direct claims to be brought by the client against subcontractors for defective performance.

2) Firms passing on information in confidence will often allow the recipient to pass on that information to other people (e.g. advisors) subject to subsidiary confidentiality agreements being signed. The new law can permit direct enforcement for any infringement of these later agreements.

3)   A franchisor may wish to have the ability to take direct action against sub-franchisees for breach of the franchise agreement made between them and the head franchisee.

Subject to the above reform, liability in these situations has traditionally been based on alternative rights provided by the law. These include:

1.   The finding of a Collateral Contract.

2.   Negligence Liability from the law of Tort.

3.   Statutory Liability based on the Consumer Protection Act 1987 (Part 1).

Non-Contractual Liability

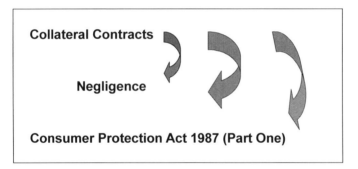

Collateral Contracts

Negligence

Consumer Protection Act 1987 (Part One)

Collateral Contracts

This involves the court discovering an implied contract, running parallel to the main one. It will be based on assurances given by a third party and which encourage the injured party to enter into a subsequent contract with a separate organisation. The assurances prove false and lead to damage being suffered. Examples include representations made by salesmen prior to a customer obtaining goods on hire purchase.

The contract is actually made between the customer and a finance company to whom the goods have been sold by the dealer in the meantime. If those representations prove false and it leads to damage (which includes financial loss), the courts have held that a collateral contract exists between the dealer and the customer, allowing a claim for damages. Another example of collateral contract is the case of:

Shanklin Pier v Detel Products Ltd.

The owners of the pier needed it to be repainted and consulted the defendants on paint which would be suitable for this purpose. The defendants assured Shanklin that a particular brand which they manufactured would be suitable and would last for at least 7 years. On this basis, Shanklin engaged contractors for the work and required them to use the paint recommended by Detel. The work was done competently, but within months, the paint began to peel badly. No action could be brought against the contractors in these circumstances. A claim was brought against Detel instead.

Held: In addition to the contract for the sale of paint, there was a second collateral contract between the claimant and Detel by which the latter guaranteed the suitability of the paint in return for the pier company specifying that the painters used it.

[In the context of construction work and subcontractors, it will be advisable wherever possible to obtain a collateral warranty from the subcontractor. This provides the purchaser with a form of guarantee regarding performance of the work and entitles him to bring a direct contractual claim based on the warranty. However, some form of payment in return, even if only nominal, is necessary to satisfy the requirements of consideration].

Negligence

Within the civil branch of the English legal system there exists a body of rights and duties known as the law of tort. Tort actions are not based on rights provided by documents (such as the law of contract or trusts), nor on status (such as family law). These rights have been created predominantly by the courts and apply to the ordinary citizen and protect him or her against such wrongs as defamation, trespass, nuisance and deceit. However, by far the most important tort action is negligence. It covers a diverse range of situations, including accidents on the roads, at work and on other people's property. It is important to realise that tort claims in general, and negligence claims in particular are more difficult to win because they require proof of blameworthiness – it is fault-based liability unlike breach of contract which is strict liability. The foundations of the modern law of negligence were laid in 1932 in the landmark case of:

Donoghue v Stevenson

Two women went into a café. One ordered some ginger beer and brought it back with two glasses. The bottle, which was made of dark green glass, was opened and the glasses filled. Later, the glasses were refilled and, at this stage, the

decomposed remains of a snail fell out of the bottle. Her friend suffered shock and severe gastro-enteritis as a result. Not having bought the bottle herself, she could not pursue a claim against the café-owner for breach of contract. She was advised to claim against the manufacturer in negligence – a test case, claims against a manufacturer by a consumer not having been brought before.
Held: The manufacturer owed a duty of care on the facts and had failed to take reasonable care. She was entitled to succeed.

Donoghue v Stevenson is a landmark case because it created the ground rules for establishing liability in negligence across the entire spectrum. The three essential ingredients for a successful claim are:

1. **A duty of care owed by the defendant to the claimant**

2. **Breach of that Duty**

3. **Consequent Damage**

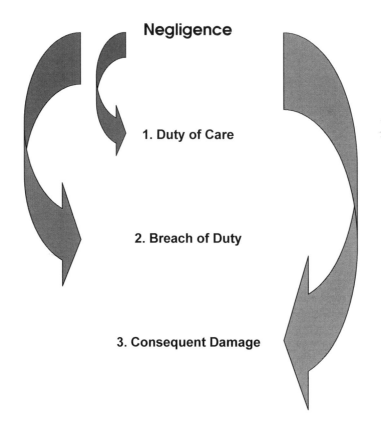

Negligence

1. Duty of Care

2. Breach of Duty

3. Consequent Damage

1. Duty of Care

Lord Atkin created a new test to decide in what situations a duty of care is owed. He said that such a duty is owed to your 'neighbour':

"You must take reasonable care to avoid acts and omissions which you could reasonably foresee would be likely to injure your neighbour. Who then in law is my neighbour? ... *any person so closely and directly affected by my act that I ought reasonably to have them in contemplation as being so affected when I am directing my mind to the acts and omissions which are called in question.*"

This test has been refined over the years and a three stage test now operates:

1. **Was the harm caused reasonable foreseeable?**
2. **Was there a relationship of proximity between the defendant and the claimant?**
3. **In all the circumstances is it just, fair and reasonable to impose a duty of care?**

The number of neighbour relationships has expanded dramatically since 1932 and covers many situations. We shall need to consider the position in three specific situations:

- **Claims by purchasers against subcontractors.**
- **Claims by purchasers against professionals (architects, surveyors, accountants etc.).**
- **Claims by consumers against manufacturers.**

Subcontractors
The duty of care is relatively straightforward between purchasers and subcontractors. Most instances of damage caused to a firm employing subcontractors would be reasonably foreseeable to the subcontractors; there would be a sufficient degree of proximity between the two; there would be no clear reasons justifying the exemption from liability on grounds of public policy.

Professionals
The leading case relating to professional negligence liability is:

Hedley Byrne & Co. v Heller & Partners

In this case it was held that a duty of care is owed by persons who occupy a special relationship of trust i.e. where what they say will be relied upon significantly by the person receiving the advice. This applies most obviously to advice provided by professional persons such as architects, valuers, surveyors and accountants. This enables claims to be brought by injured parties who have relied on negligent advice and suffered economic loss.

Clearly, where the advice was given as part of services rendered under a contract for services, the client's most likely claim would be one for breach of contract, either based on an express term agreed between the parties to this effect, or an implied term that the work must be done competently (s.13 Supply of Goods & Services Act 1982). However, there may be liability in tort if a third party can prove reasonable reliance on the advice and that the defendant should have foreseen this reliance:

Yianni v Edwin Evans & Sons

Surveyors acting for the building society valued a house at £15,000 and as a result the plaintiffs were able to secure a mortgage of £12,000. The house was in fact suffering from severe structural damage and repairs were estimated at £18,000. The basis of the plaintiff's claim was not only the surveyor's negligence but that he ought reasonable to have contemplated that the statement would be passed on by the building society to the plaintiff and that they would rely on it, which they did. It was held that a duty of care was owed by the defendants.

An important factor was that the price of the house indicated that the plaintiff was of modest means and would not be expected to obtain an independent valuation and who would in all probability rely on the defendant's survey, which was communicated to them by the building society. The court was also confident that the defendants knew that the building society would pass the survey to the purchasers and that they would rely on it.

Manufacturers
The authority for establishing liability of manufacturers to consumers of their products is **Donoghue v Stevenson** itself. Lord Atkin, after defining the neighbour test, went on to apply it to the case in question and made the following statement:

"...a manufacturer of products which he sells in such a form as to show that he intends them to reach the ultimate consumer in the form in which they left him with no reasonable opportunity of intermediate examination, and with the knowledge that the absence of reasonable care in the preparation or putting up of the products will result in an injury to the consumer's life or property, owes a duty to the consumer to take that reasonable care."

There is no limit to the type of goods covered by this rule. Cases have involved goods as diverse as cars, a pair of underpants and a hot water bottle. Since 1932 the rule has been extended from manufacturers to cover anyone who does some work on the goods, for example, a repairer. The word "consumer" has been given a wide interpretation to cover anyone who is likely to be injured by the lack of care. In one case, a successful claim was brought by a pedestrian who was injured when a wheel from a vehicle which had been badly repaired became detached and careered along the pavement.

Duty of Care

Neighbour Test (Donoghue v Stevenson 1932)

'<u>Neighbour</u>' - person so closely and directly affected by defendant's actions...

Duty to take reasonable care

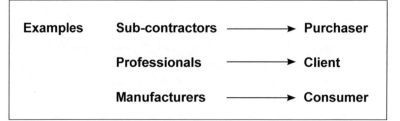

Examples	Sub-contractors	⟶	Purchaser
	Professionals	⟶	Client
	Manufacturers	⟶	Consumer

<u>Professional Liability</u>

Hedley Byrne & Co v Heller & Partners (special relationship)

<u>Manufacturers' Liability</u>

Where no possibility of intermediate inspection

2. Breach of Duty

Having established the existence of a duty of care, the second requirement is for the claimant to prove a breach of this duty - probably the most difficult problem for him to address. This means that the claimant must be able to prove that the defendant failed to act reasonably in all the circumstances. The court would decide this on the basis of comparing the defendant's actions with the usual level of competence expected from businesses engaged in the same area of activity. This will clearly vary depending on the nature of the defendant's business. Consultants will be expected to maintain a higher average level of skill and competence than semi-skilled or unskilled contractors.

In determining whether he has acted reasonably, the courts engage in a cost-benefit analysis in which they consider a number of factors. These include:

1.   **The obviousness of the risk.**
2.   **the likelihood of injury/damage.**
3.   **the potential seriousness of the injury/damage.**
4.   **the cost/practical difficulties in taking further preventative measures.**

Liability in negligence is fault based and the onus of proving that the defendant was at fault is on the claimant. This can be very particularly difficult in claims against manufacturers as usually the consumer has no means of knowing exactly what went wrong in the manufacturing process. Sometimes, however, the only reasonable explanation for the defect is that someone acted negligently: buns, for example, do not usually have stones in the middle of them.

In this kind of situation, the consumer may be able to plead *res ipsa loquitur* - the facts speak for themselves. This has the effect of reversing the normal burden of proof; the manufacturer is presumed to have acted negligently unless he can prove that he took all reasonable care.

Breach of Duty

Standard of Care

To do what a reasonable man would do or not do what a reasonable man would not do.

Factors to take into account:
- Obviousness of the Risk

- Likelihood of Damage

- Potential Seriousness of Damage

- Cost and Practical Difficulties of Doing More

i.e. A cost benefit analysis

Burden of Proof   Claimant must prove case on balance of probabilities

Exception   *Res Ipsa Loquitur* (The facts speak for themselves)

3. Consequent Damage

Even if breach of duty is established, the claimant still has to prove he has suffered consequent damage. This requires him to prove that the damage was caused by the defendant's negligent behaviour – that the damage would not have been caused but for his behaviour (the 'but for' test). If the damage would have resulted irrespective of the defendant's actions, there is a break in the chain of causation and the claim would fail. Where the damage is partly the result of the defendant's actions and partly the result of the claimant's actions, the court will allow the claim but reduce the damages awarded – by apportioning blame in percentage terms and reducing the figure by the blame apportioned to the claimant.

The damage suffered must have been reasonably foreseeable at the time of the alleged infringement – it must not be too remote. Similar (but not identical) principles apply here as with claims for damages in breach of contract actions.

There are however some important restrictions on the type of damage that can be claimed in negligence actions. Physical injury and damage to property can be claimed, but economic loss is generally not claimable This covers loss of profits and lost business. The authority for this position is:

Simaan General Contracting Co. v Pilkington Glass Ltd.

Goods supplied to the claimant by subcontractors were not up to specification and a negligence action claiming economic loss was brought.
Held: Claims for economic loss could only be made in very limited circumstances.

The case of **Junior Books Ltd. v Veitchi Co. Ltd.** suggested that where a purchaser has 'nominated' a sub-contractor (a common practice in building contracts), there is an ability to sue the sub-contractor for economic loss. This was justified on the grounds that the two parties were in closer proximity to one another, establishing a quasi-contractual relationship. The position is however unclear and the Veitchi case has been extensively criticised.

A case illustrating the limits to claimable loss is:

Spartan Steel & Alloys Ltd. v Martin & Co.

The claimant manufactured steel alloys 24 hours a day. This required continuous power. Workmen, digging a trench in a public road nearby, damaged a power cable which resulted in a lack of power for 14 hours. There was a danger of damage to the furnace so this had to be shut down. As a result, one batch of molten metal was spoilt.
Held: Damages could be awarded for the value of the spoilt metal and the loss of profit caused to that melt (i.e loss based upon physical damage). However, the claimant's claim for loss of profits for the entire period of interruption was dismissed as pure economic loss and too remote.

Consequent Damage

- **Must prove causation**

- **'But for' Test**

- **Apportionment of Blame**

- **Loss must be reasonably foreseeable**

- **Claimable Loss**

  Physical Injury - Yes

  Damage to Property - Yes

  Economic Loss - No

Simaan General Contracting Co v Pilkington Glass Ltd

Junior Books Ltd v Veitchi Co Ltd

The Consumer Protection Act 1987

For a number of reasons, including a European Directive requiring a reform, UK law introduced legislation in 1987 designed to provide stronger protection to consumers in relation to defective products. There was a recognition that the evidential problems of proving negligence in claims against manufacturers were often insurmountable and claimants either gave up or accepted settlements that were far below appropriate levels of compensation. The **Consumer Protection Act 1987** contains several parts – Part One concerns civil law and the rights of individual consumers to pursue claims against manufacturers of defective products. Part Two *et seq* are more concerned with regulation of product safety and involve intervention by public authorities and the use of criminal sanctions to deal with abuses.

The main reform was to introduce a form of strict liability into product liability. All that the claimant had to prove was that damage has been caused to him as a result of a defective product which had been produced by the defendant. It was not necessary to prove that the defect had been caused by the defendant's negligence. However, because of intense lobbying by various industrial interests in the UK, strict liability was diluted by the drafting of a 'developmental risks' defence to such claims (see later).

Part One

Section 2 (1)

Liability arises:
"Where any damage is caused wholly or partly by a defect in a product."

The claimant must prove:
> a) the product was defective.
> b) the defect caused the damage or injury.

Who is liable?
1) The producer (including component manufacturers, end product manufacturers, producers of raw materials).
2) The own brander (e.g. Marks and Spencers - St Michael).
3) An importer into the European Union.
4) Any supplier who cannot identify his source of supply.

Liability of a component manufacturer and an end-product manufacturer is joint and several - the consumer can sue one or both - each is fully liable for the damage.

When is a product defective? (Section 3)
"When the safety of the product is not such as persons generally are entitled to expect."
- Definition very similar to that of "unsatisfactory " with the word "safe" substituted for "fit".
- However, it does make clear that goods must be dangerous (not just defective) before rights are available.

Relevant factors include:
- The manner in which the product has been marketed.
- Its get-up.
- Any instructions or warnings provided.

A v National Blood Authority

A number of patients contracted Hepatitis C when they received blood transfusions where the blood was contaminated with the virus. It was held that the Authority (as supplier) was liable under the Act. The product was not as safe as 'persons generally were entitled to expect'. It was no defence that, at the time of supply, there was no effective way of screening blood products for the virus. If safer products are subsequently developed, their existence cannot be used as the sole reason for judging a product to be defective.

Defences (Section 4)

1) That the defendant did not supply the goods (e.g. manufacturer of finished product can be said not to supply component parts).

2) That the defendant did not supply the goods in the course of a business with a view to profit.

3) That the defect was not present at the time he supplied it.

4) The "developmental risks defence".

i.e. given the state of scientific and technological knowledge at the time when the product was put into circulation, no producer could have been expected to have discovered the defect. This is a particularly controversial defence and makes claims against firms in industries with close links with science and technology much more difficult e.g. pharmaceutical companies.

5) That the defendant was a component part producer and the defect was wholly attributable to its design or to compliance with instructions given by the producer of the finished product.

Damage (Section 5)

Damages are recoverable for death and personal injury, including disease or other impairment of a person's physical or mental condition. Damages are recoverable for damage to other property. Cannot claim for loss or damage to:

a) the product itself.

b) commercial property.

c) property claims of less than £275.

Limitation of action

• injured party must bring claim within 3 years of cause of action arising.

- supplier cannot be sued more than 10 years after date when product supplied.

Part Two

This part of the Act imposes criminal liability on firms which manufacture unsafe products. The Secretary of State can issue safety regulations providing more detail on how to satisfy the basic statutory duty (this has already been done for a range of items including furniture and children's night-clothes. Section 10 establishes the criminal offence of 'supplying consumer goods which are not reasonably safe.' The Secretary of State can serve a 'prohibition notice' on a supplier, prohibiting him from supplying goods which are unsafe or a 'notice to warn' which requires the supplier to publish warnings about the unsafe goods.

[Further regulation relating to unsafe products was created by the passing of the General Product Safety Regulations 1994 as part of a European Union initiative to improve safety standards]

In conclusion:

- As a general rule, contractual claims are easier to win because they are based on strict liability.

- Problems arise where no contract exists between the injured party and the organisation responsible for the damage – the doctrine of privity of contract denies third parties a right to sue for breach.

- The Contracts (Rights of Third Parties) Act 1999 has created 'potential' inroads to the doctrine.

- A collateral contract (implied contract running parallel to the main contract) can sometimes be identified, giving a contractual claim on the basis of an assurance received.

- Negligence actions are from the law of tort and fault-based – it is necessary to prove that the defendant was to blame (culpable) for the damage.

- There are three ingredients to a successful negligence claim – a duty of care, breach of duty and consequent damage.

- The modern law of negligence was founded in the case of **Donoghue v Stevenson**, which created the neighbour test for identifying duty of care situations.

- Breach of duty is determined using a cost benefit approach, weighing the degree of risk involved against the costs of doing more than is already being done.

- Consequent damage does not normally extend to economic loss.

- The Consumer Protection Act 1987 (Part One) introduced a form of strict liability to claims involving defective products which have caused damage.

- This 'strict liability' was weakened by the 'developmental risks' defence allowed in the Act.

- Part Two of the Consumer Protection Act 1987 imposes criminal liability on organisations manufacturing unsafe products.

Chapter Fourteen

Agency, Assignment & Bailment

This chapter covers a couple of miscellaneous issues relating to contracts and third parties.

Agency involves using another person or organisation to act on your behalf and possess the power to bind you to contracts negotiated with third parties. This can be achieved 'externally' where, for example, an organisation employs a commercial agent to sell its goods abroad or an employment agency to provide it with temporary staff. It also applies 'internally', where employees represent the organisation and make contracts on its behalf e.g. sales or purchasing staff entering into deals in the course of their employment.

Assignment involves the transfer of contractual rights and/or obligations to a third party after the contract was first concluded.

The chapter covers the following legal principles:

- Agency – types of authority (actual, apparent).
- Ratification.
- Doctrine of undisclosed principal.
- Relevance of the Commercial Agents (Council Directive) Regulations 1993.
- Rules relating to assignment of contractual rights and obligations.
- Types of assignment – legal, equitable and by operation of law.
- Novation.

Agency

Agents can be created by express agreement, by implication or by necessity. There are no formal requirements relating to formation of an agency agreement except where the agent will possess the power to execute deeds in the principal's name. In these circumstances the agent is given power of attorney and this must be in the form of a deed.

The general rule of agency is that if an agent makes a contract on behalf of his principal, the contract is treated as if it was made between the principal and the third party.

Agent's Authority to Bind the Principal

*   If an agent enters a contract with a third party and the contract is within the scope of his **actual authority** (express or implied), the principal is bound by the contract.

*   If the agent acts outside his actual authority but within the scope of his **apparent authority**, the principal is once again bound by the contract. Apparent authority is that authority which a third party would reasonably assume the agent to have in the circumstances involved.

*   If he acts outside his actual and apparent authority in making the contract on the principal's behalf, the principal is not bound by the contract unless he chooses to **ratify** it. For the principal to ratify the contract the principal must have the capacity and be identifiable at the time of the contract, the act must be capable of ratification and ratification must take place within a reasonable time.

*   If the agent contracts with a third party on behalf of his principal (where he is acting within his authority) but he does not make it clear to the third party that he is acting for the principal **(the undisclosed principal)**, the principal is still permitted to enforce the contract against the third party who is unaware of his identity. This is despite the fact that the third party did not intend to contract with the principal.
    However, this will not be possible if the terms of the contract are incompatible with agency e.g. where the agent's personality is central to the performance of the contract.
    In cases where there is an undisclosed principal, the third party may choose whether to enforce the contract against the agent or the principal.

Commercial Agents (Council Directive) Regulations 1993

Since 1994, the above regulations have been in force and form a statutory code governing the activities of commercial agents (as defined). Essentially, a commercial agent is an agent engaged on a continuing basis to negotiate contracts for sale or purchase of goods. This precludes agents involved in services contracts and agents appointed on a one of basis to conclude a contract. The Regulations considerably strengthen the position of a commercial agent by implying terms into agency agreements and by giving rights which survive the termination of the agency agreement.

They provide, for example, that the agent is entitled to compensation if the agency agreement is terminated and the agent is deprived of commission that he would have received if the agency agreement had been properly performed. Many of the statutory provisions cannot be excluded by express terms between the parties.

Contractual Assignment

A contract consists of rights and obligations. The general principle is that **rights** (the benefit being obtained from the contract) can be freely assigned (transferred). However, they must be proprietary and not personal to the original parties to the contract. Contracts in the publishing and recording industries are generally personal and cannot be assigned.

Contractual **obligations** (the burden) cannot be assigned without the agreement of the other party. This is designed to protect the party to the transaction who should not be prejudiced by a change in the identity of the person who has obligations under the contract. Sub-contracting the performance of the obligations is possible since the original party to the contract remains liable for the performance of his sub-contractor. To avoid this happening an express prohibition on sub-contracting is sometimes included in the contract terms.

There are three forms of assignment – legal, equitable and by operation of law:

1.   A legal assignment must be in writing and signed by the assignor; absolute (that is, of the whole interest and unconditional), and express notice must be given in writing to the other party or parties to the agreement (section 136, Law of Property Act 1925).

2.   An assignment that does not meet with the requirements of section 136 is an equitable assignment (provided there is a clear intention to assign). No particular formalities are required for an equitable assignment. The main difference is that an equitable assignment requires the assignee to join the assignor in any action under the contract.

3.   Assignment by operation or law arises on the death or bankruptcy of one of the parties where all the rights and obligations of that party pass to his personal representatives or trustee in bankruptcy.

Novation

A novation is a three way contract which extinguishes a contract and replaces it with another contract in which a third party takes up the rights and obligations which duplicate those of one of the original parties to the agreement.

Novations commonly arise on asset sales where the vendor wishes to assign all his rights and obligations under a contract to the purchaser. As contractual obligations cannot be assigned, the vendor can only achieve his aim if both the purchaser and the third party agree to a novation. The consent can be express (oral or written) or implied – where a customer, having received communication of the change of ownership, subsequently pays an invoice submitted by the new owner. Take-overs and mergers will produce a similar need for novation. The identity of one of the parties to existing contracts will have changed and there is a consequent need to obtain consent to this change.

Bailment

A bailee is a person who has possession of goods belonging to another person. Examples include:

- Carriers of goods (road haulage companies, shipping companies, airlines etc).
- Repairers.
- Warehouse owners.
- Hirers of plant and equipment (and consumers who are purchasing goods under hire purchase).
- Buyers who acquire goods under sellers' terms which contain a retention of title clause (Romalpa clause) – until payment has been made.
- Buyers who receive goods and subsequently reject them upon finding they are defective (ownership immediately reverts to the seller when rejection is communicated).

Where a bailee is involved, there is a legal duty to take reasonable care of the goods whilst in his/her possession. This requires the bailee to take appropriate steps to ensure the goods are not unnecessarily damaged or deteriorate in condition. Failure to satisfy this duty can allow the owner (the bailor) to claim damages for the lost value.

Most bailments arise through agreement i.e. voluntarily. Very occasionally, a person may find that he has come into possession of goods without his consent.

The law then lowers the duty and the bailee will only be liable for damage caused deliberately or by gross negligence.

In conclusion:

• Agents are used as intermediaries to represent organisations and conclude contracts on their behalf.

• Agents can be external to the organisation (specialist agencies) or internal (employees purchasing or selling goods for the organisation).

• Agents must possess the authority to act on behalf of their principal.

• Authority can be actual (express, implied) or apparent (that which a reasonable third party would assume exists in the circumstances).

• Assignment involves the transfer of rights and/or obligations under a contract to a third party.

• Assignment of contractual rights does not require the consent of the other party whereas the assignment of contractual duties requires this consent.

• Novation is an extreme form of assignment and involves the replacement of the original contract by a new one under which the rights and duties of one of the parties have been assumed by another organisation e.g. upon a take-over or merger.

• Bailment (where one person has possession of another person's goods) requires the person in possession (bailee) to take reasonable care of the goods.

Chapter Fifteen

Competition Law

Competition law has proved itself to be one of the most dynamic legal topics in recent years. The European Community provisions relating to cartels and abuse of a dominant market position have been subject to a number of significant amendments. Our own UK law on competition has been radically overhauled since 1998, bringing us into line with the EC approach. Some differences still exist, especially in the area of monopolies and mergers.

This chapter covers the following issues:

European Regulation:

* Underlying principles of EU competition law.
* Article 81 (regulation of cartels) – ingredients for infringement.
* Horizontal & vertical agreement – difference in approach to enforcement.
* Exemptions (block & individual).
* Market analysis – approach.
* Article 82 (regulation of abuse of dominant market position) – ingredients for infringement.
* Case law examples.
* Enforcement procedures.

UK Regulation:

* Competition Act 1998 – changes to previous position.
* Chapter One prohibition.
* Chapter Two prohibition.
* Exclusions and Exemptions.
* Procedures for enforcement.
* Monopolies and mergers – Enterprise Act 2002.
* Regulatory bodies – roles and responsibilities.

Reform of Competition Law

The **Competition Act 1998** introduced the most radical changes to UK competition law for more than a quarter of a century.

Was this change necessary?

Critics of the UK approach to regulation of competition abuses point to the track record. It was estimated that cartels were adding up to 10% on prices of both industrial and consumer goods. Overall it was estimated that the cost of anti-competitive practices and abuse of market power amounted to about 1% of GDP – in other words, several billion pounds. It had been argued that the main weaknesses of the U.K approach were a lack of bite in enforcement (inadequate powers of investigation coupled with weak penalties) and poor drafting of the main legislation which often concentrated on the form of agreements rather than their economic significance.

What has been the solution?

It was decided to adopt, with minor variations, the regime operating across the European Union for abuses that affect trade between member states – in particular the provisions found in Articles 81 and 82 of the European Treaty. This was partly an on-going process of harmonisation intended to free up barriers to trade between member states. However, it was generally recognised that the European model was far more effective in suppressing abuses. Although it had its critics (which led to recent proposals for reform) it possessed stricter controls both in terms of powers of investigation and enforcement of sanctions against abuses.

Continuing Reform

U.K. competition law was further reformed with the passing of the Enterprise Act 2002. This repealed the Fair Trading Act 1973 and brought the approach relating to monopolies and mergers closer to the one used for anti-competitive practices under the Competition Act 1998. The Enterprise Act 2002 also 'criminalised' cartel activities by making it possible for individual directors and managers to be prosecuted for their involvement in the illegal practice. This follows the U.S. policy and clearly in intended to have additional deterrent effect.

Further reform of the European Union policy on competition law includes the abolition of the system of notification, exemption or clearance of restrictive agreements as required under Article 81 of the European Treaty. It has been replaced by a system of self-regulation where businesses are expected to assess their own position and decide if there is a potential infringement of competition law provisions.

With the expansion of the European Treaty as a result of the Treaty of Nice, the European Commission has transferred a significant amount of its competition law work to the domestic enforcement agencies of individual member states. In this country, it is the Office of Fair Trading that is dealing with the delegated work.

European Community Approach

The basic purpose of European Union competition policy is:
- to encourage free trade between member states.
- to break down barriers which inhibit such free trade.
- to ensure commercial undertakings do not prevent, distort or restrict competition or abuse their position in the market to the detriment of their competitors and/or consumers.

Articles 81 & 82 attempt to apply the above principles by setting out a body of detailed prohibitions and procedures.

Article 81

Regulates *"all agreements between undertakings which have the object or effect of preventing, restricting or distorting competition."*

Article 82

Regulates unilateral action by undertakings, prohibiting abuses of a dominant position. In addition, the Merger Regulation (Regulation 4064/89) attempts to deal with the issue of potential abuse by 'concentrations' being created within the common market.

ARTICLE 81

Article 81(1) prohibits all agreements between undertakings, decisions by associations of undertakings and concerted practices which may affect trade between member states and which have as their object or effect the prevention, restriction or distortion of competition within the European Union.

Article 81(2) states that such agreements are automatically void.

To infringe Article 81 requires a degree of <u>collusion</u> between <u>independent undertakings</u>, an <u>impact of trade which applies to more than one country within the common market</u> and either an <u>intention</u> or a <u>consequence</u> of <u>impeding competition</u> in a market.

Undertakings includes limited companies, partnerships, sole traders, trade associations and public utilities operating in commercial markets. Subsidiary companies are treated as part of the group and their holding company i.e. as one entity. Thus, agreements made between these companies would not be subject to Article 81 which requires 2 or more independent undertakings.

Companies which are based outside the European Union will still be subject to Article 81 if the consequences of their agreement affect trade within the common market.

Agreements have been interpreted widely and covers written and oral, formal and informal (gentleman's agreement), decisions of trade associations which may be no more than recommendations to be observed by members, and concerted practices. 'Concerted practice' has been defined as a form of co-operation between undertakings which, without having reached the stage where an agreement properly so called has been concluded, knowingly substituted practical co-operation for the risks of competition. Some active contact needs to have taken place e.g. discussions or exchanging of information. Parallel behaviour is strong evidence of a concerted practice but not conclusive.

Effect on Trade between Member States

It is possible for agreements between businesses located in only one country, and which only operate in that country, to infringe Article 81. The ECJ has decided that such agreements can have the effect of encouraging the partitioning of the common market along national lines, which clashes with the overall policy of the European Treaty – that of removing barriers to intra-state trade.

Object or Effect of the Collusion

The following examples (non-exhaustive) of prohibited agreements or practices is provided in Article 81(1):

- Directly or indirectly fixing purchase or selling prices.
- Limiting or controlling production.
- Dividing markets or sources of supply.
- Applying dissimilar conditions to equivalent transaction with other parties.
- Imposing supplementary obligations which have no connection with the subject of the contract involved.

Specific Examples

Directly or indirectly fixing purchasing or selling prices:
- Fixing the components of a price

- Setting a minimum price below which prices are not to be reduced.
- Establishing the amount or percentage by which prices are to be increased.
- Establishing a range outside which prices are not to move.

Indirect fixing includes arrangements relating to:
- Discounts or allowances to be granted.
- Transport charges.
- Payments for additional services.
- Credit terms or the terms of guarantee.
- Adherence to published price lists.
- Consultation with potential competitors before quoting a price.
- Not charging less than any other price on the market.

Sharing markets or sources of supply:
- Collusive tendering ('bid-rigging').
- Agreements between purchasers as to with whom they will deal.
- Agreements between sellers by which they boycott certain purchasers.
- Exchange of price information leading to price co-ordination and elimination of competition (information on pricing policy, discounts, costs, terms of trade, rates & dates of change.

Applying dissimilar conditions to equivalent transaction with other parties
- Aggregated rebates – the granting of better terms to a customer the more business he places with all the parties to the scheme.

These prohibitions apply to both **horizontal** and **vertical agreements**. Horizontal agreements occur when firms at the same level of trade are the parties e.g. agreements between two manufacturers or between two distributors. Vertical agreements occur when firms which are at different levels of trade are the parties e.g. between a manufacturer and a distributor.

Vertical agreements are generally seen as less of a threat to competition policy and are treated somewhat more leniently, although they can still fall foul of Article 81:

Consten & Grundig v Commission (EC)

A German manufacturer of TV sets and tape recorders etc. established an exclusive dealing network for the distribution of its products throughout the European Union. In 1957 G. appointed Consten as exclusive distributor in France. G. agreed not to sell directly or indirectly to anyone else in France; G's other national distributors were bound not to sell outside their allotted territories – so they could not sell in France; and C. agreed not to deal in competing products nor to sell outside France.

UNEF and other French firms managed to import G's products into France and undercut C's prices. C. sued these parallel importers in French law for 'unfair competition.' The validity of the exclusive distribution agreement was challenged as an infringement of Article 81 (then Article 85).
Held: Article 81 was infringed to the extent that the agreement's aim of securing absolute territorial protection for C. against parallel imports partitioned the European Union along national frontiers, thereby distorting competition. It gave rise to different prices for the same goods in different member states.

'Appreciable Extent'

Article 81 does not apply to agreements which have a minimal effect (de minimus) on the market i.e. insignificant collusions. This is partly a recognition that some agreements are simply not worth pursuing because of their lack of impact and partly a recognition that the European Commission has limited resources to monitor every instance of collusion. Guidance is provided by the Commission in the **'Notice on Agreements of Minor Importance' (OJ 1997 C372/4)**[2]. It makes a distinction between horizontal and vertical agreements and indicates that for the former, where the aggregate market share of the parties does not exceed 10%, the agreement will not contravene Article 81. A more tolerant minimum is then indicated for vertical agreements, set at 15%. There are some 'hardcore' exceptions though:

- Horizontal agreements which fix prices or limit production or sales, or involve market sharing;
- Vertical agreements which fix resale prices or allocate geographical territory to particular businesses.

An example of the de minimus doctrine in operation is **Volk v Vervaeke**, where an exclusive dealership agreement escaped violation of Article 81 because the total market share involved amounted to 0.2%.

---

2 Notices are official publications issued by the Commission which set out a viewpoint and contain general guidance, but are not definitive. The ECJ does not regard itself as bound to follow the position taken by the Commission in a Notice.

Exemptions

The Commission has been given the power to exempt agreements, either on an **individual basis** or according to the category of agreement (the **block** exemption). Essentially, this has the effect of granting an immunity to the agreement, which otherwise would have been void under Article 81. There is also a process known as **negative clearance**, whereby the Commission, if requested by the parties, can declare that the agreement does not infringe Article 81 at all.

In order to obtain an exemption it is necessary to prove that the agreement/ practice:

- **contributes to improving production & distribution of goods and promoting technical progress;**
- **allows consumers a fair share of the resulting benefit;**
- **provided it does not enable the firms to eliminate competition in the relevant product market.**

Examples of **improvements in production or distribution** are:
- **Lower costs** from longer production or delivery runs.
- **Lower costs** from changes in the methods of production or distribution.
- Improvements in product **quality.**
- Increases in the **range** of products produced.

Examples of **promoting technical or economic progress:**
- **Efficiency gains** from economies of scale or increased specialisation in research and development.
- Increased pace of **innovation** as a result of shared R&D.

If the agreement leads to faster development of new products, new markets or to better distribution systems, the resulting benefits will be felt by the consumer. This would satisfy the second requirement above.

Relevant Market

An analysis of the relevant market to which the agreement relates has to be carried out by the Commission. It attempts to identify the potential boundaries of competition and therefore the relative size and strength of the parties to the agreement (and that of their competitors). Two basic concepts are used in the analysis:
1. **Relevant product market**
2. **Relevant geographical market**

1. Relevant product market involves identifying all the products/services which can be regarded as readily interchangeable or substitutable by the consumer. Relative characteristics, price and intended use are all relevant in arriving at a conclusion. These substitute goods would be included in the market if they would prevent prices of the products relevant to the investigation from rising above competitive levels.

2. Relevant geographical market involves identifying the territory in which the parties to the agreement carry on business in competitive conditions which are sufficiently similar and yet clearly differ from those operating in neighbouring areas.

Market Analysis

Relevant Product Market

Relevant Geographical Market

Product Market

Identify all Readily Substitutable Products

- **Characteristics**

- **Price**

- **Intended Use**

Demand Substitutability   **Supply Substitutability**

Ease of Entry into Market

Geographical Market

Identify the Territory

- **Sufficiently similar competitive conditions**

- **Clearly different from neighbouring areas**

Once the relevant market has been defined, the Commission can then decide whether exemption is appropriate.

Exemption can be either on an **individual** or a **block** basis. Individual exemptions require formal notification of the agreement to the Commission and all the attendant paperwork and problems of disclosure

For these reasons, firms usually try to fit the agreement within a block exemption which does not require such notification. This may not be easy, the agreement having to fit within the correct class and the terms be acceptable according to defined and detailed criteria. The following are the most important examples of block exemptions:

•	**Vertical Agreements**	**Regulation 2790/1999/EC**
•	**Research & Development**	**Regulation 2658/200/EC**
•	**Specialisation**	**Regulation 2659/200/EC**
•	**Technology Transfer**	**Regulation 240/96**
•	**Motor Vehicle Distribution And Servicing**	**Regulation 1475/95**

The whole area of block exemption has been criticised as being over-formal and legalistic. There is pressure to make decisions on exemption more related to the economic implications/consequences of the agreements and less on the form in which the agreement is drafted on paper.

If it seems impossible or over-complex to fit the agreement within the boundaries of a block exemption, it may be necessary to seek **individual exemption**. Apart from the problems already mentioned *(paperwork; disclosure of confidential information)* there could be a *lengthy period of investigation* with *no guarantee* of formal exemption. Limited resources mean that the Commission gives a formal decision in less than 10% of applications. For the remainder, a **'comfort letter'**[3] is the likely outcome unless it has grounds for objection. Although such comfort letters will be regarded by the Commission as binding on its own future actions (unless new information comes to light which will affect its view on the matter) they are not binding on the courts when asked to decide on validity under Article 81.

Article 82

Once an undertaking has reached a dominant position in a given market, it becomes subject to regulation by Article 82. Dominance on its own is not an infringement but its abuses are:

---

3 An informal, administrative letter indicating that the Commission considers there is no need for it to oppose the agreement. [Occasionally, the Commission will issue a Discomfort Letter where it indicates that the agreement does infringe Article 81, but as a matter or internal priorities, it will not be taking the matter further].

"Any abuse by one or more undertakings of a dominant position within the common market or in a substantial part of it shall be prohibited as incompatible with the common market."

There is no possibility of an exemption from Article 82, unlike Article 81.

Dominant Position

The essence of dominance is the power to behave independently of competitive pressures. The classic definition of dominant position was provided in **United Brands v Commission**:

"… a position of economic strength enjoyed by an undertaking which enables it to prevent effective competition being maintained on the relevant market by giving it the power to behave to an appreciable extent independently of its competitors, customers, and ultimately, of its consumers."

The same criteria are used to decide dominance as were seen applied to Article 81 – an economic analysis of the relevant product and geographical markets. Key indicators are:

- **Market share**
  There is a general presumption that a 50% market share amounts to occupying a dominant position. However, each case will be considered on its own merits and dominance has been held to exist even where the market share falls below 50%. In United Brands, the share amounted to between 40-45% but dominance was established.

- **Time**
  Dominance requires that a position of power has existed over a sufficiently long period of time.

- **Barriers to entry**
  The extent of potential competition will be a consideration, with the economic and financial difficulties involved in entering the market being examined e.g. how much capital investment would be needed?

  Examples of barriers are:
  - Intellectual property rights such as the need to obtain licences or permits.
  - Preferential access to important inputs such as denial of access to the only port available for a particular market.

- The presence/size of sunk costs[4] - highly competitive market conditions will make sunk costs more likely and thus deter entry.

  Barriers to entry tend to be more prevalent in static markets rather than dynamic ones which are highly innovative.

- **Conduct**
  The actual pattern of behaviour of a company (its track record) can provide significant evidence of a position of dominance e.g. discriminatory pricing or selective distribution.

Another factor influencing dominance of a supplier in a market is the extent of buyer-power in the market. If there are relatively few buyers this could affect the ability of an dominant supplier to abuse its position.

Abuse of a Dominant Position

Simply occupying a position of dominance does not, it itself, amount to an infringement of Article 82. There must be an abuse of that position. Article 82 provides a non-exhaustive list of abuses:

(a)   *imposing unfair prices (or other unfair trading conditions).*
(b)   *limiting production, markets, technical developments.*
(c)   *applying dissimilar conditions (discriminatory).*
(d)   *imposing unconnected supplementary obligations e.g. tie-in sales.*

Article 82 is concerned with market structure and the effect it has on the level of competition. It is realised that where an undertaking occupies a dominant position in a market it will be able to weaken competition by manipulation of its influence in that market, and thus de-stabilise normal competitive practices.

Examples of Anti-Competitive Behaviour

These include expelling or excluding competition from a market:

Selective distribution   where a manufacturer supplies only a limited number of retailers who must satisfy specified conditions (exclusive distribution involves supplying only one retailer).

Exclusive purchasing   where the retailer agrees to purchase, or deal in, goods from only one manufacturer.

---

4 Those incurred when entering a new market which cannot be recovered on exit.

Tie-in sales	where the manufacturer makes the purchase of one product (the tying product) conditional on the purchase of a second (tied) product (a set of tied products is called a bundle).
Full-line forcing	an extreme form of tie-in sale where the retailer must stock the full range of the manufacturer's product range.
Quantity Forcing	where the retailer is required to purchase a minimum quantity of a certain product.
Fidelity discounts	where the retailer receives discounts based on the proportion of its sales which come from the manufacturer.

Case Law Examples

(The original cases were decided when the relevant Article numbers were 85 & 86. Since ratification of the Treaty of Amsterdam 1997, they have been re-numbered 81 & 82. The case details below use the current Article numbers.)

United Brands v Commission

UB were charging different prices in 6 different countries for identical bananas. The ECJ held that this pricing policy infringed Article 82(c) [discriminatory pricing] because it amounted to an artificial price differential which distorted trade between member states.
N.B. The agreements with their distributors could also have been declared an infringement because they prohibited parallel importing from low to high price countries. This amounts to a restriction of trade between member states.

Hugin v Commission

Hugin were manufacturers of cash registers and new spare parts for their registers. Lipton was a distributor repairer of these machines. Hugin terminated the distribution agreement for what amounted to a minor infringement by Lipton and refused to supply it with spare parts in the future. The ECJ held that, although there was a highly competitive market for the supply of cash machines, Hugin had a dominant position in the *separate market for Hugin spare parts* and was found to be abusing it.
N.B. Hugin is frequently cited as authority for the proposition that Articles 81 & 82 can only be applied when the alleged abuse affects trade in more than one member state. In Hugin, it only related to part of the south east of England. This would not however prevent the domestic laws of the affected country from being used to deal with an abuse.

Tetra Pak v Commission 1997 (Tetra Pak II)

Tetra Pak required purchasers of its machines to agree to a range of support facilities (spare parts, maintenance and the purchase of its own cartons). This prevented other firms who produced cartons capable of being used in the machines from competing in the relevant market. The ECJ held that this was an abuse of Article 82(d). Tetra Pak were fined 75m Ecu.

ARTICLES 81 & 82 – Enforcement by the European Commission

The Commission possesses wide powers of enforcement of Articles 81 and 82. Complaints can be made by businesses affected by the alleged infringement and by member states. The Commission can also initiate action itself. The following powers exist:

- **To demand information relevant to an investigation.**
- **To search premises.**
- **To take copies or extracts of records.**

[These powers have been largely adopted under the Competition Act 1998 for investigations by the Office of Fair Trading into infringements which operate only inside the UK. We shall look at the powers in more detail when considering the new Act.]

Apart from ordering an agreement or practice to be declared void, the Commission may also, by decision:

- Require a company to terminate any infringements resulting from the agreement.
- Order the parties to refrain in future from similar conduct *(Polypropylene cartel, 1986)*.
- Order the parties to inform interested parties that the infringement has been brought to an end *(Tetra Pak II, 1992)*.
- Order the parties to make information periodically available to the Commission *(United Brands, 1976)*.

The Commission's main weapon, however, is its power to impose fines where companies have intentionally or negligently breached the articles. The following page provides some further detail on this sanction.

Penalties

- The Commission can impose fines of up to 10% of the total turnover in the previous year of each of the undertakings concerned or 1 million Euros, whichever is the greater.

- Failure to terminate an infringement can result in continuing fines of up to 1000 Euros per day.
- Fines of up to 1000 Euros per day can be imposed against undertakings which :
  - refuse to provide information requested by the Commission, or
  - refuse to co-operate in the course of an investigation.

All Commission decisions, including decisions to investigate, enforcement decisions and details of fines imposed, will be published. This can clearly have serious repercussions on the business involved in terms of business reputation and standing.

Recent Examples of Fines

- Intel were fined 1.06b euros in 2009 (the largest fine to date) for abuse of a dominant position by using illegal sales practices to ensure that computer manufacturers carry its computer chips.

- Computer games company Nintendo was fined 149m euros in November 2002 for seeking to prevent parallel imports of its game from the UK (where they were 65% cheaper) to other EU states where they could be sold by parallel importing companies at a higher price.

- The European Commission fined Sotheby's 20.4m euros for a seven year price fixing arrangement with their main auction-house competitor, Christie's. The latter was given total exemption from any fine because it had come forward and exposed the activity to the Commission (whistleblowing). The fine was equal to 6% of Sotheby's annual turnover.

The Merger Regulation (Regulation 4064/89)

Clearly, the merger of two or more undertakings within a market can have significant repercussions on trading practices and the level of competition that will continue to exist. Although the European Treaty does not itself regulate such 'concentrations,' **Regulation 4064/89** requires notification of concentrations with a common market dimension.

'Concentrations' include take-overs and full function joint ventures.[5]

---

5 Where the joint venture performs on a long-standing basis all the functions of an autonomous economic entity – See Commission Notice OJ 1998 C66/01 for detailed guidance on this concept.

Once notification has been received, the Commission has 3 weeks in which to decide whether an investigation is required and inform the parties (and the member states affected). If an investigation is carried out, a decision must be made within 3 months whether the proposed merger is approved. The basic question being asked is:

"Is the concentration creating a dominant position within a market which could impede effective competition within the common market?"

The Competition Act 1998

What is the new Act achieving?

It brought UK law into line with EC competition law by adopting a very similar approach, principles and procedures to those found in Articles 81 & 82 of the European Treaty. To do this it was necessary to abolish a number of UK Acts which previously governed the position:

- Restrictive Trade Practices Act 1976.
- Restrictive Trade Practices Act 1977.
- Resale Prices Act 1976.
- (Substantial parts of) the Competition Act 1980.

The monopolies and mergers provisions found in the Fair Trading Act 1973 (FTA) continued to apply until 2003 when the Enterprise Act replaced it.

The Act came fully into force in March 2000, but a number of transitional arrangements began to apply from 1998. One of the first changes to be brought into effect under the Act was the abolition of the Monopoly & Mergers Commission and its replacement by the Competition Commission (CC). The latter continues to carry out the investigative role previously held by the MMC on monopolies and mergers but with enhanced powers. There are two sets of provisions dealing with anti-competitive practices:

Chapter One Prohibition (Section 2)

This is essentially concerned with anti-competitive agreements between independent undertakings within a market (cartels etc.). These used to be governed by the Restrictive Trade Practices Act 1976 as amended.

Chapter Two Prohibition (Section 18)

This focuses on abuse by one undertaking (occasionally by more than one acting in concert) of a dominant position within a market. Previously, UK law in this area had been governed by the Competition Act 1980 (and by the FTA 1973 where the dominant position amounted to a monopoly as defined).

Chapter One Prohibition

The approach and content of Article 81 of the European Treaty are closely followed. The same position is taken relating to:

*   Definitions of agreement (including decisions and concerted practices).
*   'Appreciable effect' on competition.
*   Specific examples of infringements e.g. price fixing, market sharing cartels, bid-rigging, resale price maintenance).

'Appreciability' will be determined by reference to the combined market share of the undertakings involved. The same market analysis will be used to decide the 'relevant market' (product market, geographical market etc.). However, the Office of Fair Trading (OFT) will **generally** consider a combined market share of **less than** 25% to lack the 'appreciable effect' required for an infringement. However, if the agreement relates to any of the following hardcore abuses, it will be potentially an infringement even if it falls below the 25% threshold:

"Market-sharing, price fixing, resale price maintenance or a network effect caused by the cumulative impact of several smaller agreements."

There is no requirement to notify the OFT of agreements which lack an appreciable effect on the relevant market.

N.B. Non-price fixing 'small agreements' (defined by reference to UK turnovers) will not need to be notified and provide immunity from fines.

Exclusions

Vertical Agreements

As we have seen, UK competition law recognises that vertical agreements do not generally give rise to competition concerns unless one of the parties enjoys considerable market power or an agreement forms part of a wide network of similar agreements. Vertical agreements are thus excluded from the Chapter One prohibition[6], unless they relate to price fixing.

Exemptions

The same criteria for granting exemption apply as for Article 81. It is possible to obtain exemption under the Competition Act in any of the following ways:

6. By the Competition Act 1998 (Land & Vertical Agreements Exclusion) Order 2000

1. **Individual exemption by the OFT.**
2. **Block exemption on a UK basis.**
3. **Parallel exemption based on Article 81(3) of the European Treaty.**

Individual exemptions require prior notification and approval. Block exemptions automatically apply without the need for notification. Parallel exemptions do not apply where the European Commission has merely issued an informal comfort letter. However, it is unlikely that the OFT will disagree with the Commission's view on a request for individual exemption.

[For a short time, under UK law, vertical agreements were excluded from the provisions of the Competition Act 1998. However, this was seen to be too significant a departure from the European Treaty approach of allowing them exemption, subject to the usual requirements. They are now covered by a block exemption]

Chapter Two Prohibition

Again, the same basic approach and content found in Article 82 is adopted, including the list of non-exhaustive infringements (excessive or predatory pricing, refusal to supply, applying dissimilar terms to equivalent transactions etc.). As a general rule, the Competition Act **presumes** a market share of **50% or above** involves a position of dominance within that market. Where the undertaking holds **less than 40%** it will be **presumed not** to have such a position unless special factors make it unusual.

Conduct of Minor Significance

Where the dominant undertaking engages in conduct of minor significance (based on UK turnover) it will not reach the appreciability threshold and will not be subject to fines. It need not notify the OFT of the conduct.

Exemptions

There are no exemptions permitted (consistent with Article 82) and the limited exclusions apply only to horizontal restraints.

Powers of Investigation

Under the Competition Act, the Office of Fair Trading has the following powers:

- To require production of specified documents or specified information (s.26).

- To enter premises without a warrant (s.27).
- To enter and search premises with a warrant (s.28).

The Act amends the existing powers of investigation held under the Fair Trading Act 1973 relating to the investigation of monopolies. The OFT can investigate activities only if it has <u>reasonable grounds for suspecting</u> an infringement of either the Chapter One or Chapter Two prohibitions.

What can provide evidence to create reasonable suspicion?
- Copies of secret agreements.
- Statements from employees or former employees.
- A complaint by a rival business.

These can trigger the formal powers of investigation. There is nothing to prevent the OFT from obtaining information through informal enquiries e.g. through written correspondence, over the phone or at meetings. Although firms are encouraged to co-operate, the OFT does not possess statutory powers when carrying out such informal contact and cannot force responses.

Powers to Require Production of Specified Documents and Information

The OFT can require the production of relevant material and stipulate when and where it must be made available. This includes such material as:

invoices   *sales data*   *agreements*

minutes of meetings   *diaries of specified personnel*

It can require the content of specified documents to be explained at a meeting arranged for this purpose. An example would be technical data which includes codes. The instruction to provide the specified material can apply to any organisations connected to an alleged infringement, not just those under suspicion. Therefore, complainants, suppliers, customers and competitors can be ordered to provide documents or information.

The OFT can take copies or extracts from any document produced. It has the right to see records held on computer e.g. invoices or sales figures.

Power to Enter Premises without a Warrant

The OFT has power to carry out **on-site investigations** where it has the same reasonable grounds for suspicion we identified above. Normally, two days written notice must be given to the occupier of the premises but this can be dispensed with:

- If the premises involved were being occupied by the party under investigation (or there were reasonable grounds for suspecting this), or

- The investigating officer has been unable to give notice to the occupier, despite all reasonable steps.

Upon entering the premises, the investigating officer possesses the same powers as were identified above for the production of specified documents.

'Premises' does not include domestic premises unless the home is used partly for business purposes. It does include any vehicles used by the business.

The occupier must be informed in all cases of his right to have a **legal adviser** present. A short period of time will be allowed for a legal adviser to be contacted and arrive on the premises. Such delay will be kept to an absolute minimum because of the risks of evidence being tampered with or other organisation being alerted. Certain security measures can be imposed in the meantime. These include the sealing of filing cabinets, closure of external e-mail systems and the restriction of movement of key personnel involved. If there is an in-house legal adviser, no such delay will be allowed.

Power to Enter and Search Premises without a Warrant

A High Court judge can issue such a warrant where there are reasonable grounds for suspecting the presence of documents on the premises involved:

(a)   which the OFT had previously required to be produced either by written request (s.26) or in the course of an on-site investigation without a warrant (s.27), and which have not been produced; or

(b)   which, had the OFT required their production under s.26, would have been concealed, removed, tampered with or destroyed; or

(c)   which could have been required by the investigating officer in a previously attempted on-site investigation where he was refused entry.

The officer can use reasonable force (but no more) in an effort to gain entry to the premises, but not against any person who may resist.

The usual powers operate once entry has been obtained, including taking copies. It can also take possession of documents where it appears to be necessary for preserving the documents or preventing interference with them (or where it would not be reasonably practicable to take copies). Where originals are taken, which would be exceptional, they must be returned within three months.

Documents/Information which can be withheld

Organisations can refuse to produce **'privileged communications'** i.e. those between a professional legal adviser and his client or those made in connection with legal proceedings. Professional legal advisers includes in-house lawyers such as those employed in an organisation's legal department.

There is also a defence against **self-incrimination** which means that the OFT cannot compel the production of any document or information which might involve an admission by an organisation of the existence of an infringement. It will be for the OFT to have to find evidence by other means.

Confidential information relating to an individual or specific business activities of an organisation should not be disclosed without the consent of the person who originally provided the information. If potentially confidential material has been required by the investigating officer, it should be clearly marked as such and put into a separate confidential annex.

Enforcement

The OFT has the following powers available for enforcement of the Act:

1. To issue directions to discontinue an infringement.
2. To issue interim measures whilst an investigation is being carried out.
3. To impose penalties in appropriate circumstances for an infringement of either Chapter One or Chapter Two.

Directions

The OFT has a discretion to issue appropriate directions to bring an infringement to an end. This could require a modification of the existing agreement or practice or its complete cessation. The direction (which could be addressed to a parent company of a subsidiary which has committed the infringement) could require further action to be taken. Examples include informing third parties of the cessation or periodically reporting back to the OFT on specified points.

There is a right to inspect the OFT file relating to the proposed direction (except for confidential information or the OFT's internal papers). An appeal is available against a direction and would be heard by the Appeals Tribunal of the Competition Commission. In the meantime, the direction would remain effective. The direction will be published on the register kept by the OFT and on a website on the Internet.

If necessary, the OFT can apply to the High Court for an order requiring ompliance. This would be successful if an organisation is failing to comply without reasonable excuse and will require compliance within a specified time. Refusal to observe the order amounts to contempt of court and can result in fines and/or imprisonment. Additionally, court costs will have to be paid by the organisation(s) in default.

Interim Measures

- This administrative power (which did not exist before the Act) is designed to prevent serious damage being caused by the suspected infringement during the course of the investigation.

The damage can be either to other businesses or to the general public. This includes the possibility of a smaller competitor being put out of business in the immediate future or where a competitor is suffering from a considerable competitive disadvantage. The interim measures can require an agreement to be terminated or conduct to be discontinued or for them to be modified.

Penalties

The OFT can impose a financial penalty of up to 10% of the UK turnover of the infringing organisation for each year of the infringement, up to a maximum of 3 years. This is a considerably heavier sanction than any previous fine available in the UK for breach of UK domestic competition law and brings the UK into line with the penalties available to the European Commission for breach of Articles 81 and 82. The severity of the penalty is partly intended to act as a deterrent to other organisations who may otherwise be tempted to engage in anti-competitive practice.

The track record of the organisation may prove relevant in deciding intention or negligence e.g. previous infringements of the Restrictive Trade Practices Act 1976 or the Competition Act 1980. It is no defence to plead ignorance of the technical requirements of the new law.

Where an organisation has participated involuntarily in an infringement e.g. by being a reluctant member of a cartel, it could still be found to have acted intentionally or negligently but have the penalty imposed against it reduced because of this mitigating factor.

Small Agreements and Conduct of Minor Significance

Provided the above do not relate to price fixing, there is an immunity from financial penalties for organisations which satisfy the relevant criteria for the above concepts. These will be defined by UK turnover figures. This immunity applies only to penalties however. The agreements can still be declared void and third parties can still sue for damages.

Guidance on Penalties

The OFT is required to publish guidance as to the appropriate amount for any penalty. The following sets out the framework for decisions on levels of penalties:

Step 1
Assess the gravity and duration of the infringement.

Step 2
Assess whether there should be an increase based on aggravating circumstances, and if so, what level it should be.

Step 3
Assess whether there should be a reduction based on mitigating circumstances, and if so, what level it should be.

Step 4
Take into account a number of objective factors such as economic and financial benefits obtained by the infringing organisation.

The presence of a suitably drafted compliance programme which is being effectively operated by an organisation is a mitigating factor which can reduce the penalty imposed.

Another mitigating factor applies to the case of whistleblowers who co-operate during an investigation into the existence of a cartel. This can result in either an exemption from financial penalty or a reduction in the fine imposed. The OFT will have regard to a Notice published by the European Commission in 1996 which relates to 'secret cartels between enterprises aimed at fixing prices, production or sales quotas, sharing markets or banning imports or exports.' In such cases, the Commission will seriously consider reducing the penalty or even granting exemption for undertakings that are prepared to provide information and co-operate in their investigation.

Although this only operates in relation to Article 81, the OFT is expected to follow the same approach in Chapter One cases.

Appeals
Appeals against the decision to impose a fine or against the level of a fine will be heard by the Appeal Tribunal of the Competition Commission. The Appeal Tribunal

can impose, revoke or vary the amount of a fine. A further appeal on the level of fine decided by the Tribunal can go to the Court of Appeal.

Recent Examples of Fines

*   Argos and Littlewoods were fined £22.5m for fixing the prices of toys and games.

*   Ten companies including Manchester United and the Football Association were fined a total of £18.6m – the second highest fine imposed by the OFT – for a price fixing arrangement on team shirts.

The Enterprise Act 2002

The Enterprise Act 2002 had several objectives. One was to reform the law on monopolies and mergers - previously governed (not very effectively) by the Fair Trading Act 1973. Another objective was to strengthen the Competition Act 1998 in a number of specific ways. The new approach the Enterprise Act has taken on monopolies and mergers is examined in some detail in the next section.

Strengthening the Competition Act 1998

*   The **structure of the Office of Fair Trading** was altered and it was given wider powers to carry out its investigations.
*   The OFT was given power to bring about the **prosecution of individuals** (e.g. senior management, sales personnel etc) for breach of the cartel rules. The case would be referred to the Serious Fraud Office which would take the matter to court. The maximum penalty is 5 years imprisonment and/or an unlimited fine.
*   **Class actions** (brought by a representative organisation on behalf of a large number of individual consumers) are now permitted. The Consumers Association is one example of such organisations.
*   Aggrieved companies who have been the victims of anti-competitive practices can now pursue **civil actions for damages** against the organisations guilty of these practices (either in the Competition Appeal Tribunal or in the ordinary civil courts).

Apart from these provisions, the Enterprise Act brought about several other developments, including the **creation of the Competition Appeal Tribunal** which allows companies to appeal against decisions of the OFT of the Competition Commission.

Monopolies and Mergers

UK Position

The UK law on monopolies and mergers was significantly reformed in 2003 by the bringing into force of the Enterprise Act 2002. Amongst other matters not relating to competition law, the 2002 Act repealed the Fair Trading Act 1973 which had regulated monopolies and mergers since the 1970's. It was the one example of U.K. competition legislation that had not been abolished by the Competition Act 1998. What follows is a brief summary of its main provisions.

Monopolies

Part Five of the **Enterprise Act 2002** makes provision for a system of market investigations by the Competition Commission (a body that replaced the Monopolies and Mergers Commission in 1998 with enhanced powers). The purpose of these investigations is to inquire into markets where it appears that the structure of the market or the conduct of suppliers or customers is harming competition.

These market investigation references replace the earlier monopoly inquiries, and the Act repealed the relevant parts of the old Fair Trading Act 1973 that used to govern monopolies.

Making a Reference

The OFT may make market investigation references to the Competition Commission (CC). When making a reference, it must have reasonable grounds for suspecting that one or more features of a market prevents, restricts or distorts competition in relation to the supply or acquisition of goods or services in the UK (or part of the UK).

The OFT may accept undertakings in lieu of a reference from appropriate personnel in order to remedy the adverse effects on competition. In other words, the matter is resolved on a voluntary basis without the need to enter formal procedures involving the CC.

Competition Commission - Investigation and Remedies

A detailed investigation (with a maximum period of two years to complete) is carried out by the CC. If an adverse effect on competition is identified, the CC must decide how best to remedy the situation - either in the form of voluntary undertakings or compulsory orders. Orders could include requirements to modify existing trading arrangements, including a break up of the company structure into independent trading concerns.

Appeals

There is a new right to apply for a review of decisions taken by the CC (or the OFT) in connection with market investigation references. The case would be reviewed by the Competition Appeal Tribunal (CAT). The CAT is not allowed to substitute its own decision on the merits of the case, but can review the lawfulness and fairness of the decision and if necessary, require the CC or OFT to reconsider its decision.

Mergers

In the context of mergers and take-overs, UK competition law is now based on the **Enterprise Act 2002** (which replaced the Fair Trading Act 1973 in 2003).

Part Four allows proposed mergers to be subject to investigation if they would result in:
* the value of the assets taken over exceeding £70m, or,
* a monopoly (25% or more of the relevant market)) being created.

The OFT must consider (within a maximum period of four months) whether the merger may be expected to result in a 'substantial lessening of competition'. If the OFT believes that this test is, or may be, met, then it must either refer the merger to the Competition Commission (CC) or, if appropriate, seek undertakings from the merging parties.

If the merger is referred to the CC, it will conduct a full investigation to determine whether it will result in a substantial lessening of competition. It must complete its investigation within 24 weeks.

The Enterprise Act 2002 has made some significant changes to the previous position e.g.

* the Commission makes its own decisions, with no political involvement from the DTI.
* the criteria has ceased to be based on public interest and become more competition-based – will the merger have the consequence of distorting competition within the relevant market - similar to the Competition Act 1998 approach for anti-competitive practices.

The Commission has the power to prohibit the merger. Alternatively it could impose remedies in the form of undertakings which would be subsequently monitored by the OFT.

EU Position

The Merger Regulation (Regulation 4064/89)

Clearly, the merger of two or more undertakings within a market can have significant repercussions on trading practices and the level of competition that will continue to exist. Although the European Treaty does not itself regulate such 'concentrations,' **Regulation 4064/89** requires notification of concentrations with a common market dimension.

'Concentrations' include take-overs and full function joint ventures.[7]

Once notification has been received, the Commission has 3 weeks in which to decide whether an investigation is required and inform the parties (and the member states affected). If an investigation is carried out, a decision must be made within 3 months whether the proposed merger is approved. The basic question being asked is:

"Is the concentration creating a dominant position within a market which could impede effective competition within the common market?"

Competition Law Institutions

The Office of Fair Trading

- Established in 1973.
- Given statutory status in 2003 (Enterprise Act 2002).
- Non-ministerial department of government.
- Main role – to protect consumers and to enforce UK competition policy.
- Governed by Chair & Board.

Two main Divisions:
1)   **Consumer Affairs Division.**
2)   **Competition Policy Division.**

Both Divisions provide legal advice on competition legislation and publish a wide range of guidance literature.

Competition Policy Division seeks to protect customers and suppliers by monitoring abuses of market power:

---

7. Where the joint venture performs on a long-standing basis all the functions of an autonomous economic entity – See Commission Notice OJ 1998 C66/01 for detailed guidance on this concept.

- **Monopolies**

  If potential distortion of trade within a market, OFT can refer 'monopoly situation' to Competition Commission for formal investigation or encourage voluntary undertakings from business involved. OFT can monitor subsequent activities of the organisation if the Commission has obtained undertakings.

- **Anti-competitive Practices**

  Using the new powers under the Competition Act 1998, OFT can investigate and take action where restrictive agreements or abuse of a dominant position can be identified. OFT can either seek voluntary undertakings, act under its own powers or refer matter to Competition Commission (see earlier material on new powers).

- **Resale Price Maintenance**

  Imposition of minimum resale prices to the public are unlawful except in highly unusual circumstances where it can be argued to be in the public interest (no continuing examples of such exceptions now exist). OFT monitors business markets to ensure compliance.

- **Mergers**

  OFT seeks to identify impending mergers (or ones that have already occurred). May seek voluntary undertakings from the undertakings concerned or refer the merger to the Competition Commission.

  OFT liaises with European Commission and can be used to assist in investigations on European competition law infringements.

- **(For investigation powers and enforcement sanctions, see earlier notes).**

The Competition Commission

- Replaced the Monopolies and Mergers Commission (MMC) in 1999.

- Initially acquired an appeal function from decisions of the OFT. This responsibility was transferred to the newly formed Competition Appeal Tribunal in 2003.

Reporting function:
- Similar to the MMC pre 1999.
- Based largely on Enterprise Act 2002 (replacing the Fair Trading Act 1973) and privatisation statutes.

- Concerned with monopolies, mergers and regulatory inquiries.
- Each inquiry will have 4 or 5 members of the Commission.
- Time limits – maximum 24 weeks for mergers.
- normally 6 months for a utility case.
- normally 9-12 months for a monopoly inquiry (max of 2 years)*.
- Monopoly inquiries and merger inquiries are referred to CC by the OFT (occasionally by the Secretary of State for DTI).
- Cannot initiate own inquiries.
- Power to make own decisions and use enforcement techniques.

* it is anticipated that these will focus heavily on complex monopolies in future (Scale monopolies are effectively banned under the Competition Act 1998).

The Competition Appeal Tribunal

- Created in 2003 by the Enterprise Act 2002.
- Consists of a President, panel of Chairmen, and ordinary members.
- Hearings will consist of Chairman and two other members.

Functions:
- Hearing appeals from decisions taken by the OFT or sectoral regulators under Chapter One or Chapter Two of the Competition Act 1998 with the power to confirm, set aside or vary the decision, or remit the matter to the OFT or regulator.

- Hearing claims for damages where an infringement of competition law has been established under Chapters 1 or 2 of the Competition Act 1998 or Articles 81 or 82 of the European Treaty.

- Reviewing decisions on mergers or market investigation (monopoly) references taken by the OFT, Competition Commission or regulators.

- Further appeals proceed to the Court of Appeal and House of Lords.

Department of Business, Enterprise & Regulatory Reform
- Responsible for regulating and supporting trade and industry.
- Seeks to ensure fair standards of business practice.
- Seeks to protect consumer.
- Contains various agencies including Companies House and Patents Office.
- Divided into Directorates, including:
    - Corporate & Consumer Affairs
      [company affairs including competition & fair trading company investigations consumer matters including consumer safety].

The above includes the Competition Policy Directorate.

*   **Objective**
    To create and maintain effective markets free of abusive practices.

*   Can refer mergers to Competition Commission for investigation and decision.

European Commission
See Page 135.

In conclusion:

*   Competition law concentrates on two forms of abuse – agreements between independent organisations to manipulate market conditions (cartels) and abusive behaviour by individual organisations in a dominant position.

*   UK competition is regulated by a combination of domestic and EU measures.

*   The UK approach to regulation is largely modelled on the European measures with some differences.

*   The main EU measures are Article 81 of the European Treaty (cartel regulation) and Article 82 (abuse of a dominant position).

*   The main UK domestic measures are Chapter One of the Competition Act 1998 (cartels) and Chapter Two (abuse of a dominant position).

*   The Enterprise Act 2002 now regulates the position on monopolies and mergers in the UK.

*   Definitions of collusion and dominant market position, criteria for exemption, analysis of market power, and enforcement techniques are largely identical between the EU and UK provisions.

*   The EU measures only apply when the abuse affects trade between member states.

Chapter Sixteen
Intellectual Property Rights

Intellectual Property Rights (IPR) cover a wide range of 'intellectual' assets based either on creativity (inventiveness) or on protection of existing reputation. Both have significant effects on competitiveness and business success, achieving or maintaining a cutting edge in the market or relying on a strong well-recognised image. Patents, design rights, confidentiality and copyright clearly relate to inventiveness whereas trade marks and the tort action of passing off relate to protection of reputation. IPR are vigorously protected by a combination of statutory and common law principles and by contractual terms and conditions.

The chapter covers the following legal issues:

- Justification of IPR.
- Classification of IPR.
- Remedies for infringement.
- Patents - requirements of successful claim.
- Patents – employee rights.
- Trade marks – changes introduced in 1994.
- Trade marks – requirements for successful application.
- Trade marks – enforcement rights.
- Trade marks – community trade mark.
- Passing off – requirements for successful claim.
- Passing off – case law.
- Confidential information – requirements for successful claim.
- Confidential information – basis of action (contract, equity).
- Confidential information – position of employees.
- Design rights – classification (registered, unregistered).
- Design rights – requirements for successful application/claim.
- Design rights – exclusions.
- Copyright – changes introduced under the Copyright, Designs & Patents Act 1988.
- Copyright – requirements for successful claim.
- Contractual provisions relating to IPR.

What are Intellectual Property Rights?

It is an area of law that concerns itself with legal rights connected with **creative effort** or **commercial reputation and goodwill**. The law attempts to deter other people or firms from either copying or taking unfair advantage of the work or reputation of another by providing remedies.

The main remedies involved are :

> **Copyright**
>
> **Law of confidence**
>
> **Patent**
>
> **Registered design**
>
> **Design right**
>
> **Trade marks**
>
> **Passing off**

Intellectual Property Rights (IPR) are **'property'** in the legal sense. They can be **owned, assigned or licensed**. They belong to that category of property where rights can only be enforced by legal action (choses in action) as opposed to land and other tangible property where rights can be enforced by taking physical possession. Intellectual property is the most basic form of property – a man uses nothing other than his mind to produce it.

How are IPR justified?

*   A man should own what he produces – that which he brings into being. If what he produces can be taken away from him, he is no better than a slave.

*   Strong protective laws should exist to encourage investment in research and development. This, in turn, increases general wealth, employment and prosperity.

- The strong laws can be made a vehicle for the dissemination of new ideas and innovation by requiring their general publication in exchange for providing the protection. This facilitates the expansion of further R&D leading to yet more discoveries and innovation.

How can IPR be classified?

Some rights create monopolies; others merely prevent the unfair use by others of an existing work or article. Some rights require registration before they become effective (sometimes these are called **hard IPR**); others operate automatically without any need to register **(soft IPR).**

Some rights are based on legislation; others were formed by common law (judge-made).

HARD IPR	SOFT IPR	STATUTORY	COMMON LAW
Patents	Copyright	Patents	Confidentiality
Design right	Unregistered Design Right	Trade Marks	Passing off
Trade marks	Confidentiality	Registered Design Right	
	Passing Off	Unregistered Design Right	
		Copyright	

Traditionally, most of the above rights (patents, trade marks, design rights) were known as industrial property. The more modern terminology (which includes copyright) is intellectual property rights. Some contracts will still use the older expression. If they do, they should clearly specify which rights are involved, especially with regard to copyright.

Why are IPR important in business?

In the international context there is a direct correlation between investment in research and development and competitive success. Compared with their competitors, Japan and Germany generally have higher levels of long term investment and awareness of the importance of innovation and the design process. In the domestic context it is not surprising that the two largest manufacturing industries, chemicals and aerospace, also have the highest levels of investment in research and development. Such industries are highly competitive internationally. They contribute significantly to the nation's revenue and balance of trade, employ large numbers of workers and make considerable profits for their shareholders.

The impact on the consumer of the legal protection of intellectual property is enormous. Where products are protected by intellectual property, whether it be by patenting, reputation or trade marks, the manufacturer is able to charge a premium. Brand names in the fashion industry are an obvious example of this phenomenon. This trend is growing and many sizeable undertakings now find that the value of their IPR may well be significantly greater than their other, more tangible assets.

Remedies

The range of remedies available for infringement of IP rights are:

Injunctions

Damages

Account of Profits

Court orders for seizure of infringing articles etc.

Patents

Some introductory points

* Governed by the **Patents Act 1977**, which is based on the European Patent Convention.

* A patent creates a **statutory monopoly** in an invention with the exclusive right to use/exploit it for up to **20 years**.

* After 20 years, the invention falls into the public domain and can be used by any competing organisation.

- The justification for a strong patent monopoly is that it provides a reward to the inventor for effort, encourages innovation and enables recovery of research costs, and is a form of payment for allowing the invention to be published and technological understanding improved in general.

- Few patents last the full 20 years – they either fail to make enough money or they are overtaken by technological advance.

- Most patents are created by employees working in teams for large companies – not by isolated geniuses (the mad boffin image).

- Patents are stronger than trade secrets because the monopoly continues even if the secret enters the public domain.

- Competitors may attempt to break a patent by:
1. **challenge** (producing a similar product which is not covered by patent).

2. **invalidation** (proving that the product/process was not new or did not involve an inventive step).

3. **infringement** (larger organisations may risk court action in the belief that legal costs will intimidate smaller companies who hold the patent).

- Techniques available to deal with (3) above include:
1. **Licensing a larger organisation with the resources to protect against infringement.**

2. **Arranging insurance cover.**

3. **Negotiating a licence with the potential infringer.**

Governed by the Patents Act 1977

Statutory Monopoloy for 20 Years

Most lapse in the meantime

Uusually teams, not individual boffins

Stronger than Trade Secrets Proectection

Procedure

Patents require registration wherever protection is sought. There are clear advantages in multiple registration procedures where one application will cover a block of countries. An application for a patent can be made either to the European Patent Office in Munich or the British Patent Office in Newport. British applicants are obliged to file first in the U.K for reasons of national security. Approximately 27000 new applications are made each year and around 180,000 renewals.

How long will an application take?

There is a timetable for processing applications with the maximum time limits indicated below:

Patent Applications

File Application (Priority date)

Preliminary Examination and Search

Search Report

'A' Publication (18 months after priority date):
- the application
- the search report   **18 months**

Substantive Examination

Grant and 'B' Publication   **Maximum 4.5 years**

Procedural stages

Filing
The date of the invention is the date when it is first filed ("priority date") Infringement proceedings can arise from this date.

Publication
Within 18 months, the Patent Office must publish the application, allowing for public inspection. This is carried out by the government printer and is despatched world-wide.

Examination and Search

Within 6 months of publication the applicant should request that an examination and search be carried out. This involves a search through the relevant technical literature, including previous applications. Much of the material is now located on cd rom and other forms of electronic retrieval. The examiner will raise any objections and allow time for amendments. Claims are likely to be honed down during this process.

Grant of Patent

A final decision must be made within 4.5 years of the initial application. If it is granted, a notice must appear in the Official Journal (Patents) so that it has been officially published. The patent will last for 20 years subject to payment of the relevant renewal fees.

Who may make the application?

According the Patents Act 1977, the only person entitled to apply is the inventor. "Inventor" is defined as the devisor, but persons who possess property rights over the invention also can apply. This normally refers to the employer involved.

What are the contents of the application?

1. Request for grant of a patent.
2. Specification containing a description of the invention.
3. Claim or claims defining the scope of the patent.
4. Abstract summarising above.

Requirements for a successful application

Under s.1(1) of the Patents Act 1977, the following conditions are required for the grant of a patent:

the invention is new (novelty)

it involves an inventive step (obviousness)

it is capable of industrial application
+
the grant of a patent for it is not excluded (under the Act)

**Section 1(1)
Patents Act 1977**

Novelty

The Patents Act 1977 defines novelty for the first time. S.2(1) states that an invention shall be taken to be new if it does not form part of the **state of the art**. Under s.2(2) 'state of the art' is defined as **all matter which, prior to the priority date, has been made available to the public, whether in the U.K. or elsewhere**. Lack of novelty can be used as a defence to infringement proceedings (the 'Gillette defence') and can lead to revocation of the licence.

The question of novelty hinges on whether the invention has already been **'disclosed to the public'**. This can be either through published documents (forming part of the state of the art) or through being known to the public (having been seen in operation). Disclosure to a single individual can be sufficient. However, disclosures in breach of confidence will not be admissible.

Laboratory use and testing in secret does not undermine novelty. Disclosure can take place even if the audience is unaware of its significance at the time.

Windsurfing International v Tabur Marine GB

A patent had been sought for a navigational boom for a wind-surfer. It was established that an 11-year-old boy had been seen using a crude prototype off the English coast in the 1950s. This defeated the application on the grounds of lack of novelty.

Obviousness (Inventive Step)

'Invention' is not defined but s.3 indicates an inventive step involves something that is **not obvious to persons skilled in the art**, having regard to any matter which forms part of the state of the art. 'State of the art' consists of all matter that has been made available to the public before the priority date.

Obviousness is determined in court by expert witnesses being examined and cross-examined. In deciding obviousness the clearest modern test is found in the Windsurfing case. This four-fold test was restated in a more concise form in **Molnycke AB v Proctor & Gamble**:

(1)   What is the inventive step alleged to be involved?

(2)   What was the state of the art at the priority date?

(3)   In what respect does the step go beyond or differ from the state of the art?

(4)   Would the step be obvious to a skilled man?

However, a variety of tests have been used over the years. The **commercial success** of an invention has sometimes been proposed as a test of obviousness (although not a complete one – success could be the result of heavy investment in advertising). An early test which is still taken into account is whether the invention satisfied a **'long-felt want'** – where the problem had waited solution for many years. No one test will prove totally effective because of differing contexts and technological advance e.g. in the field of microbiological research. However, the Windsurfer test has resulted in a more standardised approach since its formulation.

Exclusions

A number of exclusions are found in s.1(2) and (3) of the Patents Act 1977 e.g. an application will not be accepted if the matter **falls within the natural ambit of another intellectual property right.**

The invention must be **capable of industrial application** e.g. discoveries and theories, ideas or mathematical formulae in the abstract cannot be patented. However, incorporation of a discovery into technology is patentable – a technical contribution to the art. It is the practical application of the idea or discovery that is needed.

Schemes, rules, methods for performing a mental act, playing a game or doing business, or a programme for a computer and the presentation of information are excluded. Occasionally, if a technical element is present, a patent can be obtained e.g. a method for arranging buoys for navigational purposes; a method for distributing utilities services on an housing estate; a method of teaching pronunciation of language combined with a reading machine (presence of a mechanical element).

Patent applications relating to **medical treatment** are not allowed. It is argued that no-one should have a monopoly on mechanisms which relieve human suffering (processes for medical treatment of human beings for the cure or prevention of diseases). Exceptions include a new method of contraception (pregnancy not being a disease) and new cosmetic treatments e.g. hair improvers (same argument).

Biological inventions are not patentable on ethical grounds – animals and plants should not be the subject of patents and monopoly practices. Exceptions can be found including the Onco mouse (which was developed for research leading to the improved treatment of cancer patients). However, microbiological processes and products may be patentable. Problems arise in distinguishing between biological and microbiological processes – no definitions have been formulated. One controversial area of current applications for patents relates to DNA sequences which have enormous implications for the future medical treatment of patients.

Defences to Patent Infringement Claim

A number of defences can be available to defendants in actions for infringement of a patent. The majority are contained in s.60 of the Patents Act 1977:

- Invalidity.
- Licence.
- Prior Use.
- Exhaustion of rights.
- Accidental Infringement.
- Public Policy.

Invalidity

Here the defendant will argue that the patent should be revoked. The challenge will be based on the requirements of s.1(1) on grounds of lack of novelty or inventive step. In essence it is arguing that the patent was granted in error and should be nullified (Licensees of a patent are unable to challenge on grounds of invalidity unless the licence specifically allows for this).

Licence

This is a complete defence. The alleged infringement must however come within the ambit of the licence in terms of duration (not after the licence has expired), geographical area (although this may cause problems for the licensor if the restrictions are seen to infringe competition law regulation as being anti-competitive), and extent of activities permitted (e.g. a licence to use does not extend to manufacture as well). Licences can be implied as in the case of a licence to repair where the purchaser of a patented product gives the item to a third party for repair. The purchaser of a patented product assumes ownership and will be entitled to re-sell it unless the original sale restricts this.

Exhaustion of Rights

Once a patented product has been put on the market in any EC country with the consent of the proprietor, the disposal will have exhausted his rights and no subsequent disposal will infringe.

Prior Use

A person cannot be restrained from continuing to do what has hitherto been done. If another firm has been working on parallel lines and can prove prior use, it turns the monopoly into a duopoly.

Accidental Infringement

The general principle is that it is no defence for the defendant to argue innocence. Infringement does not require fault on the part of the infringer. There are some exceptions though e.g. accidental or temporary entry of a foreign registered aircraft or vessel into the U.K.

Public Policy
If it can be shown that the alleged infringement was done for non-commercial purposes e.g. for education in private, experimental application, it will not infringe the patent.

Employee Rights

Under s.7, the applicant for a patent has to be its inventor. This is defined as its devisor or any person entitled to property in the patent. Where the invention is produced by an employee or employees working for a firm the employer will normally claim patent rights using the property argument above. This is usually based on **express provision** in the contract of employment, but even if the contract does not have a specific clause dealing with patent rights the courts have held that it contains an **implied undertaking** to hand over patent rights for inventions made during the course of employment.

The invention is said to be held on trust for the employer under the employee's implied duty of **good faith and fidelity.** Section 39 reinforces the rights of the employer. It states that any invention made in the course of employment shall belong to the employer where it was made:

a) in the normal course of the normal duties of the employee, or
b) in the course of duties falling outside his normal duties but specifically   assigned to him, and
in either case, an invention might reasonable be expected to result.

Section 40 allows employees to claim compensation where the employer has patented to invention and it has been of outstanding benefit. It allows employees to claim a fair share of this return. In fact, only a handful of such claims have been made since 1978.

Trade Marks

This section contains a description of the following features of trade mark law:

*   Background to the Trade Marks Act 1994.
*   The new definition of a trade mark.
*   Powers of the Trade Mark Registrar to refuse registration.

- Rights of a trade mark proprietor to bring infringement proceedings.
- Defences to infringement proceedings.
- Community trade marks.

The Trade Marks Act 1994

This Act made radical changes to the previous law, improving rights of the proprietor. This was achieved in the following ways:

1. Brought UK trade mark law into line with the rest of the EC.
2. Created a presumption in favour of registration.
3. Widened the definition of a trade mark.
4. Made registration of geographical names easier.
5. Overturned previous restrictions on registering shapes.
6. Extended rights to include marks on packaging.
7. Allowed three dimensional 'signs' to be registered.
8. Allowed colours to be registered.
9. Allowed smells and sounds to be registered.
10. Created a more flexible licensing system.
11. Created a number of new criminal offences.
12. Extended rights to complain about similar signs on dissimilar goods.

Duration

Marks can be registered for an **initial period of 10 years** (previously 7) with **renewal periods of 10 years** (previously 14). This provides for consistency with EC law and the Madrid Protocol.

Definition of Trade Mark

Section 1(1) of the Trade Marks Act 1994 defines a trade mark as **any sign capable of being represented graphically and capable of distinguishing the goods or services of one undertaking from those of other undertakings.**

It further states that a trade mark **may consist of words (including personal names), designs, letters, numerals or the shape of goods or their packaging.** The mark must be used **to denote the source or origin of the goods/services concerned.** "A word or words, to be really distinctive of a person's goods, must generally speaking be incapable of application to the goods of anyone else. There must be some quality in the mark that earmarks the goods so marked as distinct from those of other producers of such goods.

Trade Marks

'Any sign capable of being represented graphically and capable of distinguishing the goods or services of one undertaking from those of other undertakings'

May consist of:

- Words (including personal names)

- Designs

- Letters

- Numerals

- Shape of goods

- Packaging

- Must denote source or origin of the goods/services

Refusal to Register

Under Part 3 of the Act it is the duty of the Trade Marks Registrar to maintain a register and scrutinise applications for trade marks. He must ensure that successful applications comply with the requirements of the Act and that owners of existing marks are protected. There are a number of absolute grounds for refusal to register found in section.3 e.g.

- **if a sign does not meet the requirements of s1(1) of the Act (see above).**

- **if the mark is devoid of distinctive character (being merely descriptive).**

Invented words are more likely to satisfy the second barrier, although problems can still arise here. In **SF & O Hallgarten's Application,** the word 'Whiskeur' was refused for a product that combined liqueur and whisky. It was regarded as merely descriptive of the product rather than a trade mark. The courts are cautious with invented words where they are attempting to get around the restrictions on the character and quality of the goods (again becoming descriptive).

In the **ORWOOLA case,** the court held that the mark was a misspelling of "all wool" and did not form a distinctive mark. This could in fact be misleading if the goods were not entirely made of wool. Misspelt words are not treated as invented, although a combination of two misspelt words may be seen to acquire distinctiveness.

Section 3 also allows for refusal if the mark would be **contrary to public policy** or morality. An example of such a refusal is **HALLELUJAH TRADE MARK** where the name 'Hallelujah' was to be used to sell women's clothes.

Section 4 bans trade marks which consist of or contain a representation of a **national flag of the UK** if it appears to the Registrar that its use would be misleading or grossly offensive. A mark which is applied for in **bad faith** or with no honest intention to use will be refused registration.

Refusal under Section 5

Any person is entitled to **oppose an application** for registration of a trade mark. This may be done by arguing that s.5 has been infringed. This permits the Registrar to refuse registration of a mark:

1.   which is identical or similar to a mark for identical goods;

2.   which is identical or similar for similar goods and there is a likelihood of confusion;

3.   which is identical or similar and is applied to goods which are dissimilar but the mark has a reputation.

Where the opposition is based on similarity and confusion (2 above) the established test is as follows:

Is there a real likelihood of deception amongst a number of people between normal use of the previous trade mark registration and normal use of the proposed registration?

An example of a challenge under s.5 is **Portakabin v Portablast.** The totality of the impression was stressed with the sound as well as the visual appearance being relevant. As the first five letters in both words looked and sounded the same the application was rejected as the rest of the words did not diminish the initial impression. Some cases have suggested that similarity between the first two syllables of two words is of most significance in deciding the issue.

The nature of the target audience is taken into account – does it consist of experts and trade professionals or ordinary members of the public – consumers? However, the ultimate purchasers of goods are not presumed to be unusually unobservant. In **Morning Star v Express Newspapers (1979)** it was said that "only a moron in a hurry" could have confused the two titles.

Infringement Proceedings

The proprietor enjoys **exclusive rights** in a registered trade mark (s.9). It becomes part of his personal property and entitles him to bring infringement proceedings. **Section 10** sets out the grounds for complaint i.e. where a mark has been used without consent which is:

1.   identical on the same goods for which the mark was registered; s.10(1).

2.   identical or similar on the same or similar goods where there is a likelihood of confusion; s10(2).

3.   identical or similar on goods which are dissimilar but where the trade mark enjoys a reputation, and use of the mark will be detrimental to its reputation; s.10(3).

The marks will be compared on a mark by mark basis. A case illustrating the approach is:

Wagamama Ltd. v City Centre Restaurants

The plaintiff had a successful Japanese restaurant in London under the registered trade mark 'Wagamama,' a Japanese word. The defendant, in April 1995, opened a restaurant in London selling Indian food under the name Rajamama. The court considered both the look and sound of the name in deciding there was an infringement under s.10(2).

Damage can take a number of forms where infringement has occurred. **Confusion leading to wrong association** with another company can affect issues such as the quality of goods sold, the type of business carried out, the ability to obtain credit and the inconvenience of confusion caused by suppliers making mistakes as to identity.

In some situations it is a defence to infringement proceedings (or opposition to an application for registration) to argue **concurrent existing use.** In the latter case, this allows the Registrar to permit two identical marks to be registered. The Act provides that the Registrar shall not refuse an application because of an earlier trade mark unless objection for this reason is made by the earlier registered proprietor. If an **objection** is raised, however, it would appear that **refusal is automatic.** [s.5(3) is relevant here – a trade mark cannot be registered for dissimilar goods if the previous mark has an established reputation].

What is honest, concurrent use?

The court will consider whether "there was really only some fictitious or colourable use and not a real or genuine use."

Community Trade Mark System

Under the "Harmonisation Directive," regulations have been passed bringing a common trade mark system into operation since April 1996. This enables a single application for registration to cover all member states of the EU. It provides protection across the 15 countries and the ability to enforce trade mark rights under the relevant legal system where the infringement took place. Very similar rules apply to granting registration as under the Trade Marks Act 1994.

The benefits of Community registration are the saving of time and money and the greater ease of enforcement if infringements take place. It also avoids having to identify slight but significant differences in registration requirements in individual member states. The significance of such registrations is bound to increase in time with the expansion of international markets.

A Community trade mark is renewed every 10 years and will be cheaper than multiple renewals in individual countries.

Passing Off

This section will provide you with a description of the following aspects of the law of passing off:

- Basic definitions of passing off.
- Meaning of goodwill.

- Meaning of 'get-up'.
- Prospective goodwill.
- Deception, not mere confusion.
- Common field of activity.
- Target audience.
- Types of 'damage'.
- Use of own name.
- Future of passing off.
- Additional cases.

A trader must not "...sell his own goods under the pretence that they are goods of another man."

The essential elements of this common law action (an economic tort) were identified in **Erven Warnink bv v Townend & Sons (Hull) Ltd** as:

1. A misrepresentation;

2. made by a trader in the course of trade;

3. to prospective customers or ultimate consumers of goods/services supplied by him;

4. which is calculated to injure the business or goodwill or another trader; and

5. which results in damage to a business or goodwill of a trader or is likely to do so.

(per Lord Diplock)

Another formulation was put forward in **Reckitt & Colman v Borden (1990)** by Lord Oliver. He suggested that passing off contains 3 elements:

1. goodwill or reputation attached to the goods or services supplied with an associated 'get-up';

2. a misrepresentation by the defendant to the public leading or likely to lead to the public believing that the goods/services offered by him are those of the plaintiff; and

3. actual or likely damage by reason of the erroneous belief engendered by the defendant's misrepresentation.

Essentially, the tort consists of three ingredients – **reputation** (or goodwill) acquired by the plaintiff in his goods, name or mark; **misrepresentation** by the defendant leading to confusion; **damage** to the plaintiff.

Goodwill has been defined as "the attractive force which brings customers in." In actions for passing off, the plaintiff must prove that the goodwill is linked in the public imagination to a 'get-up' – a distinctive mark or name. An early example is **Birmingham Vinegar Brewery C. v Powell** where 'Yorkshire Relish' was a widely known sauce manufactured by the plaintiff. It had attained the necessary distinctiveness even though the precise identity of the manufacturer was not so well known.

Names, fancy or invented words, shapes and colours can all constitute a 'get-up'. In **Hoffman La Roche v DDSA** the defendants imitated the colouring of a specific brand of tranquilliser. This was held to be passing off, even though many people did not know the name of the specific manufacturer involved. The 'get-up' of the tablets had created in the mind of the public a particular source of manufacture. Most cases involve names or invented words.

The goodwill may be limited geographically but, equally, it is possible for the trade to take place abroad. In **Maxim's Ltd. v DYE:**

The plaintiff, an English company, owned a world famous restaurant in Paris known as 'Maxim's'. The defendant opened a restaurant in Norwich and also named it 'Maxim's'. It was held that the plaintiff had goodwill in England derived from the business in France which might be regarded as prospective. The plaintiff might want to commence trading in England in the future and should be able to rely on the goodwill he had in connection with the name.

Mere confusion in the mind of the public is not enough. There must be a **degree of deception** – a false representation, whether fraudulent or otherwise.

There must be a common field of activity between the plaintiff and the defendant.

McCullogh v Lewis A May Ltd.:

The plaintiff was a well known children's broadcaster who used the name 'Uncle Mac'. The plaintiff had some physical infirmities. The defendant sold cereal under the name 'Uncle Mac' with indirect reference to the plaintiff's infirmities without the plaintiff's permission. It was argued that the public might draw certain conclusions harmful to the image of the plaintiff e.g. that he was prepared to receive large payments for commercial advertising which conflicted with the image he had cultivated with the public.

Held: The claim must fail as there was no common field of activity such as would cause confusion in the minds of the public. He was in public broadcasting. The defendants were in the manufacture and marketing of cereals (questionable reasoning here).

The same principle was applied in **Wombles Ltd. v Wombles Skips Ltd.:**

The plaintiff company owned the copyright in the books and drawings of the Wombles. Its main business was granting licences in respect of the characters; for example, it granted one such licence for waste paper baskets for children. The defendant formed a company to lease builders' skips. He decided to call the business 'Wombles Skips Ltd' because of their association with tidying up rubbish. **Held:** There was no common field of activity and therefore no danger of confusion (even allowing for the licence relating to waste paper baskets.)

Sometimes, however, the facts are less clear-cut and the decision more difficult to anticipate:

Lego v Lemelstrich

The well-known Lego company, which makes coloured plastic construction bricks for children, was granted an injunction preventing the use of the name Lego by the defendant who was planning to use it for its plastic irrigation and garden equipment. It was held that the name had become so closely associated with the plaintiff's business that there was a potential for confusion – the common field of activity in this case being coloured plastic.

For a claim to be successful, the plaintiff must show that a **substantial number of the public are likely to be misled**. The nature of the target audience needs to be taken into account (is it a professional audience or the general public?) However, the court will not have regard to unusually stupid people.

Proof of damage is essential – either existing or likely to be suffered. This can cover a range of matters including diversion of sales, damage to reputation, and even loss of a licensing opportunity.

An example of damage to reputation is **Harrods Ltd. v R. Harrod Ltd.:**

The plaintiff was a well known company with a banking department, but which was precluded from operating as a moneylender by the articles of association. The defendant registered a money-lending company under the 'fancy-name' of R. Harrod Ltd, that is a name having nothing to do with his own name. This fact together with his advertising style showed that he was acting fraudulently in an attempt to gain advantage from these similarities and the plaintiff was granted an injunction to restrain the defendant from using that name.

Placing **secondary goods or inferior goods** on the market, making out that they were the goods of the plaintiff amounts to damage to reputation.

Occasionally an action for passing off will lie through injurious association i.e. even though the plaintiff and the defendant are not in the same line of business, a false suggestion by the defendant that they were connected with one another could harm the reputation of the plaintiff's business. In **Annabel's Club v Schock**, it was held that there was a possibility of confusion between the plaintiff's night-club and an escort agency set up by the defendants using the same name.

Use of Own Name

No-one can claim copyright in a single word or name. It is however possible to restrain the use of a name under the law of passing off, subject to an exception – the right of a person to use his own name in business.

The right to trade in one's own name does not extend to the right to use it as a trade mark though if the result would lead to confusion.

Ultimately, the key question in each case seems to be whether the use of a name is calculated to deceive the public. Confusion in itself is not enough. English law does allow a person generally to use his/her own name honestly in the market, but not if it is being used intentionally to deceive and confuse the public. The intention behind the use of the name is therefore crucial to a claim for passing off here. In **Parker Knoll v Knoll International** (1962) Denning L.J. gave the example that a man called William John Pears cannot set up a soap business and call his soap 'Pears Soap'.

Future of Passing Off

An important feature of this tort is that its boundaries are never static. It moves with the times to accommodate new situations and problems. This can make accurate definition of the tort a dangerous activity. One example of recent development is **Lego v Lemelstrich** where, despite there being no apparent common field of activity, it was held that the claim would be successful and the damage included the loss of a licensing opportunity.

The widening of the definition of a trade mark in s.1 (1) of the Trade Marks Act 1994 may seem to make actions for passing off less important in the future. Firms can register a trade mark and receive statutory protection – a stronger and often easier basis of complaint. There are however a number of reasons why this common law action is likely to remain relevant to protection of trade marks. Some organisations, by their very nature, are unlikely to wish to go to the lengths of registering a trade mark e.g. charities and other voluntary organisations. They may however wish to protect their activities through an action for passing off.

It also retains a relevance where the Registrar is considering applications for new trade marks. He is obliged, under the Trade Marks Act 1994 to consider the rights of proprietors of earlier unregistered marks and should not allow any marks which would infringe a passing off claim. Also, because of a number of uncertainties in the law of registered trade marks, it is always advisable to bring an alternative claim for passing off in addition to an infringement claim under s.10 of the 1994 Act. This would cover the problem if the trade mark were declared invalid or was revoked.

Additional Cases

Associated Newsagents v Insert Media Ltd.

The defendant's business was to arrange advertising through inserting leaflets in newspapers. Without permission of the plaintiffs, they attempted to do this with a group of newsagents (the *Daily Mail* and *Mail on Sunday* were affected) **Held:** An action for passing off successful. The public would be confused and assume the inserts had the support and approval of the newspapers. There was a misrepresentation and a risk of loss of goodwill and reputation by the plaintiffs.

Bollinger v Costa Bravo Wine Co.

"Spanish Champagne" declared an infringement. "Champagne" has to come from a particular part of France.

Erven Warninck v Townend

The plaintiffs made advocaat (from eggs and spirits). The defendants started making an egg flip (from dried eggs and Cyprus sherry) but decided to call it advocaat because of the latter's success and popularity.
Held: A claim for passing off was successful. The plaintiffs had a considerable reputation to protect and the use of the same name for a product made from different ingredients was an infringement.

Confidential Information

The following section provides you with a description of the following aspects of the duty of confidentiality:

*   Examples of confidential information
*   Requirements for a successful complaint
*   Definitions of 'confidential'
*   Definitions of where the duty is owed
*   Classification – contractual and equitable claims
*   Employee obligations – express and implied contractual terms

Some of the classic examples of intellectual property protected by confidentiality are:

*   Coca Cola (coke)
*   Chatreuse Liqueur
*   Kentucky Fried Chicken
*   Listerine Mouth Wash

Confidential information can include hi-tech processes, customer lists, prices and background financial information. The duty applies to firms engaged in negotiations that may or may not lead to a contract, and to undertakings engaged in partnering agreements. It also applies to employees (and ex-employees for a limited time).

Breach of Confidence - Requirements

1.   The information must be "confidential".

2.   The disclosure must be where there was an obligation not to confide.

3.   There must be actual or anticipated unauthorised use or disclosure.

1.   Confidential Information

Confidential information has been defined as "something which is not public property or knowledge". (Lord Green in **Saltman Engineering v Campbell Co.**) Another definition is found in **Thomas Marshall (Exports) v Guinle.** Sir Robert Megarry suggested there are 4 elements :

> (i)   the owner believes its release will be injurious to him;
> (ii)   the owner believes the information is secret (not in the public domain);

      (iii)   both beliefs are reasonable.

      (iv)   the information must be judged in the light of the particular industry's usages and practices.

2.   Obligation Not to Confide

2 tests have been developed to help define the circumstances where the duty applies :

      (i)   The Reasonable Man Test;

      (ii)   The Limited Purpose Test.

(i)   Would a reasonable man, in the shoes of the recipient, realise on reasonable grounds that the information was being given to him in confidence?

     There is a strong presumption in favour of such a realisation in business circles.

(ii)   Was the information disclosed only for a limited purpose or purposes? If this is the case it should not be used for any other purpose. There is again a strong presumption in business circles that this will be the case.

Saltman Engineering v Campbell Co.

The plaintiff owned the copyright in drawings of tools for use in the manufacture of leather punches. The defendant was given the drawings and instructed to make 5000 of the tools at 3s 6d each. After completing the order, the defendant retained the drawings and made use of them for its own purposes.
Held: There was an implied duty only to use the drawings for the limited purpose of producing the 5000 punches. The defendant had infringed this obligation of confidence.

Fraser v Thames Television

The plaintiffs had disclosed in confidence to a television company an idea for their own show. When the company tried to use the idea for a series featuring other actresses, without first obtaining the plaintiff's consent, it was held to be in breach of confidence.

Actions for Breach of Confidence

There are two possible ways to base a claim for breach of confidence:

1.   Breach of Contract, or

2.   Equity

1.   Breach of Contract

It can be covered either by an express provision in the contract (which will add clarity to what is being protected) or by an implied term relating to confidentiality. In **Thomas Marshall (Exports) v Guinle**:

The defendant was appointed as the managing director of the plaintiff company for ten years. His service agreement stated that he was not to become employed in any other business without the company's consent and that he must not disclose confidential information. Further, after ceasing to be managing director, he was not to use or disclose confidential information about the customers of the plaintiff company. When his service contract had another four and a half years left to run, he resigned.
Held: The defendant was not infringing the express provision in the contract which did not cover using the information in a business of his own. However, he was infringing the implied duty of fidelity and good faith owed to his employer and an injunction would be granted banning its continuation.

In **Schering Chemicals v Falman:**

The plaintiff was a drug company which manufactured a drug called Primodos. It had been suggested that the drug could have harmful effects on unborn children and as a result the company suffered bad publicity. It engaged the first defendant to train its executives in television techniques and to put across the plaintiff's point of view. The first defendant engaged the second defendant to help with the training courses. The plaintiff supplied a large amount of information about the drug to the first defendant which was in turn passed on the second defendant. It was acknowledged that the first defendant had received the information in confidence, but it was never established whether the second defendant gave a similar express undertaking to respect confidence.

Shortly after the training course, the second defendant proposed to make a programme about Primodos for Thames Television. Much of the information in the programme would have been obtained from the training courses information, although most of it would have been available from other public sources. The drug company applied for an injunction to restrain the use of the information.
Held: The defendant was in breach of an implied promise to use the material for only one purpose – the training courses.

2.   Equity

Sometimes information is disclosed during negotiations and no contract is concluded. Here the recipient may be subject to an equitable duty not to breach confidentiality. In **Coco v A.N. Clark (Engineers) Ltd.:**

The plaintiff entered into informal negotiations with the defendant for the latter to manufacture a moped he had designed. These negotiations broke down but only after certain confidential information on the design had been disclosed. When the defendant decided to build its own engine to a design which bore a close resemblance to that of the plaintiff, Coco brought an action against it. He was not granted an injunction on the grounds that his case was too weak for this remedy to be awarded. However, he was granted a right to receive royalties on any future engines made and sold by the defendant to the design in question.

In **Seager v Copydex Ltd.:**

Negotiations for a carpet grip foundered. Before this, the plaintiff had disclosed his design for a second grip and suggested a name - "Invisigrip." The defendants marketed a carpet grip later which they called "Invisigrip" and had a close resemblance to the plaintiff's design.
Held: Breach of confidence - unauthorised use of confidential information - too many coincidences and similarities.

Employees

Employers are entitled to protect **genuine proprietary interests** - where the employee has access to **trade secrets** or **influence over clients**. Restrictive covenants can be included in the contract of employment. However, there is a danger that attempts to restrict employees freedom of action (either during the lifetime of the contract or after its termination) will fall foul of the law on restraint of trade.

Employers cannot restrict general knowledge and skills acquired whilst working for them. Even when trade secrets or trade connection are involved, the restraint must be **reasonable** both in terms of **time** and **geographical area.**

More recently, employers have started using **long periods of notice** (with a transfer to less significant work) or **garden leave** arrangements (a commitment to leave the employer and not work for another rival business for a defined period in exchange for full pay) as an alternative to restrictive covenants. They are subject to similar requirements of reasonableness by the courts.

Implied Duty of Fidelity

Even where the contract possesses no express restraint there is an implied duty to act faithfully and with the best interest of the employer in mind. This obligation is more demanding on existing employees (not for example, to work for rival businesses in their own time), than on ex-employees who continue to be subject to its coverage for a brief time afterwards. Again, passing on confidential information would involve a breach of this implied duty of fidelity. Employers will find using the implied duty more difficult when dealing with ex-employees after the case of **Faccenda Chicken Co. Ltd. v Fowler (1986)** where the court seemed to restrict its operation significantly. Issues to be considered (when establishing whether a duty of confidentiality still exists) include:

(1)   the nature of the employment;
(2)   the nature of the information;
(3)   awareness of the employee re confidentiality of the material;
(4)   the extent to which it is possible to separate secret information from non-secret material.

The facts of the case were as follows:

Faccenda Chicken Co. Ltd. v Fowler

The employer's business consisted of supplying fresh chickens from itinerant refrigerated vans to retailers and caterers. The defendant was employed by the business as a sales manager. He left the company to set up business on his own account , taking eight of the plaintiff's employees with him. He started selling fresh chickens from refrigerated vans in the same area. A claim for breach of confidence was brought by his ex-employer, alleging that he was misusing confidential information which he had access to whilst employed by them. This consisted of sales information, including customers names and addresses, routes to customers, prices charged, and details of customers' usual orders.
Held: the information was within the scope of confidential information which could be covered by an express clause and would possibly be implied into the contract of an existing employee. However, it was not sufficiently important to allow an ex-employer to curtail its use by a former employee under a claim for breach of the implied duty of fidelity.

N.B. Consultants are generally subject to more demanding duties regarding confidential information, which will normally be covered by express provision. In the absence of express provision there is an implied duty in their contracts not to disclose, with a heavy presumption in favour of material being confidential.

Design Rights

The following section provides you with a description of the following aspects of the law on design rights:

- Classification of design rights – registered design, design right, design copyright.
- Registered Design Right.
- Definition.
- Duration.
- Requirements – novelty, industrial application, eye appeal.
- Exclusions (including must match/must fit designs).
- Defences.
- Remedies for infringement.
- International registration.
- Design Right (Unregistered).
- Comparison with registered design right.
- Duration.
- Definition.
- Exclusions (including must match/must fit designs).
- Remedies.

Legal protection of designs comes in three forms:

1. **Registered designs** (governed by the Registered Designs Act 1949 as amended).

2. **Design right** (dealing with unregistered designs, and regulated by the Copyright, Design and Patents Act 1988).

3. **Copyright law**, which overlaps with the above measures.

Designs can be for functional articles e.g. can opener, tool box, exhaust pipe. These will normally by governed by the design right (2 above).

Some designs may relate to **decorative** articles e.g. an attractive table lamp, a pattern for porcelain pottery. Such visually attractive designs are intended to appeal to the eye and are more appropriately covered by **registered design** protection (1 above). In some cases, a design could be patentable (provided all the essentials are present). However, if any one is missing (e.g. lack of novelty), the above provisions would form the basis of intellectual property protection.

The registered design has much in common with a patent whereas the design right is more like a copyright.

Registered Design (Registered Designs Act 1949)

The most common kinds of designs which have been registered are for toys, games and electrical goods. The distinguishing feature is that of **eye appeal.**

Whereas the design right applies mainly to functional designs, registered design applies to aesthetic articles.

Section 1(1) of the Registered Designs Act 1949 states that a design consists of **"… features of shape, configuration, pattern or ornament applied to any article by an industrial process, being features which in the finished article appeal to and are judged by the eye."**

The design must be **'new'** (not previously registered or published in the UK prior to the date of application for registration). This does not mean that the design must be unlike any previous design. It does not have to exhibit 'novelty of a startling or groundbreaking variety to be valid'.

The design has to be **applied** to the article by **'an industrial process'.** The law of registered design is aimed at industrial designs, being designs applied to manufactured articles which are mass produced. Regulations define industrial application as application to more than 50 articles.

The design must **appeal to the eye** of the prospective purchaser of the article, who is not deemed to be an expert in the field. It must have a material bearing on his decision to buy the product. In **Lamson Industries Ltd's Application**, it was decided that a design for computer print-out paper having alternative coloured bands upon it was not registrable because the reason customers would buy the paper was that it would be easier to read, and because information could be printed out on the paper more closely spaced. Customers would buy the paper because of its utility and not because of its appearance.

Some designs may be disqualified for registration under s.1. These are:

(a)   methods or principles of construction; or
(b)   features of shape or configuration which are:
      (i)   dictated solely by the article's function, or
      (ii)   dependent upon the appearance of another article or which the article is intended by the design's author to form an integral part.

These exclusions are justified in terms of preventing the right (effectively a monopoly) from becoming too strong and **hindering** the **development of new designs** for similar articles. Also, it enables **free competition** to operate for the **manufacture of spare parts** by **other organisations** (the must match exception).

The importance of maintaining a free market in spare parts was stressed in **British Leyland Motor Corp. Ltd. v Armstrong Patents Co. Ltd.** If a vehicle manufacturer was allowed to register the body panels of his cars he could charge exorbitant prices for replacement panels and refuse to grant licences to third party parts manufacturers or only in return for hefty royalties.

The must-match exception is fairly narrow and applies only if the design features are dependent on the appearance of another article and it is the author's intention that his articles form an integral part of the other article. It has been suggested that spare parts can be classified into two groups:

(i)   Main body panels, doors, bonnet lids, windscreens (excluded).
(ii)   Wing mirrors, wheels, seats, steering wheels etc. (not excluded).

It was argued that the latter can be made in a variety of designs to fit a particular vehicle as substitutions for the original parts while leaving the shape and general appearance of the vehicle unaffected. Under rules passed in 1995, a number of further exclusions exist e.g. portraits of the royal family, flags of any country, insignia etc. without the consent of the appropriate authorities.

Registration gives its owner certain **exclusive rights:**

a)   to **make** or **import for sale or hire or use** for business purposes articles to which the design is attached.
b)   to **sell, hire etc.** such articles.

If anyone else does any of the above without a licence, it is an infringement.

Defences

There are a number of defences to an action for infringement, often based on attacking the validity of the registration e.g:

*   The design was not new when registered.
*   The registration has expired.
         (The 'Gillette' defence argues that either the alleged infringing design is not within the registered design or the registered design is invalid for lack of novelty.)

Registration

Applications are processed by the **Designs Registry** (a branch of the Patents Office). The current fee is £60 but other expenses are inevitable e.g. preparation of drawings or photographs. Many firms employ an agent for this work. The Registry carries out an examination and search. Simple applications could be dealt with in 3-4 months.

Duration

The initial registration period is **5 years** but it can be renewed for a **further four periods of 5 years (total of 25 years).** Most designs have a limited commercial life, often 10-15 years maximum.

International Registration

If protection is required in another country, application must be made in each country involved. However, under the Paris Convention for Industrial Property 1883, a person who has applied for registration of a design in any of the Convention countries is given a priority with respect to applications to other Convention countries made within 6 months of the first application. Most of the industrialised counties in the world have ratified the Paris Convention.

Design Right
(Copyright, Designs and Patents Act 1988)

Until 1968 there was a gap in the protection of designs which were primarily functional. Copyright protected artistic works, patents covered new inventions and designs with eye appeal could be protected by registration. However, a design with none of the above features had no protection e.g. an overflow pipe for a washing machine.

A number of changes were made, culminating in the creation of the design right – a right which **automatically attaches** to certain designs without the need for registration. It has been described as a weakened form of artistic copyright, which can be contrasted with the patent-like protection afforded registered designs. The duration of the design right is shorter, effectively **no more than 10 years** (and licences of right can be applied for in the last 5 years).

Examples of articles that can be protected include exhaust pipes (and other parts of motor vehicles), tools, kitchen equipment, office equipment and packaging.

Section 213(2) of the Copyright, Designs and Patents Act 1988 defines a design as **"the design of any aspect of the shape or configuration (whether internal or external) of the whole or part of an article."**

For the design right to apply to an article it must be **original** (not commonplace) and be in some **tangible form** e.g. recorded in a design document or by an article made to the design.

Exclusions exist which are similar to (but not identical with) those for **registered design**. The same justification applies i.e. preserving opportunities for development and a free market for spare parts. Surface decoration is also excluded because it is the natural preserve of registered design.

New and attractive designs can be the subject of the design right protection as well as registered design. However, an **advantage of registration** is that the period of **protection is longer** - a maximum of 25 years as against 15 years (or 10 from the product's first marketing). The form of **protection** is also **stronger**. Registering a design also provides **proof** that the owner is **taking his legal rights seriously** – something which can be made clear by attaching the fact of registration and the registration number on each article put on the market. It is also **relatively inexpensive** to register a design.

Because of the requirement for eye appeal, internal features relating to shape and configuration cannot be registered (although they receive protection under the design right).

Exclusions

The following are excluded from protection – **Section 213(3)**:

(a)   methods or principles of construction.

(b)   features or shape or configuration which:

      i.   enable the article to be connected to, placed in, around or against another article so that either article may perform its function (the 'must-fit exception), or

      ii.   are dependent upon the appearance of another article of which the article is intended by the designer to form an integral part (the 'must match' exception).

(c)   surface decoration.

The must-fit and must-match exceptions have significant implications for the manufacturers of replacement parts (and to manufacturers of accessory parts e.g. a lamp to fit on a bicycle mounting or a dust-cover for a typewriter). Because of the must-fit exception, the features that must be a certain shape or configuration can be made without infringing the design right e.g. a television set and stand manufactured by a manufacturer. The connection between the two is not protected, but other design features of both the television and the stand are capable of protection.

An example of the must-match exception are replacement car doors. The external features must match the sweep of the bodywork. However, the inner skin (hidden from view by upholstery) is usually made of plastic. It often has holes for lightness and ribs for strength. The position of the holes and configuration of the ribs, if the design is original, could well be protected by the design right.

Design Copyright

Where a drawing forms the basis of a functional design it can be protected by copyright, provided it meets the requirements of originality and that a person who was not an expert could recognise the article as being reproduced from the drawing. The Copyright, Designs & Patents Act 1988 sought to rationalise the overlap between copyright and design rights:

- Where a work consists of or includes a design that is protected by copyright, the design right is suppressed in favour of the copyright (copying the drawing);

- Where the design is recorded in a drawing and a person makes an article using that drawing, he does not infringe copyright in the drawing although he does infringe design right (making the product);

- Where a person makes a photocopy of the drawing instead, copyright is infringed, but any subsequent making of articles from the copy will infringe design right only.

Copyright

This section will provide you with a description of the following features of copyright law:

- Background to the Copyright, Designs and Patents Act 1988 (CDPA).
- Duration of copyright.

- Meaning of 'original' work.
- Meaning & examples of literary work.
- Exclusive rights gained through copyright.
- Nature and classification of infringements (primary & secondary).
- Meaning of 'substantial part' of a work.
- Exceptions to law of copyright (including 'fair dealing').

Objectives of the CDPA 1988

1. To restate and amend earlier statute law on copyright (e.g. Copyright Act 1956).

2. To take into account developments in new technology.

3. To rationalise design law where it overlapped with copyright.

4. To introduce the concept of moral rights for authors.

New technology includes such everyday items as photocopiers, fax machines, email, design tools and washing machines because all have computer programmes built into their composition.

Duration

Copyright lasts for the **lifetime of the author, plus 70 years** after the end of the calendar year in which the author dies (s.12).

The copyright of a work which an author enjoys is essentially of a negative character – the right to prevent other persons, individual or legal, from reproducing the work without permission. The work is deemed to possess economic value, being the result of time and effort. Competitors could gain an edge simply by copying the material and selling more cheaply.

There are, however, a number of important exceptions and qualifications which restrict the extent of an author's monopoly (see later).

An author will only enjoy rights in a literary work which is **original**. This relates to the **source** of the work. It does not mean that the work must be in substance original or possess inventive thought.

A literary work is defined in s.3 of the CDPA 1988 as **any work, other than a dramatic or musical work, which is written, spoken, sung and, therefore includes:**

(a)   **a table or compilation, and**

(b)   **a computer programme.**

The definition includes:

Lists of customers, consignment notes, business letters, balance sheets actuarial tables, directories, tables of figures and football coupons. Drawings of engineering equipment may still be included, although, since 1988, these are more likely covered by design rights.

For a **'work'** to be involved, **some measure of skill and effort** must have been invested in its creation. In one case, the copying of tables showing the values of leases and annuities was held not to be an infringement of copyright – the work could have been recalculated in a few hours and was relatively easy to have been reproduced.

Copyright cannot exist in a **single word** or **title** such as 'Hitachi' or 'Kojak'. The case of **Exxon v Exxon Insurance Ltd.** is authority for this principle, where it was decided that, although Exxon was able to prove that it had gone to considerable time and trouble to decide on the name 'Exxon', it could not prevent copying through the law of copyright.

Under s.16, the author of a work enjoys exclusive rights to:

- Copy the work.
- Issue copies of the work to the public.
- Perform, show or play the work in public.
- Broadcast the work or include it in a cable programme.
- Make an adaptation of the work or do any of the above.

Infringements are defined as the doing of any of the above acts in relation to the work either 'as a whole' or 'any substantial part of it' either directly or indirectly. Strict liability applies to the acts listed in s.16 and it is no defence to plead ignorance, or that one genuinely believed that there was an entitlement to copy. There are two types of infringement:

(a)   Primary infringement – usually making the infringing copy.

(b)   Secondary infringement – dealing with the infringing copy.

Copying the whole or a substantial part of a work can be an infringement. The question of what may be a **substantial part** of a protected work is one of fact in each case. Defining what is substantial is problematic though. A three-part test is employed:

(1)   Has a qualifying work been copied?
(2)   What is 'substantial' with reference to the quality of what has been taken?
(3)   What is the value of what has been taken compared to the original?

The value of what has been copied has been addressed in a number of cases in terms of whether it identifies the earlier work or encapsulates it, and whether the labour and skill of an author has been unfairly appropriated. As a result, the courts will look beyond the volume of material reproduced and assess it in terms of the skill, labour and effort applied by the author.

Exceptions

Copyright is only a partial monopoly. There is no tort of copying and a number of important exceptions exist which permit a person to reproduce parts of the work of another. Some 50 sections of the 1988 Act provide a system of general rights to copy. The rationale for the permitted acts can be seen as a way of limiting the strength of the rights associated with copyright. It provides a fair balance between the rights of the copyright owner and the rights of society at large. Most of the permitted acts do not unduly interfere with the commercial exploitation of the work.

Two of the exceptions relate to **'fair dealing'**. Under s.29, it is fair dealing with a work to copy it for the purposes of **private research and study**. Section 30 permits the copying of a work for the purposes of **criticism, review and reporting of current events.**

The 1988 Act does not define 'fair dealing' and few cases have examined the concept. The courts have often held that taking a relatively small amount of a work is sufficient to be an infringement. They will look at a number of factors including the quantity and significance of the matter taken, whether the activity is in competition with the claimant, whether the work is published and whether the defendant acted maliciously.

Contractual Provision

IP rights can be strengthened by the drafting of suitable express contractual terms and conditions. Take the following example:

Infabrics Ltd, a private company with limited resources, has designed a new technical product which it wishes to develop. It has not registered any IP rights in the product. It decides to make a contract with A&G Manufacturing Ltd by which the latter agrees to manufacture the product on Infabrics behalf. Infabrics provide A&G

with design drawings and technical specifications for this purpose. A&G will then produce all the specialist tools needed for manufacture.

Infabrics could, provided it has sufficient bargaining leverage over A&G, include the following terms which would enhance its position and reduce the risk of potential misuse of the confidential information made available to A&G:

- A **confidentiality clause** highlighting which information is regarded as confidential and stressing the limits to its legitimate use.

- Clauses relating to **ownership of tools, plans and designs** relating to the product (which could include the right to insist on their return upon completion of the contract – the value of the tools manufactured by A&G being taken into account in the initial pricing agreement).

- A clause concerning **ownership of the finished products,** including defective ones which fail quality control checks.

- A clause permitting **periodical inspection of the production site** to ensure compliance with the above contractual arrangements.

clauses to improve IPR!

The presence of a general IP rights clause would certainly increase the awareness of A&G of its IP obligations and the fact that Infabrics are taking its rights seriously.

The above situation could well be covered by an implied duty to use confidential information only for authorised purposes even in the absence of express contractual provision. In **Saltman Engineering v Campbell:**

Confidential designs for new tools were given to the defendants so they could manufacture the tools exclusively for the plaintiffs. The defendants started to manufacture and sell them on their own account.
Held: Breach of confidence.

Contract provisions relating to IPR need to cover three issues:

1. Definition.
2. Ownership.
3. Protection.

1. **Definition** provisions will identify clearly the type(s) of IPR covered by the agreement. They may refer to know-how and define knowhow in terms of patents, design rights, copyright, guidance manuals etc.

2.   **Issues of Ownership** of IPR in a contract become more complicated where new IPR is to developed during the life-span of the contract. This involves **background** and **foreground** IPR. Pre-existing rights are known as **background IPR** – rights which each party already possesses and which it will be contributing to the successful performance of the contract. Intellectual property rights which are created during the course of the contract are called **foreground IPR.**

3.   **Protection** is achieved through the inclusion of **warranties**. These need to cover both fitness for purpose (that the software, patented invention etc. does the job it is supposed to do) and potential third party claims. The latter relates to possible claims by the holders of existing IP rights that the purchaser is infringing these rights i.e. that the seller had no right to supply the product without the appropriate permission.

In conclusion:

•   Intellectual Property Rights (IPR) are based on either protection of creative effort or commercial reputation.

•   It can be classified into either hard IPR (requiring registration) or soft IPR (granted automatically).

•   Remedies for infringement are injunctions, damages, account of profits and seizure of infringing goods.

•   The relevant forms of IPR are patents, trade marks, passing off, breach of confidence, design rights and copyright.

•   Attempts to modernise the law on IPR has resulted in the Patents Act 1977, the Copyright, Patents and Designs Act 1988, the Trade Marks Act 1994 and a range of EU Directives covering most of the above forms of IPR.

•   There still exists important common law protection – the actions for breach of confidence and passing off.

•   Contractual provisions can strengthen the rights of a party by explicitly defining issues relating to coverage, ownership and protection against infringement of IPR.

Chapter Seventeen

International Trade

The long distances involved in international sale of goods means that the parties usually have little opportunity to engage in active or detailed negotiation. There is consequently a need to rely on standard documentation containing well-established trade terms with which both parties are familiar. The following set of notes outlines the main documentation involved.

Documentation for Import and Export

Up to 4 separate contracts can be involved in buying goods from abroad:

1.   the actual purchase contract.

2.   a contract of carriage.

3.   a contract of insurance.

4.   a contract of finance (often involving a letter of credit - see later).

Each involves costs and the parties need to decide how they are to be allocated. This is done by choosing from a range of standard contractual provisions known as Incoterms. Over many years a number of trade terms were developed to deal with the special conditions of international trade. They were subsequently codified by the International Chamber of Commerce (ICC) and now provide a widely accepted uniform system. Incoterms consists of agreed explanations of many of the terms used in international trade and defines the duties of the seller and buyer. The 2000 edition covers 13 such terms including ex works, FOB and CIF.

Incoterms must be expressly incorporated into the contract if they are to apply. There is no automatic incorporation by operation of law. The parties will need to agree on which one of the 13 possible Incoterms is the most appropriate for their particular contract. The benefit of using Incoterms is to minimise the risk of ambiguity and misunderstanding between the parties. Amongst other things, the choice of which terms to use will affect who is responsible for making the arrangements for carriage, who bears the cost and who bears the risk of accidental damage .

Commonly used Expressions

CIF Contracts

The initials stand for cost, insurance and freight as these stand for the three main items of expenditure incurred by the seller in shipment of the goods. Therefore, if A purchases goods from B on CIF terms, the price quoted by B will include all necessary expenditure involved in the shipment of those goods, i.e. the price of the goods themselves, the premium for insuring them in transit and the freight costs for their carriage by ship to their port of destination.

It should be noted that the terminology used by the parties should not be treated as conclusive. It is feasible for the parties to nominate a contract cif, but on examination of all the circumstances, for it to become apparent that this description is inaccurate. Property in the goods (ownership) normally passes when the documents are handed over to the buyer. CIF contracts are sometimes described as 'document driven' transactions. If the seller has handed over the correct shipping documents, he is entitled to be paid, irrespective of where the goods are at the time, or their condition.

In other words, the seller performs the contract by delivery up of the shipping documents (effectively the bill of lading) – not the delivery of the goods. The buyer cannot defer payment until after inspection of the goods. However, this in no way prejudices the buyer's right to reject the goods as defective once they do arrive.

Manbre Co. v Corn Products Ltd.

The sale contract (c.i.f.) was for a number of 280 lb. bags of starch. Bags of 140 lb. and 220 lb. were actually shipped aboard the ship, which was later sunk by a German submarine, with the loss of all the cargo aboard. The defendant seller, knowing of this, two days later tendered documents including a letter which declared that the goods were insured, but no policy of insurance. The buyer refused to accept the documents and sued the seller for damages for breach of the sale contract (the market value of equivalent goods having risen considerably above the original price).

Held: As a general principle, a c.i.f. seller is able to tender bills of lading for goods, even though he knows that the goods had been lost at sea.

[N.B. The buyer in this case was in fact able to resist the claim of the seller because of the failure to tender the insurance policy and because the goods were the wrong size. It was for these reasons, however, and not because the goods had been lost at sea, that the buyer was able to reject the documents tendered].

Generally, this causes no hardship to the buyer who has a remedy against the insurers or the carrier. If, however, the goods were lost without the fault of the carrier and due to an uninsured risk, the buyer must still bear the loss – he is the one at risk from the time of shipment.

The seller's main duties can best be summarised as follows:

1.   make out an invoice of goods sold.

2.   ship at the port of shipment goods answering the description in the contract.

3.   procure a contract for freighting the goods by ship to the destination referred to in the contract.

4.   arrange for insurance of the goods during shipment.

5.   within a reasonable time send to the buyer the shipping documents concerned (i.e. invoice, bill of lading, policy of insurance etc.).

In addition, he will be required to obtain export clearance. However, the buyer will be expected to bear the cost of unloading and import duties.

It is a duty on the seller to conclude contracts on the best terms available for the buyer.

FOB Contracts (or strict fob)
The initials stand for free on board. The seller places the contract goods on the agreed vessel at the agreed port of shipment and all the costs of carriage are borne by the buyer. It is therefore not the seller who is the shipper, but the buyer, who receives the bill of lading directly through his agent.

This will obviously affect the passing of property and risk. Normally property in the goods passes to the buyer the moment the goods go on board. It is important to note, however that there are exceptions to this rule which are quite significant. For example, if the goods are loaded as part of a larger consignment of goods of the same description, so that at point of loading they are unascertained, then property will only pass when there is an unconditional appropriation of suitable goods in a deliverable state.

Since risk usually passes with ownership, any damage occurring prior to shipment is the seller's responsibility. Once the goods are over the ship's rail the buyer assumes responsibility for any damage. The buyer is required to nominate an effective ship (one which is ready, willing and able to carry the goods in question) and this should be notified in reasonable time to the seller. If the nominated ship proves unsuitable, the buyer can re-nominate another ship provided this leaves the seller with enough time to carry out his responsibilities.

The seller is required to nominate a shipping date and notify the buyer of that date. Note that some contracts are designated "fob - additional services". Under such contracts, the parties may re-allocate their obligations. In particular certain duties, normally those of the buyer, may be undertaken by the seller as the buyer's agent. It does not normally, however, make any difference to the passing of property in the goods.

Usually the fob seller's duties may be summarised as follows:

1. make an invoice of the goods sold.

2. to ship at the port of shipment, goods of the description in the contract.

3. to nominate a shipping date and notify the buyer of that date.

4. to tender to the buyer the invoice and the bill of lading.

The seller is responsible for all expenses and costs incurred in getting the goods over the ship's rail e.g. if the ship is delayed, he will have to bear the additional storage costs.

Where the contract is **fob - additional services**, and the seller acts as agent for the buyer, he will often undertake duties such as procuring appropriate insurance - but of course this will be at the buyer's expense.

Free Alongside Ship
The seller performs his duties when the goods have been placed alongside the ship on the quay (or in lighters) at the port of shipment named by the buyer on the correct date or within the agreed period. The buyer then assumes responsibility for all costs and risks from that point.

Ex Works (EXW)
The seller fulfils his duties when he has made the goods available at his premises. He is not obliged to load them on the lorry provided by the buyer or for arranging export clearance (unless otherwise agreed). The buyer incurs all the costs and risks connected with the transit. This is the minimum commitment from the seller's point of view and should be reflected in a lower price for the contract. Specifically, the seller is required to:

- Supply goods in conformity with the contract of sale.

- Place the goods at the disposal of the buyer at the point of delivery named by the buyer.

- Package the goods suitably to allow for their collection.

- Give reasonable notification to the buyer of when the goods are available.

- Bear the risk and costs connected with the goods until collection.

The buyer, in turn, is required to:

- Take delivery of the goods as soon as they are placed at his disposal.

- Make arrangements for the carriage of the goods from the seller's premises.

- Bear all risks and costs from the time they have been placed at his disposal, including the costs of any export/import documentation.

DDP (Delivery Duty Paid)

DDP contracts are the most favourable available to the buyer. It means that the seller bears all costs, expenses and risks in getting the goods to the place specified by the seller, usually his place of business in the country of importation. This involves obtaining the necessary export and import licences, and paying port taxes, export duties, and miscellaneous other charges.

- Carriage to be arranged by the seller.

- Risk transfer from the seller to the buyer when the goods are placed at the disposal of the buyer.

- Cost transfer from the seller to the buyer when the goods are placed at the disposal of the buyer.

Bills of Lading

"A document signed by the shipowner or by the master or other agent on behalf of the shipowner, which states that certain goods have been shipped on a particular ship or have been received for shipment." (Charlesworth's Business Law - Sweet & Maxwell).

It sets out the terms on which goods have been delivered to and received by the shipowner. Once signed by/on behalf of the carrier, it is handed to the shipper (usually the owner; usually the exporter). The law relating to bills of lading is contained in both common law and legislation, especially the **Carriage of Goods by Sea Act 1992.**

Characteristics

Document of Title

This amounts to conclusive proof of ownership. Upon receipt of the bill of lading, the carrier must transfer the goods to the importer as owner. Bearer bills (made out to 'consignee', or 'to shipper's order' or 'bearer') can be transferred to another person by assignment which enables the purchase/sale of goods whilst in transit. The assignee can claim the goods by presenting the bill on the vessel's arrival at the port of destination. Transfer of a bill of lading amounts to a symbolic delivery of the goods (a constructive transfer of possession).

Receipt

The bill is issued by or on behalf of the carrier to acknowledge receipt of the goods. It provides evidence of the identity, quantity and condition of goods, and usually includes details of identification marks. This enables the buyer to identify defects acquired in transit which become the responsibility of the carrier. It will contain a statement on the condition of the goods at time of shipment. If the bill of lading says the goods are in apparent good order then this is a **"clean"** bill; if the carrier has any reservations then the bill will be **"claused"**.

Evidence of Terms

The bill also provides proof of the terms of the contract of carriage - the contract between the shipper and the carrier. This can be either a charterparty ("a contract whereby the charterer hires the use of a ship from the shipowner.") or a contract of carriage on a general ship where an entire ship is not needed.

A bill of lading may be of several different types. It may be in **complete form,** containing all the clauses, or an abbreviated version - a **'short form bill'** - containing only the more important clauses.

It may be a **'containerised bill'** where the shipped goods are packed in containers or a **'combined transport bill'** where the shipment requires not only carriage of the goods on board ship, but other modes of transport as well. **"Received for shipment" bills** indicate that the goods have been received by the carrier and held under his control whereas a **"shipped"** bill indicates that the goods have actually been placed on board ship.

Contracts of Carriage of Goods

Charterparties

These are contracts involving the hire of an entire ship (either for a defined period of time, or for a particular voyage). The document sets out the duties of the shipowner and the rights and duties of the hirer. It will identify the vessel, indicate its carrying capacity and tonnage, specify its availability, state the hire fee and the period of hire. Most charterparties will be arranged on the basis that the master and crew remain the servants of the shipowner (technically described as a charterparty not by way of demise). The division of responsibility between shipowner and charterer has been described as follows:

"The charterer might direct where the vessel is to go and with what she is to be laden but the shipowner remains in all respects accountable for the manner in which she may be navigated."

Demurrage & Lay Days

The charterparty will normally specify a set number of days when the vessel will be engaged in loading and unloading cargo – the lay days. If this number is exceeded, the charterer will usually be required to pay compensation for the delay caused. The amount will be set out in the charterparty and is known as 'demurrage'. It is a form of liquidated damages and must satisfy the rules relating to penalties.

Contracts of Carriage on a General Ship

When an entire ship in not needed, a contract of carriage on a general ship will be arranged. Once the goods have been placed on board the vessel, the shipowner will issue the shipper with a bill of lading to cover his goods and no others. Such contracts need to strike a balance between the interests of the carrier and the interests of the shipper on such matters as risk of loss or damage to the goods. Various international conventions have been negotiated to specify the obligations of the carrier and at present two such conventions operate across the world.

A protocol was agreed in Brussels in 1968 which created the Hague-Visby Rules, the latter being incorporated into English law by the Carriage of Goods by Sea Act 1971. Some countries felt that the Hague-Visby Rules favoured the carrier too much and another set of rules were formulated in 1978 known as the Hamburg

Rules. Today, both sets of rules exist with some countries favouring one and other countries preferring the alternative:

Hague-Visby Rules	Hamburg Rules
UK	US
France	Germany
Netherlands	Spain
Sweden	Australia
Belgium	and others
& others	

We shall focus on the Hague-Visby Rules for obvious reasons. These imply a set of duties which are imposed on the carrier. The Rules do not automatically attach to contracts of carriage involving UK companies, but will apply in the vast majority of cases e.g. any voyage where the port of shipment is in the UK, voyages where the port of shipment is in a country which is a signatory to the Hague-Visby Rules, voyages where the contract refers explicitly to the Hague-Visby Rules.

There are three main duties imposed on the carrier:
1.   To provide a seaworthy ship.

2.   To properly load, stow, carry and discharge to goods.

3.   To issue a bill of lading on the demand of the shipper.

1.   To provide a seaworthy ship
This is not an absolute duty. The carrier is required to exercise due diligence to provide a seaworthy ship. This includes issues such as the design, structure and condition of the vessel and equipment, the competency and sufficiency of the crew, and the manner in which the cargo is stowed

2.   To properly load, stow, carry and discharge to goods
These tasks must be properly carried out i.e. a recognised system must be used and one which is suitable to the particular requirements of the cargo involved e.g. cargoes which may taint each other should not be stowed near each other. The standard of care required is one of reasonableness.

This duty, with regard to loading of goods, is subject to significant exclusions available to the carrier. If goods are damaged or destroyed owing to fire (unless caused by the carrier), perils, dangers and accidents of the sea, Acts of God, strikes & other industrial stoppages and various other events the carrier will not be liable. Liability for loss or damage is limited to a maximum level, details of which are set out within the Hague-Visby Rules.

3.   To issue a bill of lading on the demand of the shipper

The carrier is obliged, after receiving the goods, to issue a bill of lading containing specified details (e.g. loading marks necessary for identification of the goods, number of packages or pieces, apparent order and condition of the goods) on the demand of the shipper.

Payment Methods and Instruments

As we have indicated, additional complications exist when international trade is involved:

*   distances.

*   risks of international transportation.

*   limited direct contact.

*   different legal systems.

All affect the seller's confidence in receiving payment. Some form of greater security is required and this is achieved through the use of banks as intermediaries. Although collection agreements are possible whereby the seller will obtain payment from a bank in the buyer's country, documentary credits have been the most popular method of payment in international contracts – "the lifeblood of commerce" according to more than one judge. The most common form of documentary credit is the letter of credit.

Letters of Credit

This in an undertaking by a bank to a seller, made on behalf of a purchaser, that payment will be made on presentation of the appropriate documents. Once the seller delivers the documents of title (e.g. an invoice, a bill of lading and an insurance certificate) to a bank is his own country, payment will be made. The bank in the seller's country remits the documents to the buyer's bank in his country, which passes them on to the buyer in exchange for the sum paid (+ commission).

SELLER ◄─── ADVISING BANK ◄─── ISSUING BANK ◄─── BUYER

*   Buyer instructs bank in his own country (issuing bank) to open a credit with bank in seller's country (advising bank) in favour of the seller.

*   Seller will be able to draw on this credit (i.e. obtain funds from advising bank) upon delivery to the advising bank of any documents specified by the buyer (e.g. clean bill of lading).

- Advising bank hands over the documents to issuing bank and is reimbursed for sum advanced.

- Issuing bank presents the documents to the buyer in return for payment.

Benefits

Using this technique, risks (of non-delivery or non-payment) are minimised. The bank will not pay the seller unless the appropriate documents of title are produced. The seller, in return, has the assurance that payment will be made before the buyer assumes control of the goods. Additionally, payment will be in his own country.

Disadvantages

Delay because multiple parties are involved e.g. goods can arrive at the port of destination before the buyer has received the bill of lading from the issuing bank.

Types of Letters of Credit

Revocable & Unconfirmed

There is no commitment on the part of either the issuing bank or the advising bank. This offers little protection to the seller that the money will be paid. The buyer will be able to terminate the arrangement at any time.

Irrevocable & Unconfirmed

The issuing bank is bound to honour the credit even if the buyer has attempted to revoke the payment. However, if the issuing bank refuses, it will be necessary to pursue a complaint in the country where the bank is located.

Irrevocable and Confirmed

Both banks are committed to honouring the payment. If either refuses, the seller can pursue an action against the advising bank in his own country.

Even where fraud is involved, e.g. the shipment itself is fraudulent or the documents are forged, there must be clear evidence before the banks can refuse payment.

Banks insist on strict compliance in relation to the documents to be handed over and will refuse to make the payment where even minor discrepancies are involved.

Transferability

Letters of credit can be transferable, permitting the seller to finance the acquisition of the goods from his supplier. Having received the credit, he can simply reduce the amount to be transferred (keeping his profit) and hand it over to his supplier. However, it can only be transferred once.

The credit must be made available to the seller at the beginning of the shipment period.

The Shipping Documents

Commercial invoice

The invoice is a claim by the exporter for payment from the importer under the terms of the sales contract. It should include a description of the goods, together with unit prices, if appropriate, amount payable, shipping marks and shipping terms. All these details must also match exactly the information stipulated in the letter of credit. Normally several copies of the invoice are required by the customs authorities overseas. The invoice should also state the price of the goods as agreed by both importer and exporter, using the standard price terms (Incoterms).

Bill of Lading

This document is the receipt given to the exporter by the shipping company for goods accepted for transport by sea. It conveys title to the goods when in negotiable form. The bill of lading names the shipper and the consignee (importer) or the consignee's agent and it is signed on behalf of the carrier. If it is issued to order, it is transferable by the party named as shipper or, if issued to the order of a named party, it is transferable by that party, in both cases by endorsement.

Bills of lading are normally issued in sets of two, three or more originals, any one of which may be used to obtain delivery of the goods. The number of originals in a set is shown on each document. As soon as one original is presented to the carrier at the port of destination in order to obtain release of the goods, the carrier's liability is discharged even if the true owner were to present another original. For complete control over the goods, therefore, it is necessary to possess a full set. Non-negotiable copies, which are unsigned, are not documents of title and are used only for record purposes. Most letters of credit call for full sets to be presented to the bank before the exporter is paid.

Insurance policy or certificate

Proof that the goods are covered for risk of damage or loss during transit is often asked for in the letter of credit, which will call for either an insurance policy or an insurance certificate. (However, certificates issued by insurance brokers are not acceptable unless specifically permitted by the credit).

Regular exporters can arrange to cover all exports over a particular period, thereby avoiding the need to take out a fresh policy with each shipment. In this case individual insurance certificates are issued for each shipment - either by the insurers or by the exporter.

Certificate of origin

Most countries require a certificate that shows evidence of the country of origin of the goods being imported. Letters of credit often stipulate the presentation of this document, which may be issued by the exporter himself or by a Chamber of Commerce or Consular authority, as specified.

Bills of exchange

A bill of exchange is legally defined as 'an unconditional order in writing, addressed by one person to another, signed by the person giving it, requiring the person to whom it is addressed to pay on demand or at a fixed or determinable future time a sum certain in money to, or to the order of, a specified person or to bearer'.

In the case of a letter of credit transaction, it is drawn up by the exporter (the drawer) and is an order to the importer or the paying bank (the drawee) to pay a specified amount of money immediately (a sight bill) or at a future date (a usance bill). In the case of a usance bill, the drawee acknowledges and accepts liability for the exporter's claim for payment by signing an acceptance across it. The wording on the bill of exchange must match exactly the terms of the credit.

A single bill of exchange (called a sola bill) may be presented, provided that the credit does not stipulate that bills are required in duplicate.

In conclusion:

- International trade involves the use of a number of specialised documents and terms and conditions that are recognised throughout the commercial world.

- These include bills of lading, charterparties, the Hague-Visby Rules, Incoterms and letters of credit.

- Bills of lading fulfil a number of functions, namely, constituting a document of title to the goods, proof of receipt of the goods by the shipping company and evidence of the terms of the contract of carriage – the charterparty.

- The charterparty, if subject to English law, will often include the Hague-Visby Rules which impose a number of duties on the shipper and the carrier.

- The charterparty will usually include the definitions contained in Incoterms relating to relevant obligations such as CIF, FOB, FAS etc, thus reducing ambiguity or misunderstanding between the parties.

- Letters of credit (or documentary credits) are frequently used to facilitate payment in international transactions.

Chapter Eighteen

International Sale of Goods

There have been several attempts to harmonise or align contractual regulation of contracts involving businesses from different countries. At present, the UK has ratified the Hague Convention and implemented its provisions in 1967.

This short chapter identifies the main provisions of the Hague Convention as implemented through the Uniform Laws on International Sales Act 1967 and the approach adopted by the Rome Convention on the Laws Applicable to Contractual Obligations. There are a number of **international conventions** that attempt to achieve a greater degree of uniformity of rights and obligations where companies from different countries enter into sale of goods contracts with each other.

The **Uniform Laws on International Sales Act 1967** was passed to give effect to two Conventions signed at a conference at The Hague in 1964. The two Conventions are incorporated in the Act as schedules:

Schedule 1   **The Uniform Law on the International Sale of Goods.**

Schedule 2   **The Uniform Law on the Formation of Contracts for the International Sale of Goods.**

The Act is part of the English law and, whenever English law governs a contract, the provisions of Schedule 1 apply if the parties expressly state that this is their wish. The benefit is that a set of terms that are well-recognised in different countries will then decide rights and duties between the parties.

Schedule 1 contains provisions governing the seller's obligations as to:
- the time and place of delivery.
- the insurance and carriage of the goods.
- the conformity of the goods with the contract.
- the giving of good title.

Other provisions relate to:
- the passing of risk.
- the buyer's obligations as to payment and taking delivery.

There are some significant differences with English contract law. The Uniform Laws do not recognise the concept of 'condition,' breach of which entitles the buyer to reject the goods. An alternative concept is used – that of 'fundamental breach.' The consequences of the breach would have to be assessed in order to establish whether the buyer has a right to reject.

Schedule 2 applies to the formation of contracts and its provisions are concerned with the rules of offer and acceptance:

- An offer is generally revocable until the offeree has despatched his acceptance.

- An offer is not revocable if it either states a fixed time for acceptance or else indicates that it is irrevocable.

- A qualified acceptance will normally be construed as a rejection of the offer and a counter offer.

- (However), if the qualification consists of additional or different terms which do not materially alter the terms of the offer, it will constitutes a binding acceptance unless the offeror promptly objects to the discrepancy.

- A late acceptance may be treated by the buyer as having arrived in time, provided the offeror promptly informs the acceptor that he regards it as binding.

- A late acceptance which suffers from unusual delay in transit and which would in normal transit have arrived in time is regarded as being in time unless the offeror promptly informs the acceptor that he considers his offer lapsed.

The UN Convention on Contracts for the International Sale of Goods ('Vienna Convention')

The Vienna Convention is a further development of the attempt to unify the law here. It is founded on the two Hague Conventions of 1964 and is intended to supersede them. The Vienna Convention combines the topics treated in the two Hague Conventions into one document.

However, although many countries have now ratified it, the UK has not as yet given effect to the Convention. The earlier Conventions continue to apply in the meantime.

International Contracts – Which law governs the contract?

Problems can arise over which law applies to a contract where the two parties operate from different countries. The position is now governed by the **Contracts (Applicable Law) Act 1990** which adopted the **Rome Convention on the Law Applicable to Contractual Obligations 1980** – again a measure intended to harmonise the position across all member states.

Essentially, it is for the parties to choose which law applies to the contract. This can be achieved expressly in the contract (either by specific provision stating which law applies, or by reasonable deduction from the terms of the contract) or established from the circumstances of the contract e.g. the previous course of dealing between the two parties.

If the above approach cannot decide the issue, it is a matter of deciding which law is most closely connected to the contract. There is a presumption in favour of the performer's habitual residence being the most closely connected e.g. the seller in a contract for sale of goods. 'Habitual residence' means generally the place of business of the party performing the contract. This presumption can be rebutted if the law of another country would be more closely connected to the country e.g. the country in which a construction contract is taking place.

In conclusion:

- The Hague Convention 1964 was an attempt to harmonise the laws governing international contracts.

- Its main provisions on contract and formation of contract were ratified in the UK by the passing of the Uniform Laws on International Sales Act 1967.

- There is significant commonality between these provisions and UK law of contract but there are also differences.

- The Vienna Convention 1980 was an attempt to improve on the earlier document, but has not yet been ratified by the UK.

- The law governing a contract is regulated by the Contracts (Applicable Law) Act 1990, adopting the Rome Convention 1980.

Chapter Nineteen

Dispute Resolution

The traditional approach to disputes has been to avoid litigation by using arbitration where negotiation has failed to achieve settlement. There were strong arguments for this preference in earlier years but these had become weaker for a number of reasons. Some reform of arbitration procedures was carried out in 1996 to address the problem. There has still been a growing trend towards the use of mediation in recent years, combined with an increase in another alternative – adjudication.

The chapter contains an explanation of the following legal issues:

- Classification of alternative dispute resolution procedures.
- Identification of main concerns/requirements of parties involved.
- Comparison of mediation and conciliation.
- Comparison of adjudication and arbitration.
- Reform of arbitration – the Arbitration Act 1996.
- Litigation.

There are a number of alternative methods to deal with conflicts:

1.   **By agreement.**

2.   **By intervention.**

3.   **By third party determination.**

4.   **Through litigation.**

What do organisations want from a dispute resolution procedure?

Recent research suggests the following preferences (in descending order):
- Speed.
- Commercial pragmatism.
- Fairness and equity.

- Low cost.
- Confidentiality.
- Protection of business relationships.

Speed is by far and away the most important issue (which would explain the preference for arbitration over litigation and partly the increasing use of adjudication over arbitration). It would clearly seem that speed and cost are the essential ingredients desired by organisations wishing to resolve a conflict. Whether these specific objectives are critical to the organisation will depend on the situation involved. Future trading relations, the protection of its public reputation, the need to be seen to be enforcing its rights (for future deterrent purposes) also can play an important role in business objectives.

Resolution by Intervention

These methods occupy an intermediate position between negotiation and third party determination. Their more recent title is alternative dispute resolution (ADR). They consist of two basic approaches:

- **Mediation**
- **Conciliation**

Both involve a third party being brought in to facilitate discussion and resolution. It is sometimes called assisted negotiation.

What is the difference between mediation and conciliation?

The mediator merely facilitates discussion whereas the conciliator provides the parties with a recommendation based on his opinions.

In 1990, the CBI created the **Centre for Dispute Resolution (CEDR)** to encourage mediation (and other methods of dispute handling).

The mediation process is somewhat like shuttle diplomacy – the parties meet in joint and separate meetings, the mediator moving between them, attempting to find points of common ground and build on them. It has to be treated as an entirely voluntary exercise, and either side can withdraw at any stage. It does not require pre-agreed contractual terms for it to be adopted but if such a provision has been drafted into the contract (e.g. an alternative dispute resolution clause) it can oblige the parties to use the process, even though one of both have changed their minds. However, there is some doubt on this point, as it would seem improbable that the courts would enforce a non-binding negotiation method on the parties. Although a settlement is initially not legally binding on the parties it is usual for it to be documented and signed as a contractually enforceable agreement.

There is considerable similarity between mediation and conciliation. Conciliation is entirely voluntary and is undertaken on a confidential basis. The parties prepare statements of their view on the disputed issue to send to the conciliator. He commences an investigation by interviewing the parties. Unlike an arbitrator he does not have to observe the principles of natural justice (see later). He adopts an inquisitorial method, controlling the collection of evidence and questioning the parties involved.

A meeting is then arranged at which the conciliator begins to form an opinion (possible with an 'expert' present to assist and advise on technical issues). He will express his views on the strengths and weaknesses of the parties' cases and offer an opinion of how an arbitrator may view the dispute. This is partly being done to encourage a possible settlement between the parties. Failing this, the conciliator will issue his own recommendation. The following points can be made about this recommendation:

- It is only the opinion of the conciliator.

- It is not justified with reasons (unless specifically requested).

- It is not binding ('without prejudice').

- It is a practical solution, not necessarily in strict accord with the relevant law).

The process may take about 3 months to complete.

Adavantages of a Mediation/ Conciliation

- Speed (for mediation just a few days; for conciliation not exceeding 2-3 months).

- Inexpensive (sometimes less than 1% of disputed amount).

- Confidential.

- Non-binding.

- Parties able to agree settlement.

- Flexible outcomes (commercial trade-offs etc).

- Encourages future trade relations with other party.

Third Party Determination

This part of the spectrum of conflict resolution methods contains the following approaches:

- Adjudication.

- Arbitration.

- Litigation.

All involve a third party presiding on the issues and pronouncing a judgement of his own i.e. the parties lose control on the outcome.

Adjudication and arbitration have much in common - the parties agree who shall play the judicial role, present their cases and receive a judgement. However, there are significant differences in approach. Nevertheless, there remains widespread confusion in business as to their respective meanings. In fact the terminology used in the contract is not conclusive as to which process would apply in the event of a dispute. For example, the contract may specify that 'adjudication' would operate. If it then proceeded to describe procedures which were essentially arbitral, the courts would insist on arbitration being used.

Arbitration is a process by which it is agreed by the parties that an independent third party is brought in to make a decision which is binding on the parties. The power (jurisdiction) of the arbitrator will be derived either from the consent of the parties or from a court order or from statute clearly indicating use of arbitration. The choice of arbitrator will be for the parties to decide, or according to a method to which they have consented. He must act impartially and fairly, applying the principles of natural justice to the proceedings.

Bearing these points in mind, some clear differences can be identified from adjudication. The term "adjudication" is used almost exclusively for dispute resolution under Part II of the Housing Grants, Construction and Regeneration Act 1996 (HGCR). Under the Act construction contracts must include a provision for adjudication, with the adjudicator giving a decision within 28 days of referral. The adjudicator's decision is binding until a final determination reached by agreement, arbitration or litigation, or the parties may take the adjudicator's decision as final. He examines the evidence and makes appropriate enquiries, Being an expert, he uses his own skill and judgement in order to formulate a decision. An arbitrator, conversely, makes an award which is final and binding, after receiving presentations from both parties according to the principles of natural justice[8]. The latter process is therefore more thorough and time-consuming.

Why has adjudication emerged in recent years?

It was a reaction to some of the growing failings of arbitration. Originally, arbitration was established to provide a more informal, quicker and cheaper method of resolving disputes to the courts. By the early 1990's opinion viewed it as increasingly formal, slow and expensive, partly as a result of increased lawyer involvement ('wigless litigation'). Among other criticisms it was argued that procedure imitated High Court actions which made hearings as lengthy as litigation and could cost even more. It was also relatively easy to appeal against the decision of the arbitrator and the subsequent appeal case could take years to reach a decision.

It was argued that, although there were some occasions where disputes are so important and/or complex to justify elaborate arbitration proceedings, there were many others which did not require such thoroughness. What was more important was a speedy resolution to the dispute, even if it was achieved at the expense of detailed scrutiny. Adjudication provided this alternative, albeit more superficial, approach[9]. Something had to be done to improve the arbitration process in the face of all these mounting criticisms.

Reform of Arbitration

Parliament passed the **Arbitration Act 1996** in an effort to make arbitration more attractive. The Act intended to improve the position in the following ways:

- It redrafted and codified the law on arbitration in clearer language.

- It placed the arbitrator in firm control of the proceedings.

- It placed a duty on the arbitrator to operate cost-effective methods, depending on the size and complexity of the dispute.

- It reduced the ability of appeals to the court.

8. The rules of natural justice require that the 'judge' be impartial (e.g. by having no personal interest in the dispute or connection with the parties) and that he provides both parties with a fair opportunity to present their cases. This requirement has implications for ensuring adequate time for preparation and the right to legal representation when presenting the case.

9. Because it is a quicker and cheaper approach, it would not be appropriate to make the decision final and binding. However, the parties can elect to make it so by agreement.

This has improved the attractiveness of arbitration in comparison with litigation in the courts. However, it has to be remembered that the civil court system has also been significantly reformed in the last few years. The cost and time involved in many civil actions will now often be less off-putting since the recommendations of the Woolf Report have been implemented (see section on Litigation).

The Arbitration Act 1996 made a significant number of other improvements:

Procedures

- Arbitration no longer has to follow High Court procedures closely. It is no longer possible to appeal simply because court procedures were not carefully observed. Appeals will only be possible for serious procedural irregularities.

- Linked to the above, arbitrators are expected to adopt procedures which are suitable to the particular case before them. The only underlying requirement is that they give both parties a reasonable opportunity to put their case.

- Linked to this, arbitration should become shorter and cheaper in many disputes.

Powers of Arbitrator

The arbitrator now has the right to decide all procedural issues, subject to agreement by both parties. This has simplified and clarified the previous position.

Court Intervention

- The courts now hold a predominantly supportive role in connection with arbitration.

- Courts can assist by making orders for the attendance of witnesses, to enforce orders and to appoint a new arbitrator if one resigns or dies.

- Courts, in certain situations, can grant an interim injunction in support of an arbitration.

Removal of an Arbitrator

The courts can only act to remove an arbitrator if:

214

Any available recourse to a relevant arbitral body has been exhausted, and one of the following is involved:

- there are justifiable doubts as to the impartiality of the arbitrator.

- he is incapable of conducting the proceedings.

- he has failed to conduct the proceedings properly or reasonable quickly, and by doing so, has caused substantial injustice.

Appeals

1. Appeal on the Merits

The arbitration agreement may exclude any right to challenge the decision on its merits. If it does not, appeal must have the consent of all the parties or leave of the court. The court will only give its consent if the award is obviously wrong, or, where the question is one of general public importance, is open to serious doubt

2. Appeal on Procedural Grounds

There must be a serious irregularity, which includes failure to give reasons (unless agreed beforehand) and ambiguity in the detail of the award.

Costs

This can be agreed between the parties themselves (but only after the dispute has arisen). Otherwise, the arbitrator will decide on the allocation of costs. This will normally be on the general principle that the winner will have his reasonable costs paid for by the loser. The arbitrator may assess the costs to be awarded, or, failing this, the court will decide the matter. The general rule is that the winner will be able to recover a reasonable amount for costs reasonable incurred.

Arbitration Fees

The fees involved, including the hire of suitable facilities, will frequently far exceed those paid to the court in litigation.

Litigation

Advantages:
- it is possible to bring an unwilling party into the procedure.

- it can set a precedent to establish future rights and duties.

- the solution will be enforceable without further agreement.

Disadvantages:
- potentially lengthy and costly.

- adversarial process likely to damage business relationships.

- the outcome is in the hands of a third party, the judge.

Remember the court can now refer parties to mediation or another form of alternative dispute resolution, if appropriate.

International Arbitration

Some special features only operate where international arbitration is involved.
Clearly some of the earlier advantages still apply:
- Cost.

- Speed.

- Confidentiality.

- Expertise.

- Influence over selection of arbitrator.

Some other benefits of international arbitration include:
- Control over where (which country) it takes place.

- Control over which law governs the proceedings.

Additional disadvantages include:

- *Potential legal complexity.*
  In theory, three different legal systems can be relevant in international arbitration. The disputed contract could be governed by the laws of one country; the arbitration procedures could be governed by the laws of another; the interpretation of the arbitration agreement itself (e.g. its scope) could be governed by another. It is obvious that considerable confusion can be caused in such situations. In practice, it is normal for the law

governing the disputed contract also to be the law governing interpretation of the arbitration agreement and for the law governing procedure to be that of the country where the hearing is being held.

- *Enforcement of the Award.*
  Clearly there can be problems attached to enforcing arbitration awards where the other party is situated in another part of the world. To assist enforcement, the succinctly named New York Convention on the Recognition & Enforcement of Foreign Arbitral Awards 1958 (between friends - the New York Convention) was agreed. Convention awards are enforced in the same manner as an English award where the agreement was made in a country which has acceded to the Convention. Over 80 countries have already done so.

- *Complications of Appeal to the Courts in another country.*
  The usual procedure is for such appeals to go to the courts in the country where the arbitration hearing took place. Thus, the case could be decided according to a legal system which had nothing to do with the parties who agreed the contract.

- *Language problems and obtaining suitable legal assistance.*

In conclusion:

- In dispute resolution, the main requirements of the parties are speed, the adoption of a pragmatic approach, fairness, low cost, confidentiality and the protection of business relationships.

- Dispute resolution methods include third party intervention and third party determination (other than courts).

- These are sometimes referred to as Alternative Dispute Resolution (ADR).

- Third party intervention comprises mediation and conciliation.

- Third party determination comprises adjudication and arbitration.

- Arbitration procedures have been extensively amended by the Arbitration Act 1996 in the light of heavy criticism.

- The popularity of arbitration (over litigation) has been waning in recent years, with mediation and adjudication becoming more extensively used.

Chapter Twenty

Legal Aspects of Tendering and Outsourcing

The following chapter contains a number of issues which have one theme acting as a common denominator – outsourcing. A general awareness of these issues is important even though they are not considered in great detail.

Issues to be considered in this lesson include:

- Specific & general tenders – a legal interpretation of the process.

- The EC Procurement Directives & UK Regulations on public sector tendering.

- The Acquired Rights Directive (98/50) & TUPE Regulations 1981.

- Some practical implications of outsourcing from a legal perspective.

- Redundancy & entitlement to compensation.

Tenders

Almost all adverts requesting tenders to be submitted for the supply of goods or services are regarded as invitations to treat. The tenders themselves are seen as the offers, capable of being accepted or rejected by the buyer involved.

There are two types of tender:

- **specific tenders** i.e. one off transactions (quantity/delivery etc fixed and known in advance).

- **general tenders** (orders to be submitted if and when the goods/services are required - no fixed quantities/deliveries etc.)

With specific tenders, a binding contract comes into existence as soon as the successful tender is accepted. Both parties then have to fulfil their obligations to supply and pay for the goods/work done. With the approval of a general tender, the offer is said to stand and will only be changed into a contract when an order is submitted.

Each order is seen as an acceptance of this standing offer and separate contracts are concluded over the coming weeks or months. It is therefore possible for the firm who submitted the tender to revoke the offer at any time, although they will still have to perform any existing contracts agreed before the revocation.

Sometimes the firm which has submitted the tender commit themselves for a stated period of time but this will only be binding if consideration has been given in return or a deed (which does not require consideration) was concluded and signed.

Duties of the Buyer

- There is no obligation to accept any tender at all (unless this is stated at the time).

- There is no obligation to accept the lowest tender (unless this is stated at the time).

- There is no obligation to order goods or services under a general tender. If the buyer has promised to obtain the specified goods only from the successful tenderer, he cannot however go elsewhere during the period in question.

- There is no general obligation to order in line with suggested estimates referred to at the negotiation stage.

- There is a legal obligation to give due consideration to all properly submitted tenders which are received by any set deadline **(Blackpool BC case)**.

- The process of awarding tenders is subject to a fundamental test of reasonableness. There can be exceptional circumstances where the procedure that was followed shows a degree of unfairness which the courts will find unacceptable **(Camelot Case)**.

Blackpool & Fylde Aero Club Ltd v Blackpool Borough Council

The Aero club submitted a tender just before the deadline by placing it in the postbox at the town hall. However, the box was not opened by the council until several hours later. The council refused to consider the submission on account of it being passed the deadline.

Held: The council was in breach of the above implied undertaking and liable to pay damages.

Camelot Group Plc v National Lottery Commission (2001)

The National Lottery licence initially awarded to Camelot had run its seven years. Tenders had been requested by the Commission for the award of a new seven year licence. Two contractors submitted bids – Camelot and the People's Lottery (TPL). Having announced that both bids were considered unsatisfactory, the Commission decided that a new process would operate. There would be only one bidder – TPL. Camelot challenged this decision.

Held: The action of the Commission (in deciding to negotiate exclusively with TPL) was so unfair as to amount to an abuse of power. It fell outside the range of decisions which a reasonable and properly informed decision-maker would take.

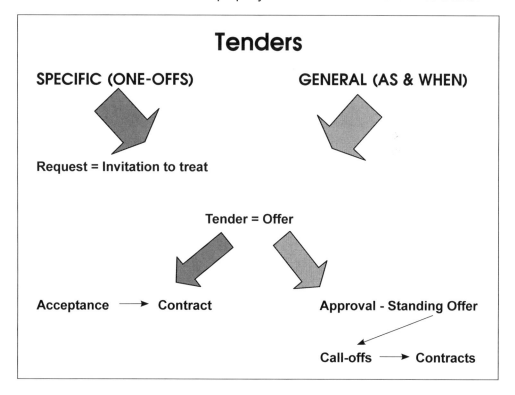

EU Public Procurement Rules

The above rules are based on a European Union Directive and subsequent UK Regulations implementing it. The current Directive is 2004/18/EC[10]. It consolidated three previous Directives and was intended to ensure greater consistency in the operation of the rules. It also took into account changes in procurement practice, including the greater use of electronic trading and ICT (information & communication technology). The UK regulations were brought into operation in 2006[11]. The purpose of the rules is to open up the public procurement market and to ensure the free movement of goods and services within the EU. In most cases they require competition.

The EU rules reflect and reinforce the value for money focus of the government's procurement policy. The rules apply to purchases by public bodies (government departments and agencies, local authorities, NHS trusts etc) and where the purchases are above set monetary thresholds. Where the Regulations apply, contracts must be advertised in the Official Journal of the EU (OJEU) and there are other detailed rules that must be followed. The rules are enforced through the courts, including the European Court of Justice.

Directive 2004/18/EC sets out the legal framework for public procurement. It applies when public authorities seek to acquire **goods, services or works** (the last relating to construction & civil engineering). It sets out procedures that must be followed before awarding a contract when its value exceeds thresholds, unless it qualifies for an exemption (e.g. on grounds of secrecy).

The current threshold figures (until January 2010) are *approximately*:

Central government departments and agencies		Local Authorities and Hospital Trusts
Supplies	£90,000	£140,000
Services	£90,000	£140,000
Works	£3.6m	£3.6m

(handwritten annotation: ✳ no longer accurate! slides!)

The utilities (chiefly water, energy & transport) are governed by a separate Directive which, in general, allows more flexibility in the buying process. The threshold figures are also much higher in this sector too, reflecting the tendency for contracts to involve far higher financial levels.

---

10. A separate Directive governs procurement in the utilities sector e.g. water, energy, public transport – 2004/17/EC.

11. The Public Contracts Regulations 2006 (the equivalent for the utilities sector are the Utilities Contracts Regulations 2006).

Aggregation

When deciding whether a procurement need falls above or below the threshold figure, it is sometimes necessary to aggregate purchases over a period of time. For example, where there is a recurring need for goods or services within the same financial year (such as purchase of stationery and other routine requirements) it is necessary to calculate the likely total spend over that period (to aggregate it). If the total falls above the threshold involved, then the rules must be followed. It is wrong to treat the orders independently as separate contracts. A similar rule applies to purchase of goods or services that all relate to a single project e.g. provision of security, maintenance and cleaning for a new office block. Where a large government department has been divided into a number of units with independent authority to decide which procurement contracts shall be undertaken, then aggregation need only be applied at unit level – not across the whole department.

The OJEU Advertising Rules

As soon as possible at the start of the financial year, public authorities can publish a **'Prior Information Notice'** (or 'periodic indicative notice'), usually referred to as the 'PIN'. This provides an estimate of likely procurement requirements over the coming 12 months and allows potential suppliers to become aware of possible business.

As specific needs arise during the year, the authority is required to publish a **'Contract Notice'** giving specific information regarding the actual goods/services/ works required, the procedure to be followed to award the contract and what criteria will be used to decide the award.

After the contract has been awarded, it is then required that the authority issues an **'Award Notice'** indicating who has been awarded the contract and some information regarding why the successful tender was successful.

Choice of Procurement Procedure

The time allowed for responses or tenders depends on which award procedure is used. Four award procedures are now provided for:

Open procedure, under which all those interested may respond to the advertisement in the OJEU by tendering for the contract;

Restricted procedure, under which a selection is made of those who respond to the advert and only they are invited to submit a tender for the contract. This allows purchasers to avoid having to deal with an overwhelmingly large number of tenders;

Negotiated procedure, under which a purchaser may select one or more persons with whom to negotiate the terms of the contract.

Public authorities have a free choice between the open and restricted procedures but may only use the negotiated procedure in the limited circumstances set out in the Regulations. This tends to be where the contract is a very complex one. PFI, PPP and major IT contracts are examples. Under restricted procedures and negotiated procedures there must be a sufficient number of participants to ensure genuine competition, with a minimum of five for restricted procedure, and a minimum of three for negotiated procedure.

Competitive dialogue procedure

The use of negotiation has been liberalised by the introduction of a new competitive dialogue procedure for complex contracts. Complex contracts involve situations where it is not possible to objectively define the technical means of satisfying the buyer's needs (the solution) or it is not possible to specify the legal and/or financial make-up of the project. This allows discussion with the selected suppliers of the details of the contract in order to clarify the requirement and allow suppliers to formulate a more complete bid. Discussions post tender will still however be limited to clarification (as it is for the open and restricted procedures).

Stages in the Procurement Process

The Regulations set out detailed criteria that are designed to avoid discrimination on grounds of origin in a particular member state and to ensure that all suppliers or contractors established in countries covered by the rules are treated on equal terms. The criteria cover:

Specification stage – how requirements must be specified, avoiding brand names and other references that would have the effect of favouring or eliminating particular providers, products or services. There is a requirement to accept equivalence too. (e.g. 'ISO 9001 or equivalent').

Selection stage – the rejection or selection of candidates based on:
*   evidence that they are not unsuitable on grounds e.g. of bankruptcy, criminal conviction or failure to pay taxes;

*   their economic and financial standing e.g. that they are judged to be financially sound on the basis of their annual accounts;

*   their technical capacity e.g. that they will be adequately equipped to do the job and that their track record is satisfactory.

Award Stage – the award of contracts either on the basis of 'lowest price' or a range of criteria referred to as 'most economically advantageous tender' (or MEAT). This allows other issues to be considered, including quality, after sales service etc. The latter is almost always the one adopted, allowing the achievement of best value for money.

Post-Tender Negotiations

There are restrictions on the use of post tender negotiation under the open and restricted procedures. No fundamental aspects of contracts may be the subject of negotiation as they are likely to distort competition. However, discussions with candidates may be held for purposes of clarification or supplementing the content of their tenders.

Enforcement

It is for **aggrieved suppliers to pursue individual actions in the High Court**. This can result in the **suspension of an incomplete contract award** procedure or the **setting aside of a pre-award decision** taken by a public authority. **If the award has already been made** before the case comes before the Court, **damages will be awarded** to the aggrieved supplier. However, the **award will not be quashed.**

*P.S. As a result of the above limitation on the rights of aggrieved suppliers post-award, there has been a change in the EU rules that has to be complied with as from February 2006. In line with the so-called **ALCATEL** decision of the European Court of Justice, public authorities are required to notify all short-listed tenderers of the outcome of the process **but then wait 10 DAYS before declaring the award officially concluded**. This enables aggrieved tenderers to take legal action at the 'pre-award' stage and thus stand a chance of winning the contract if the court orders the authority to return to an earlier stage of the process.*

European Union Public Procurement

Reforms in 2006

More technical stuff - would be section B.

- The Commission has passed a single Directive to make the rules simpler, clearer and more up to date, without substantial changes to principles.

- The current strong preference for European standards has been reduced by encouraging the use of performance based specifications and stressing that equivalent means of meeting the requirement must be considered.

- There is also provision for the use of eco-labels to certify compliance with environmental requirements subject to certain safeguards.

- Purchasers are able to let contracts with or though a central purchasing body to the extent that the body itself complies with them. This provision has been added to the proposal in order to remove doubts about consortia purchasing, following the case of **Teckal** in the European Court.

- In the past, the public sector directives specified the information that may be used to select suppliers but did not specify, in restricted and negotiated procedures, the standards or criteria to be used in selecting suppliers. The new Directive requires that these be made clear to suppliers in the contract notice.

- Once an offer has been sought, the factors to be applied in the assessment of the 'most economically advantageous tender' must be made more transparent. Where possible the weighting of the factors must be disclosed in advance; if not then the relative ranking of the factors must be given. As before, disclosure is allowed in the contract documentation or in the contract notice.

- In the past the Commission has been concerned that in the public sector the unregulated use of frameworks, where typically a contract is only completed when/if a user calls-off from the agreement, would distort competition and lead to disguised preferences for particular suppliers. The new Directive 'legitimises' the use of frameworks, whilst introducing safeguards reflecting good practice.

  Thus, the normal duration of a framework is normally to be 4 years or less, multi-supplier frameworks should include at least 3 suppliers and where mini-tenders are used to determine which supplier to use these must include all with the capacity to carry out the work and the award criteria must be explicit.

- Purchasers are allowed to require parts of the process to be electronic, provided it does not restrict access to the contracts concerned and there will be safeguards to preserve confidentiality and probity. Electronic means can reduce timescales by up to 12 days.

- It is made clear that electronic reverse auctions are permitted subject to certain safeguards, including a requirement to inform suppliers in advance of the intention to use the auction method and provide information about the conduct of the auction in the contract documents.

• A new type of approach – 'dynamic purchasing systems' – has also been introduced. This is a type of multi-supplier framework agreement which allows amendment to the details of the offers by suppliers displayed in the system. Before placing call-off orders, users of the system must allow all suppliers 15 days to make an application to join the system. The user would then seek formal tenders from all suppliers admitted to the system, awarding the call-off on the basis of the award criteria in the original notice advertising the system.

• The use of negotiation has been liberalised by extending it to supplies contracts in certain cases provided there has been a call for competition and by the introduction of a new competitive dialogue procedure for complex contracts (e.g. major IT or PFI contracts). This allows discussion with the selected suppliers of the details of the contract in order to clarify the requirement and allow suppliers to formulate a more complete bid. Discussions post tender are still however limited to clarification (as it is for the open and restricted procedures).

The above changes were implemented at the beginning of February 2006.

Outsourcing - Legal Aspects

We shall need to consider two legal topics where outsourcing of a service is being adopted – whether at the initial stage of contracting out for the first time, or whether at later stages when changes in the contractors are taking place:

1. the requirements of the TUPE Regulations 2006.

2. the requirements relating to redundancy based on the Employment Rights Act 1996 and related regulations.

1. Transfer of Undertakings (Protection of Employment) Regulations 2006

The Transfer of Undertakings (Protection of Employment) Regulations 2006 (referred to below as TUPE 2006) is now the main piece of legislation governing the transfer of an undertaking. The Regulations are designed to protect the rights of employees in a transfer situation enabling them to enjoy the same terms and conditions, with continuity of employment, as they had with their previous employer. The Regulations are based on the requirements of the European Union Acquired Rights Directive 2001. TUPE 2006 entirely replaces the previous regulations – TUPE 1981.

What is a relevant transfer of an undertaking?

TUPE will apply to what are known as **'relevant transfers'** which may occur in a wide range of situations. Since 2006, the two broad categories are *business transfers and service provisions changes (outsourcing)*.

Business transfers
This relates to such business activities as take-overs, mergers, amalgamations or compulsory acquisitions in insolvency cases. The question here is whether there is a **transfer of an economic entity that retains is identity.** This can be broken into two parts:

- Is there a 'stable economic entity' that is capable of being transferred?

- Will the economic entity retain its identity after the transfer in question? To decide whether a stable economic entity has been transferred, the factors to consider include:
    - Is the type of business being conducted by the transferee (incoming business) the same as the transferor's (outgoing business)?

    - Has there been a transfer of tangible assets such as building and moveable property(although this is not essential)?

    - What is the value of the intangible assets at the time of the transfer?

    - Have the majority of employees been taken over by the new employer?

    - Have the customers been transferred?

    - What is the degree of similarity of the activities carried on before and after?

If the answer to all (or in some cases several of) the above questions is 'yes', it is safe to assume that there has been a transfer of a stable economic entity. **These complex questions no longer arise since 2006 where the second category of transfer is involved - outsourcing.**

Service provision changes (Outsourcing)
- This category refers to the wide range of outsourcing arrangements that have become so common in recent years. A service provision change occurs when a client:

o   contracts out the service for the first time

o   changes contractors at some future time (second generation contracting)

o   brings the service back into the organisation (contracting in)

Since 2006, outsourcing <u>is to be treated</u> in the same way <u>as a TUPE transfer</u> i.e. *there is a presumption that TUPE applies to an outsourcing event.*

TUPE is presumed to apply:
*   where a 'service provision change' is involved; and

*   there are assigned employees (not temporary);

*   to an organised grouping, and;

*   its principal purpose is to carry out the service activities for the client involved.
         i.e. there must be an identifiable (dedicated) team of employees working for the client from whom the work is transferring.

Service provision changes will, however, not be treated as TUPE transfers if:
*   the contract is wholly or mainly for the **supply of goods** for the client's use, or
*   the activities are carried out in connection with a **single specific event or a task of short-term duration.**

The law on relevant transfers in the case of contracting out and changes of contractors for labour intensive activities, such as security, catering, refuse collection and cleaning, has given rise to considerable confusion in the past. Many of these difficulties should now have been resolved by TUPE 2006.

Impact of a breach of the TUPE regulations

If a TUPE transfer applies, all terms and conditions of work and continuity of employment should be preserved. This principle applies to all employees who were employed in the entity transferred immediately before the transfer; and those who would have been so employed if they had not been unfairly dismissed for a reason connected with the transfer.

Subject to a one year qualifying period, such a dismissal will be automatically unfair for a reason connected with the transfer unless it is for an 'economic, technical or organisational' (ETO) reason (see below). An employee who has been unfairly dismissed could recover up to £11,400 (basic award) and up to £66,200 (compensatory award)1. If a transferor triggers liability for unfair dismissal that liability will usually transfer to the transferee unless there was an ETO reason for the dismissal.

Dismissal for ETO reasons

An exception is allowed where the dismissal is for **economic, technical or organisational reasons** entailing **"changes in the workforce" - Regulation 8(2) (an ETO reason).**

The meaning of this expression ('changes in the workforce') has proved difficult to interpret clearly but it seems to require changes in either the numbers employed or some re-definition of job functions. The problem is that although it may be argued that organisational reasons were behind dismissals they do not entail changes in the workforce. This makes it very difficult indeed for a transferee employer effectively to harmonise terms and conditions after a transfer. Simply changing pay rates or working conditions in themselves do not amount to changes in the workforce.

The case of **Berriman v Delabole Slate Ltd.** illustrates this problem well. An employee suffered a reduction in his weekly wage. He resigned and claimed constructive dismissal. The Court of Appeal held that the dismissal was automatically unfair as there was no economic, technical or organisational reason entailing changes in the workforce. For a change in the workforce within the meaning of Regulation 8(2) there had to be a change in the composition of the workforce. As we have seen, this meant a change in numbers or possibly job functions.

Information

From 6 April 2006, transferors became obliged to give the transferee written information about the employees who are to transfer and all the associated rights and obligations towards them. This information includes, for example, the identity and age of the employees who will transfer, information contained in the employees' written particulars of employment under section 1 of the Employment Rights Act 1996 and details of any claims that the transferor reasonably believes might be brought. If the transferor does not provide this information, the transferee may apply to an employment tribunal for such amount as it considers just and equitable. Compensation starts at a minimum of £500 for each employee in respect of whom the information was not provided or was defective.

Consultation and notification

The transferor has a responsibility to conduct a full and meaningful consultation

12. Financial amounts correct in October 2009

with employees at the earliest practicable time. Failure to conduct consultation results in liability for the payment of compensation which may be up to 13 weeks' pay. The transferor and transferee are both liable for any award of compensation made by an employment tribunal for failure to inform and consult.

Liability passing on to the incoming contractor

The transferee takes over the liability for all statutory rights, claims and liabilities arising from the contract of employment, for example liabilities in tort, unfair dismissal and discrimination claims. The exception to this rule applies to criminal liabilities.

Pensions

Strictly speaking, obligations relating to provisions about benefits for old age, invalidity or survivors in employees' occupational pension schemes do not transfer under TUPE. However, the provisions of the Pensions Act 2004 sections 257 and 258 do apply to transfers taking place after 6 April 2005. In effect, this means that provisions equivalent to the TUPE regulations apply to pension rights from that date. In essence, if the previous employer provided a pension scheme then the new employer has to provide some form of pension arrangement for employees who were eligible for, or members of the old employer's scheme. It will not have to be the same as the arrangement provided by the previous employer but will have to be of a certain minimum standard specified under the Pensions Act[13].

2. Redundancy

Where outsourcing is taking place, there is a real possibility that existing employees may find that their contracts of employment are terminated. We have seen that TUPE might enable these employees to bring claims for either unfair dismissal or redundancy against either the transferor or transferee. The following section looks in outline at the law on redundancy.

The Employment Rights Act 1996

This Act provides a wide-ranging series of statutory rights for employees at work. They include:

- Unfair dismissal protection.

- Maternity rights.

- Minimum notice entitlement.

---

13. Public sector employees have always had better protection relating to transfer of pension rights. Under a voluntary code of conduct operating in central government, the transferee employer has to provide a comparable pension in terms of benefits etc. Equivalent rights operate in local government and the NHS.

- Time off work for specified activities.

- Redundancy payments.

Redundancy payments

The last entitlement is based on the concept that an employee should receive compensation for loss of job security. It is not strictly there to provide a financial buffer in between jobs – the employee could find better paid employment the next day and still be entitled to the redundancy payment. The issue is that he or she is less secure in the new work and does not receive statutory protection until they have served minimum periods of continuous service (the length varying depending on which statutory right is involved).

An employee must satisfy three requirements to be entitled to a redundancy payment. There must be:

1.   Dismissal.

2.   A redundancy situation.

3.   A minimum period of continuous employment.

1. Dismissal

There are three variations of dismissal which permit claims:

- Dismissal by the employer with or without notice.

- Constructive dismissal (resignation following a breach of contract by the employer).

- Failure to renew a fixed term contract.

2. Redundancy

There are three variations that can arise:

- Complete closure of an organisation.

- Closure of one factory, branch, office or site, but the organisation's other work places continue.

Problems of entitlement to redundancy payment can arise here where an employee is required to move from one site to another. The employee may be unwilling to move and insist on a redundancy payment instead. The rights of the two parties will depend on interpreting the contract and the extent to which the employee can be seen to be mobile. If there is an express mobility clause requiring such movement, the employee cannot claim redundancy. If it does not extend as far as the required move, a payment can be claimed.

O'Brien v Associated Fire Alarms

Employee working in Merseyside was ordered to transfer to Barrow. He refused and claimed a redundancy payment. The employment tribunal looked at his contract and could find no reference to mobility. **Held:** It was an illegitimate order entitling him to resign (constructive dismissal). It was a redundancy situation – his old job was disappearing, and he possessed the minimum period of notice. He won his claim.

Some employees are deemed to possess an implied duty of mobility – those in selling or marketing roles and staff occupying management responsibilities. Employers need to be careful here – the mobility requirement is limited to a test of reasonableness – and it would be far safer to draft an explicit clause into the contract.

- Where, although there is no closure of any factory, office etc, there is a reduction in the needs of the organisation for work of a particular kind.

Problems arise as to what is 'work of a particular kind'? The needs of businesses can require all employees to be adaptable to a reasonable extent and to develop new skills and competencies as the work develops. If an employee fails to adapt to changing circumstances to a reasonable extent, any dismissal may be seen as fair (on the grounds of incapacity) and not redundancy – the job still exists, even though it has changed some of its appearance.

North Riding Garages Butterwick

Senior management decided to change emphasis of work in chain of garages from repair/maintenance to car sales. Each garage manager was given minimum sales targets to meet. The manager of one garage failed to meet the target and, after warnings, was dismissed. He claimed redundancy - the needs of the employer for work of a particular kind (manager of repair/maintenance garage) had diminished. The employment tribunal held that the job still existed – that of being a manager of a garage. All that had changed was the stress being given to different aspects of that work. The manager had proved incompetent in one of those aspects – selling.

Redundancy & Outsourcing

In the context of outsourcing, if the number of employees needed to carry on the outsourced activity is fewer (possibly because of different working methods or greater use of capital equipment), those who find their contracts terminated may well have a claim for redundancy payment.

Offers of Alternative Employment

Employees, instead of being given notice of redundancy, will sometimes be offered alternative work – their existing work no longer being required. This could be caused by newer technology or diversification into different areas of business. Can an employee refuse to transfer to the new work and claim a redundancy payment? This depends on considering the suitability of the new job compared with the old one. Refusal to accept the offer of a suitable alternative job will render the employee unable to claim a redundancy payment.

What is suitable? This is a matter of 'substantial equivalence' between the two jobs, taking into account:

- The type of work involved.
- Pay levels.
- Status of the two jobs.
- Overtime opportunities.
- Shift work requirements.
- Fringe benefits.
- Travelling time.

Some degree of adaptability and moderate financial loss may be expected, depending on the circumstances of the business in question.

An offer of suitable alternative work can be reasonably refused on grounds such as ill-health, dependent relatives, schooling problems where a move to another area is involved.

Continuous Employment

The employee has to have been continuously employed by the employer for two years in order to claim a statutory redundancy payment – private schemes may allow for claims at an earlier stage.

The Payment

The compensation is calculated according to a formula based on three criteria:

1.   Age of employee at time of dismissal.

2.   Length of continuous service.

3.   Gross pay at time of dismissal.

•   For each year of relevant employment between the ages of 18-21 – compensation of 0.5 week's pay.

•   For each year of relevant employment between the ages of 22-40 – compensation of 1 week's pay.

•   For each year of relevant employment above the age of 41 – compensation of 1.5 week's pay.

A maximum of 20 years service is allowed under the formula. Gross pay above £380.00 per week is disregarded (the maximum pay is subject to annual review – this figure is accurate at the time of writing – October 2009). This means that the maximum payment under the statutory scheme is 20 x 1.5 x £380.00 i.e. £11,400.

12,900.

Information and Consultation Requirements

We have already found a number of procedural requirements laid out by Parliament – in the Collective Redundancies & Transfer of Undertakings (Protection of Employment)(Amendment) Regulations 1999. The details have already been outlined in the previous section on TUPE.

Selection for Redundancy

Although redundancy constitutes one the gateways of reasons that can justify dismissal (thereby avoiding potential claims for unfair dismissal), unfair selection procedures override this immunity and permit such claims. The procedure must be fair and reasonable both in the way the process is conducted and the criteria used to decide selection. Certain criteria are treated as automatically unfair and include:

•   Sex, race or disability discrimination.

- Pregnancy, childbirth or maternity leave.

- Trade union representation (or health & safety representation).

In other cases, the claim is decided on the reasonableness of:

1. Selection of employees, or

2. Procedure adopted.

1. Selection

Employers are given a fairly free hand in choosing selection criteria provided that the pool from which the redundant employees will be selected is fair and the selection criteria are:

- Reasonably objective.

- Not in breach of an agreed procedure (with, for example, a trade union).

- Fairly applied.

The use of LIFO (last in/first out) is attractive to unions and employees because of its complete objectivity. It can however perpetuate weaknesses such as an ageing workforce. LIFO can be used effectively as a tie-breaker when other criteria result in a tie.

The most common selection criteria include the following:
- Skills & experience for remaining jobs.

- Key skills.

- Performance records.

- Absenteeism/length of absence.

- Disciplinary record.

Criteria referred to in a staff handbook may give rise to claims for breach of contract if not implemented at a time of selection.

Care has to be taken to ensure that the criteria chosen do not infringe the law on discrimination. Selecting part-time staff ahead of full-timers has been held to be indirect sex discrimination. Even 'length of service' has been challenged on the same grounds. The employer needs to be able to show there is objective neutral justification for choosing these criteria.

Deciding the Pool

i.e. deciding who are the affected employees (those within the job categories or departments from which the redundancies have to be made). Adherence to an agreed procedure or custom and practice is usually a starting point. Ultimately, the decision has to satisfy the test of reasonableness in the circumstances. It may be appropriate to combine two sites or departments into a single 'pool'.

2. Procedure

The case of **Williams v Compair Maxim Ltd.** identified three steps which should be taken when implementing redundancies. These are separate to any requirements relating to collective redundancies (see later). They are:

- To give as much advance warning as is reasonably practicable.

- To consult with individual employees affected.

- To consider opportunities to offer alternative suitable vacancies.

Unfair Dismissal and Redundancy - Remedies

Where an employee is unfairly dismissed during a redundancy process, the normal remedy awarded by an employment tribunal is compensation. The alternatives of reinstatement or re-engagement are not usually awarded in order to avoid the consequence of another employee then being dismissed when the successful applicant returns to the organisation.

The current maximum award for unfair dismissal at present is £51,700.

Collective Consultation

We have already found a number of procedural requirements laid out by Parliament – in the **Collective Redundancies & Transfer of Undertakings (Protection of**

Employment)(Amendment) Regulations 1999. The details have already been outlined in the previous section on TUPE.

Where 20 or more employees are proposed to be made redundant within a period of 90 days, specific rules apply requiring to employer to carry out a consultation exercise. This must be undertaken 'with a view to reaching agreement' i.e. it must represent a genuine attempt by the employer. It is not a duty to negotiate – only to inform and provide an opportunity for alternative options to be put forward. The consultation must cover:

•   Ways of avoiding the dismissals.

•   Ways of reducing the numbers to be dismissed.

•   Ways of mitigating the consequences of dismissal e.g. severance pay.

Practical Alternatives

•   Restrictions on recruitment.

•   Reductions in overtime.

•   Short-time working to cover temporary fluctuations.

•   Retraining.

•   Transfer to alternative work.

Some consideration should be applied to the above options even if they have little likelihood of implementation (evidence in defence in subsequent claims).

The employer must provide the following information:

•   The reason for the collective redundancy.

•   Numbers & descriptions of the employees the employer proposes to dismiss as redundant.

•   Proposed method of selection.

•   Proposed procedure for carrying out the redundancies.

- Proposed method of calculating any redundancy payment in excess of the statutory redundancy payment.

In conclusion:

Having read this chapter, you should now have an understanding of the following issues and principles:

- Requests for tenders amount to an invitation to treat.

- Tenders amount to offers.

- With specific (one-off) tender agreements, the contract is agreed from the start – when the successful contractor is informed.

- With general (as and when) tender agreements, contracts come into existence when individual call-offs are made – there is no continuing contract for the overall period in question.

- Organisations must give proper consideration to all tenders that have been correctly submitted within the time scale set (the Blackpool BC case).

- The awarding of tenders is subject to a requirement that the process satisfies a basic level of fairness (the Camelot case).

- Public sector tendering procedures are regulated by EC Directives and UK Regulations intended to create a more free and transparent market between member states. Various enforcement powers are held by the courts to deal with any transgression.

- The ARD & TUPE are intended to protect employees from losing their employment in the event of take-overs, mergers or outsourcing of activities. Their existing terms and conditions are preserved after the transfer. The legal position on when the Regulations apply to outsourcing is, however, very unclear at the present time.

- Redundancy payments may be claimable when jobs are lost where an activity is being outsourced. Entitlement to a payment is based on rules set out in the Employment Rights Act 1996.

- The process for redundancy and selection criteria used must be fair and reasonable. Otherwise, a claim for unfair dismissal will be available against the organisation involved.

Chapter Twenty One

The Freedom of Information Act 2000

Background to the Act

There had been growing pressure over a period of time for greater openness in government – a right for the public to have access to public records and decision making. Although there had been a voluntary code of practice operating since the early 1990's, the incoming government in 1997 announced its intention to pass legislation introducing 'freedom of information'. The Freedom of Information Act (FoIA) received the royal assent in 2000. There had been precedents in other countries, chiefly the USA, Australia, New Zealand and Ireland.

There is some overlap between the new FoIA and the Data Protection Act 1998 (DPA) in that they have a similar purpose – the right of the public to access information. However, there are differences. The DPA 1998 relates only to personal information concerning the individual applicant, whereas the FoIA 2000 is concerned with non-personal information. The applicant does not even have to possess any personal connection with the material being requested. In many cases, the applicant will be representatives of the media.

The person with overall responsibility for the operation of both Acts is the Information Commissioner.

The Basic Duties

Each relevant public body (this includes all central government departments & agencies, local authorities, NHS trusts & public utilities) must produce a publication scheme (section 19) and subsequently respond to individual requests for information (section 1).

Publication Scheme

This forms a guide to information held by the public authority and routinely available. This can be in the form of website pages, prospectuses, almanacs etc. It must set out the classes of information published, the manner of publication and any charges payable. This information is then exempt from subsequent individual requests – it is already available to the public in the above format. There are obvious cost advantages to the authority in providing extensive information in such a way – the reduction of time-consuming individual requests.

The publication scheme has to be approved by the Information Commissioner and is subject to periodic review.

Individual Requests (the right to know)

Section 1 requires the authority to confirm or deny whether it possesses the information being requested. Where it does hold the information, it must (subject to a number of exemptions – see later) provide the relevant information. The applicant does not have to be the subject of the information (unlike the DPA 1998) or even affected by it. The applicant does not have to give reasons or justify the request.

The authority can refuse the request if the cost exceeds an appropriate amount (although the initial approach has been relatively generous in interpretation here). Where the authority refuses to provide the information (based on one of the exemptions) it must give written reasons justifying its decision. There is a right of appeal, initially using an internal grievance procedure within the public authority involved but subsequently to the Information Commissioner and finally to a special Information Tribunal.

The response to the request must be prompt, and no more than 20 working days. A charge (based on fees regulations passed under the Act) can be imposed where the costs are likely to be significant.

Exemptions

There are a significant number of exemptions under the Act. Some are categorised as 'absolute', some as 'qualified'. Where they are qualified, they can only be used by the authority if it is more in the public interest to deny access than to permit it. With absolute exemptions, the right to refuse is automatic.

Absolute exemptions include court records, Parliamentary privilege & information provided in confidence.

Qualified exemptions include national security, law enforcement, & commercial interests.

From the procurement perspective, the exemptions relating to breach of confidentiality (section 41) and causing damage to commercial interests (section 43) are the most important. Clearly, these two defences have relevance to suppliers. However, their availability is much more restrictive than might be thought to be the case.

The Freedom of Information Act – a Procurement Perspective

What types of commercial information might be held by a public authority which could be the subject of a request under the Act? They include:

•   Future procurement plans.

•   Information relating to a tendering process, including information on unsuccessful bids.

•   Details of successful bids and contractual details.

•   Supplier rating on existing contracts.

Clearly, suppliers may argue that release of such information will be damaging to their commercial interests and therefore covered by the 'commercial interests' exemption. Inappropriate release of this information could result in a claim for damages being brought against the authority.

A number of questions has to be asked when any of the above information is being requested:

•   Does the information have a bearing on a commercial activity?

•   What is the level of competition within the relevant market?

•   Would its release do harm to the company's reputation?

•   Who might be affected by its release?

•   Is the information significant in revealing a company's competitive edge?

Some practical advice

- Alert suppliers to the Act and its implications.

- Consult with key suppliers on issues of confidentiality and commercial interests.

- Include paragraph on FoIA in ITT/ITQ documentation asking suppliers to identify types of information that is genuinely confidential.
- Amend existing confidentiality clauses in your standard terms and conditions.

- Consider including a schedule in contracts specifically identifying which information is confidential and not to be disclosed.

- Ensure suppliers justify their reasons for inclusion.

- Refuse blanket confidentiality clauses in suppliers terms and conditions (explain why to suppliers).

- Consider using a checklist of issues when agreeing contracts.

In conclusion

Having read this chapter, you should now have an understanding of the following issues and principles:

- All public authorities are obliged to provide information relating to their activities on request and to produce and maintain a publication scheme, making accessible much of the potential information that may be requested.

- Unlike the Data Protection Act 1998, the information involved is not 'personal information', and the applicant does not have to have a personal interest in the matter.

- The information requested should normally be provided within a maximum of 20 days and be free of cost to the applicant.

- There are a number of exemptions where a public authority can refuse to disclose information.

- The most important exemptions in relation to procurement activities are breach of confidentiality and damage to commercial interests.

- Appeals against refusal can be made.

- The person with responsibility for the Act is the Information Commissioner.

Chapter Twenty Two

Insurance Law

Insurance law is a combination of general principles of contract and mercantile practice developed over the past centuries. The latter was legally recognised initially through the law merchant and later became incorporated into the common law. There have been very few Acts of Parliament relating to the topic, chiefly the **Marine Insurance Act 1906**. Important sources of information to understand the parties' rights and obligations are always the documents of insurance – the proposal forms and policies.

The chapter examines the following legal principles and issues:

* Classification of insurance – distinction between property/liability insurance and life insurance.

* Definition of insurance and its essential ingredients.

* Formation and duration of insurance policies.

* Meaning of 'insurable interest'.

* Effect of fraud, misrepresentation, non-disclosure and breach of warranties.

* Meaning and significance of *'uberrimae fidei'*.

* Meaning and significance of 'increase of risk' clauses.

* Warranties and 'basis of contract' clauses.

* Promissory warranties.

* Subrogation.

Types of Insurance

The most basic distinction in types of policy divides policies into:

- **Property & liability insurance**

- **Life**

Property and liability insurance

The insurance company indemnifies (reimburses) the insured for the loss incurred. The policy does not specify in advance what the amount will be (although a maximum figure will be stipulated). The policy will compensate only for the loss actually suffered. Examples include fire, theft and marine insurance. Liability insurance involves the insured being covered against the risk of claims by third parties. This covers potential actions for breach of contract and negligence and includes consequential losses.

Life insurance

Here the policy provides an agreed payment upon the happening of a specified event – a contingency event. The policy stipulates in advance how much will be paid. It is not based on actual loss suffered. For this reason it has been traditional to use the expression "assurance" instead of insurance. However, the two are used flexibly today and are frequently interchangeable.

Definition of Insurance

There is no statutory definition of insurance. One standard attempt suggests that a contract of insurance:

"Is a contract to pay money or provide a service on the occurrence of a future uncertain event or a certain event, the date of which is uncertain, provided that the insured has an interest in that event."

Three ingredients seem to be required:

1) Consideration

In exchange for periodical payments (premiums) the insured will be entitled to receive payment upon the happening of a specified event(s).

2) The event must be uncertain – either as to whether it will happen (fire, flood, accident etc) or when it will happen (death).

3) The insured must have an insurable interest in the uncertain event i.e. it will affect him adversely (e.g. as owner of the property damaged or stolen, or as a seller with a retention of title clause. Otherwise it would be deemed a wager and unlawful.

Authority to conduct business as an Insurer

It is an offence to conduct insurance business without the proper authorisation. This is achieved by obtaining a licence from the Department of Trade & Industry (or by being a Lloyd's Underwriter). There are minimum capital requirements and a stipulated excess of assets over liabilities. There are further requirements including adequate re-insurance arrangements.

Formation of the Contract

The general rule relating to simple contracts applies to insurance – they can be created in writing or orally. There is a requirement with life assurance policies for the assured to be sent a statutory notice before or at the time the contract is being concluded giving him or her the opportunity to change their mind and cancel the agreement.

The offer will normally come from the applicant; the acceptance from the insurance company. With renewals of property or liability insurance, the offer will usually be made by the insurer (by sending a reminder with details of premium to be paid etc). The insured will then accept by sending payment. Cover notes are fully effective and treated as valid contracts of insurance. The only details that must be clear when the note is issued are the duration of the policy, the nature of the risk, and the premium to be paid. Most cover notes will state that they are issued subject to the standard terms and conditions of the insurer's usual policy. This attaches those terms to the arrangement with the insured.

Duration of the Contract

Leaving aside life assurance policies, most other contracts are for a fixed period of one year. A new contract must then be entered each time it is renewed. This imposes on the insured a further obligation to disclose changes in material facts between policies. The insurance company is under no obligation to renew a policy, nor to provide reasons for non-renewal. Most contracts contain conditions (for definition of this expression - see later) allowing the insurer to terminate the contract. They often relate to undertakings given by the insured such as to maintain the property insured in a reasonable state.

Once the insurer has incurred risk under the policy it will not be possible for the insured to recover any premium(s) paid under the policy. If, however, the policy becomes defective through operative mistake or misrepresentation by the insurer, he will be able to recover monies already paid to the insurer on the grounds of a total failure of consideration. The same is true where the insurance company avoids the contract for misrepresentation or failure to disclose on the part of the insured. The only exception is where the insured acted fraudulently.

Insurable Interest

One of the essentials of a contract of insurance is that the insured must have an insurable interest in the event insured against. Again, we shall be only considering non-life insurance because of its greater relevance to the business world.
There are few issues of concern here when dealing with liability insurance. The applicant will always have an interest in protecting himself against potential liability to pay compensation to a third party.

However, problems occasionally arise when considering property insurance. One 'definition' of insurable interest is to require the applicant to have " a right in the property, or a right derivable out of some contract about the property." (Lord Eldon in **Lucena v Craufurd**). Simply being affected by loss or damage to property does not give the applicant sufficient standing. If, for example, a café owner whose business depended heavily on a nearby factory attempted to insure against the factory's damage or destruction, he would lack the necessary insurable interest. Mere possession of property is not enough, unless it is being held as a bailee who has legal obligations to take reasonable care of its condition.
A leading case on insurable interest is:

Macaura v Northern Assurance Company Ltd.

M. transferred his ownership in some timber forest land to a registered company he had recently formed. It was essentially a one-man company – he was the sole shareholder. He applied for a fire insurance policy to cover the land in question but put down his own name on the policy. A fire subsequently destroyed much of the forest. When he claimed on the policy it was held that he did not possess an insurable interest in the land. It was owned by the company, and although he was a shareholder (and creditor) of the company, this did not give him any rights to claim.

Where property insurance is involved, the applicant must have the insurable interest from the date on which the policy commences. It must also identify the name(s) of any other persons who are to be covered e.g. a tenant under a policy being concluded by the landlord.

Where goods are the subject matter of the policy, it is not necessary for the applicant to have an insurable interest in the strict sense when the contract is agreed. Some other form of interest in the goods is required – some potential loss from their destruction. This facilitates a whole range of business situations where goods are being held without ownership, yet the possessor may need insurance protection e.g. goods delivered on retention of title terms, goods received on hire or hire purchase terms.

When can the Insurance Company treat the policy as Void?

Various events can allow the insurer to avoid the contract:

1.   Fraud.

2.   Other forms of misrepresentation.

3.   Non-disclosure of material information.

4.   Breach of warranties (see Warranties and Conditions on page 260).

1.   Fraud
If the applicant commits fraud on the proposal form, the contract can be treated as void by the insurer.

2.   Misrepresentation
In theory, the normal rules of misrepresentation apply to insurance contracts. The insurer has the right to avoid the contract for any mis-statement of material facts by the proposer. In practice, insurance companies tend to treat such mis-statements either as non-disclosure and therefore covered by the doctrine of non-disclosure (see next) or as breach of warranty when they are found on the proposal form (see later).

3.   Non-Disclosure
Contracts of insurance are an example (the most important example) of a class of contracts described as being *uberrimae fidei*. This translates as 'of the utmost

good faith'. One party is in a far better position to know material facts than the other (i.e. the insured will possess the salient facts such as previous medical record, or the previous record of applications for similar policies etc.). In such cases, the law imposes a fiduciary duty (essentially placing the insured in a position of trust) on the applicant and requires him to disclose all material facts.

If misleading (false) information is given, the contract is voidable and can be cancelled by the insurance company when the truth becomes known. It may not even have to return the existing premiums if it involves fraud or illegality. A classic case illustrating this principle is:

London Assurance Co. v Mansel

When completing a life assurance policy, M. was asked whether he had made previous applications on his life. He replied that he was already insured at two offices, omitting to say that he had been declined at a number of other offices. **Held:** This was a failure to disclose a material fact, allowing the insurer to avoid the policy.

Whether an omitted fact is material or not is a question of fact and each case will have to be considered on its own merits. A case which concluded that the contract could not be set aside is:

Mutual Life Assurance Co. (New York) v Ontario Metals Co.

When asked for the name of any doctor consulted during the past 5 years, the applicant stated "None". This was untrue – he had consulted a doctor who had simply prescribed him a tonic. He had had no time off work. When the doctor's opinion was subsequently sought, he indicated that, if asked, he would have recommended acceptance of the risk by the insurer.
Held: No material fact was involved in this non-disclosure. The policy could not be avoided by the insurer.

In contracts *uberrimae fidei:*

- the applicant can commit misrepresentation **by silence**. If he fails to disclose important information (material to the contract) the contract can be avoided just as much as if the applicant had told a positive untruth.

- he commits a misrepresentation even when it was true at the time he originally made it **but became inaccurate between then and when the insurance contract was concluded.**

The duty of disclosure will normally operate in practice in connection with questions to be answered on the proposal form. It does however apply to the contract as a whole. Where insurance cover is to be renewed (yearly in most cases) there is a fresh obligation to disclose each time the contract is concluded.

Lambert v CIS Ltd.

A wife had insurance cover for jewellery belonging to herself and her husband. The policy had been renewed for eight years. In 1971 her husband was imprisoned for dishonesty, a fact she did not disclose when renewing the policy in 1972. Later that year, she claimed for the theft of the jewellery.
Held: The insurer had the right to avoid the policy and refuse payment.

The duty to disclose only applies to material facts. The test to decide which facts are material is:

Would a reasonable insurer regard the fact in question as significant to his decision to agree the policy or to determine the amount of the premium?

Some facts by their very nature will be treated as clearly material. Examples include the previous history of applications for insurance by the proposer and his previous criminal record. Non-disclosure of a bad accident record or a high risk occupation are other examples.

The duty of non-disclosure was originally created in the context of marine insurance, when communications were poor and it was necessary to impose additional obligations on the party that possessed all the relevant information. It therefore pre-dated the evolution of proposal forms. In what ways do these forms affect the doctrine of *uberrimae fidei*?:

- There is a presumption that information provided in answers to questions on the form are material to the insurance contract.

- Where the insurer does not require further information to partially answered questions or those left blank, there is an inference that it is waiving any rights to claim non-disclosure subsequently.

- Where questions are asked in specific terms, this limits the field of reference and the applicant is under no obligation to provide information outside that field. If, for example the question asks for details relating to the last 5 years, events from an earlier time can be omitted. Again, this is treated as a waiver of rights by the insurer.

Once the contract has been concluded, there is no general obligation to inform the insurer about changes in material facts. However, this can be affected by the presence of **'increase of risk' clauses** in the policy. Sometimes called 'promissory warranties', the insured is under a duty to disclose all matters which permanently affect the risk covered by the policy. An example is:

Farnham v Royal Insurance Co.

Under a property damage policy, the outbuildings of a farm were covered. The farmer had informed the insurance company that metal containers were being stored in his barns. Without telling the insurer, he had then allowed welding work to be carried out in the barns.
Held: The farmer should have informed the insurer about this change of use under an increase of risk clause found in the contract. As a result, the insurer could avoid the policy.

Warranties and Conditions

Insurance contracts obviously contain a variety of terms, located in the proposal form and the policy document. Some of these terms have assumed a particular significance in insurance law and need to be considered more closely. They are:

• **Warranties**

• **Conditions**

It must be made clear at the start that their meaning in insurance law is different from their standard meaning in general principles of contract – in fact in some ways they contradict this traditional definition. Usually, warranties are defined as terms of relatively minor importance to a contract; conditions are defined as terms of fundamental importance. The remedies for breach are consequently greater for infringement of a condition. In insurance law, a warranty is considered to be more important than a condition.

Warranties

A term under which the insured promises that a particular state of affairs exists or will exist, such that if it is untrue (or becomes untrue), the insurer will have the right to avoid the contract. It is irrelevant whether the breach of warranty caused or contributed to the loss. Warranties can relate either to the present – warranting that a particular state of affairs already exists – or to the future – warranting that a state of affairs will exist or continue to exist for some future time. The latter is called a

promissory warranty. If it is becomes untrue, the insurer can avoid the policy from the date of breach.

Warranties can be established in a variety of ways:

1.   It is common for the proposal form to contain a provision indicating that the questions and answers constitute the **basis of the contract**, and any untruths will invalidate the policy. The effect of this is to enable the insurer to avoid the contract even where the untruth does not relate to a material fact:

Dawsons Ltd. v Bonnin

A lorry had been insured against fire and third party liability. In answer to the question 'State full address at which vehicle will usually be garaged', the insured had inadvertently identified their normal place of business in central Glasgow. In fact it was housed on the outskirts of Glasgow – if anything, a safer place. The proposal form finished by stating that it was to form the basis of the contract. **Held:** The insurer was entitled to avoid the policy because of this incorrect information. The clause making such answers the basis of the contract made the information a warranty.

Questions requiring an opinion by the applicant are not treated as warranties e.g. a question requiring an answer "to the best of the proposer's knowledge and belief." However, statements relating to future events can become promissory warranties even if they do not amount to statements of fact at the time the proposal form is being completed:

Hales v Reliance Fire & Accident Insurance Co. Ltd.

When answering a question on the proposal form that asked whether any inflammable oils or goods were used or kept on the premises, a shopkeeper stated that 'lighter fuel' was the only such product. In the run-up to Guy Fawkes Night, he bought a stock of fireworks. This was held to be a promissory warranty that had been infringed from the moment the fireworks were delivered. The policy could be avoided by the insurer from that moment.

2.   Where the clause uses the expression 'Warranty' or states that 'the insured warrants' it will be treated as a warranty.

3.   Where a clause indicates that the happening or non-happening of a specified event will cause the contract to become void, it will be treated as a warranty.

Promissory warranties can lead to difficult problems of interpretation. If there is any ambiguity in the clause, it will be interpreted narrowly, against the wishes of the insurance company:

Provincial Insurance Company Ltd. v Morgan

Coal merchants wished to insure a lorry and completed the proposal form. One of the questions required them to 'State (a) the purpose in full for which the vehicle will be used; and (b) the nature of the goods to be carried.' They answered "delivery of coal" and "coal" respectively. On one occasion, they transported some timber as well as coal. After delivering the timber and some of the coal there was an accident and they wished to claim on the policy. The insurance company argued that there was a breach of a promissory warranty.

Held: On a reasonable interpretation, the coal merchants had only warranted that the lorry would carry coal, which was accurate – not that it would carry coal exclusively.

Conditions

These are clauses that cover issues which are not fundamental to the risks covered by a policy and do not relate to statements of fact. They include terms giving the insurer additional rights beyond those provided by general principles. Examples are rights of cancellation and subrogation (see below).

Failure to comply with a condition in an insurance contract will only allow the insurance company to avoid a specific liability for a particular loss. Liability for other losses under the policy continue to apply where the relevant conditions have been satisfied.

Subrogation

This doctrine applies to insurance policies that have indemnified the insured against certain risks such as fire, motor, or non-payment of money (but not to life or personal accident insurance). It is designed to prevent the insured from being able to recover more than a full indemnity:

"The contract of insurance … is a contract of indemnity, and of indemnity only, … and the assured shall be fully indemnified, but shall never be more than fully indemnified." **(Castellain v Preston)**

The doctrine has two elements:

1.   The insured cannot make a profit from his loss.

2.	The insurer has a right to step into the shoes of the insured (and, in his name, pursue claims which may reduce the loss insured against).

## 1.	The insured cannot make a profit

An early example of this rule is found in:

Darrell v Tibbits

The owner of a house insured it against fire. It was leased to a tenant. Serious damage was caused to the building by an explosion caused by the local council. The council paid compensation to the tenant, who used the money to make good the repairs (as he was required to do under the tenancy agreement). The insurance company paid up under the fire policy and then sought to recover the money. **Held:** It was entitled to the return of the payment. The owner would have profited if he had been able to keep the insurance money (an example of double indemnity).

## 2)	The right to take action

This will usually involve a right to sue a third party liable to pay damages in tort or for breach of contract:

Lister v Romford Ice & Cold Storage Ltd.

A son and his father were employed as a driver and his mate. Whilst helping his son reverse the lorry, the father was injured by his son's negligent driving. The employer was held vicariously liable for the son's negligence and had to pay significant compensation. The money was in fact paid under the relevant insurance policy. The insurance company then insisted (as they were entitled to do under the terms of the policy) that a breach of contract claim be brought against the son – for breaching the implied duty to perform work competently and using reasonable care. There is an implied right in a contract of employment for an employer to be indemnified against losses caused by unlawful behaviour of employees **Held:** The insurance company was entitled to pursue this claim and secure the return of their money.

The insured must not do anything to prejudice the insurer e.g. by entering into a compromise with the wrongdoer:

West of England Fire Insurance Co. v Isaacs

A sub-tenant insured property against fire. Following a fire, he claimed on the policy and received payment. He paid this money to the tenant to execute repair work.

At the same time he undertook not to sue the tenant for a breach of the tenancy agreement – a covenant that the tenant would arrange suitable insurance cover himself. In fact he was under insured or the property in question.

Held: The sub-tenant was liable to return the equivalent money to the insurance company. He had prejudiced their potential right to use his name to sue the tenant for breach of the covenant.

Another case illustrating this principle is:

Phoenix Assurance Co. v Spooner

Mrs Spooner insured property belonging to her against fire. During the period in which the policy was covering the property, Plymouth Corporation served notice of a compulsory purchase order. Shortly afterwards, the property was destroyed in a fire. Phoenix paid £925 under the policy. Subsequently, Mrs Spooner negotiated an arrangement with the council by which it paid her the difference between the price she would have received if the property had been intact and the £925 she had received under the insurance policy. Phoenix argued that it was entitled to recover the £925 from Mrs Spooner.

Held: At the time of the fire, the risk had already transferred to the council. Mrs Spooner should therefore have been entitled to the full purchase price. As Phoenix were subrogated to Mrs. Spooner's rights, they could claim the return of the money from her.

In conclusion:

- Insurance can be broadly classified into policies covering property or liability and policies covering life.

- The three essential requirements for a valid insurance policy are consideration uncertainty of the event and an 'insurable interest' possessed by the applicant.

- Various factors can invalidate insurance policies, chiefly non-disclosure of material information and breach of warranties.

- Insurance contracts are an example of contracts *uberrimae fidei* (of the utmost good faith), imposing stricter requirements on the applicant to disclose material information.

- Increase of risk clauses can require the insured to update the insurance company on any changes of material importance which permanently affect the risk covered.

- Breach of a 'warranty' as defined in an insurance contract entitles the insurance company to terminate the contract.

- Insurance companies can 'step into the shoes' of the insured to claim rights using the doctrine of subrogation.

Appendix One

Answering Case Studies in Law Examinations

There is a tendency amongst candidates taking the Professional Stage examinations to regard Legal Aspects as one of the more difficult modules to pass. There are a number of reasons, which have led to this view – the lack of day to day contact with the subject matter - the more abstract nature of many of the principles and concepts involved. As a result many candidates lack basic confidence which sometimes affects performance. But one of the unfortunate and unnecessary features of their taking the module can be a basic ignorance of how law papers are marked – the methodology for assessing papers and allocating marks. There is in fact a distinctive technique, which, if understood, will substantially improve your chances of success.

Process, more than Conclusions

Although drawing up valid and appropriate conclusions is clearly an important element of answering law questions, the bulk of the marks are not awarded in this area. Most are awarded for the setting out of a series of stages by which suitable conclusions can be drawn. An analogy can be made to the taking of a Maths exam. Let us assume 2 students are answering a maths question worth 20 marks. Student A writes down nothing on the answer sheet except the correct answer. Result – he or she fails. Student B explains how they move through a series of stages, citing appropriate formulae and principles. However, near the conclusion, a simple arithmetical mistake is made and the wrong answer is reached. Result – a pass (possibly with distinction if the rest of the answer is well presented and explained.) The same approach applies to law questions.

Avoid Conclusions until the end

There is a natural tendency to jump straight into a case study or problem and start discussing the rights and duties of the parties involved. This is dangerous because you will tend to assume knowledge of the basic legal principles and merely apply them. Remember – the bulk of the marks are awarded for the identification and explanation of the relevant legal principles.

(N.B. When drawing your conclusions, marks can be awarded for introducing practical ideas and approaches, which reinforce your legal analysis. Remember though – these should only supplement the legal points, not replace them)

Answering a Law Problem

To avoid the above danger , the following technique is suggested:

Stage One

Read scenario and identify relevant legal issues and principles. Produce a rough list, including any statutes and cases, which come to mind.

Stage Two

Without referring to the problem, explain as fully as possible the above legal principles.
In doing so, refer to relevant legislation (including section numbers for important provisions) and case law (see later)

Stage Three

Apply the above explanation to the problem now. Draw appropriate conclusions if you can (rights/duties of the parties). Indicate when you cannot do this and the reason(s) why e.g. insufficient information in the scenario; uncertainty in the law itself.

How do you use cases?

Candidates often become anxious about revising cases – how many need to be committed to memory; what do I need to memorise; what do I do if I can't remember the name of a case. Whilst it is true to say that cases must always be studied as part of a preparation for any law exam, a balance needs to be drawn so that you can still see the wood for the trees –spending all you time learning details of cases, many of which are not of great importance to the development of the law, can cause unnecessary anxiety. You therefore need to focus on two types of case:

1.   Landmark cases – those, which have had a fundamental impact on legal development. There are nearly always one or two such cases in each

major topic in the syllabus. Some examples are Hadley v Baxendale (awarding of unliquidated damages); Taylor v Caldwell (doctrine of frustration of contract); Donoghue v Stevenson (negligence liability).

2.   Recent cases which have been decided in the last few years and which show you have the ability to keep updated in the law as it continues to develop.

Remember too that cases are not important for their facts – they are important for the legal principles which they created or are illustrating. Yes, include the facts of a landmark case, which is central to your problem, but try to relate it clearly to the principle of law involved. With cases of smaller importance, just refer to the mane and say that it illustrated the point of law being discussed.

And if you forget the name of that important case, just say "In an actual case..." and continue as you intended. You should not be penalised and you have shown a certain subtlety of approach. Do not try to remember the years when cases were decided – unless there is a particular significance to this fact e.g. it is a recent case and casts doubt on earlier cases on the same issue.

Getting to grips with Case Studies

For the longer "problem" found in Section A of the Legal Aspects paper – the case study – it is important to become very familiar with the scenario. One technique I would thoroughly recommend is to convert it into a diagram – make it more visual by creating an overview on an single sheet of A4 – names of parties in capitals and circled, events noted in concise form, arrows leading from company to company etc. Try not to clutter the page – leave as much white space as possible. Then list the potential legal principles in a column to one side – a word or short note representing each one. This activity forces you to become more aware of all the issues involved.

Constructing the Answer

Always prepare a rough plan. To those who protest insufficient time I would suggest you consider how much time is spent stopping and starting between points when no clear plan has been produced at the beginning of the answer. By creating a rough plan, a number of benefits result. You cast your mind wider before becoming locked into specific issues and therefore tend to remember more. You become aware of what is coming later in your answer – which helps your presentation of ideas. You write continuously which improves the fluency of your style.

For these reasons, the following technique is suggested:

1. Read the question closely (and establish what it is really asking – not the question you have prepared for and would like it to be asking).

2. List all the legal points and principles you feel to be relevant until you cannot add to it.

3. Re-read the question and check if all the points are relevant.

4. Re-arrange the remaining points into a better sequence – one which answers to question more directly.

5. Decide which of the points are 'core' issues, which need to be developed more fully. Asterisk them to remind yourself as you start to write the answer in full.

This takes time, but remember, you will make up for this later. And you will be convincing the examiner that you are an intelligent candidate capable of adapting the material to the needs of the question.

Some basic exam guidance

1. Draw up a timetable: remember that in addition to testing your knowledge and understanding of a subject, exams are testing your ability to use a limited amount of time efficiently and effectively. You must therefore plan how much time you have for each question and sub-question. Look at the weighting next to the questions for help here.

2. Best questions first: tackle the questions in descending order of preference. Go for your best one at the start and gain the confidence a good start can provide. This could well be from Section B of the paper – it does not matter in which order you answer the questions from the examiner's point of view.

3. Provide ammunition: remember that the examiner is on your side and will want to find marks from you script. Therefore, give him/her the opportunity to locate them by answering all the questions and sub-questions you are required to answer or have chosen to answer. Do not opt out of any because you don't think you know enough. There are always some 'easy' marks going at the start of each answer and you may well be able to pick them up by writing generally about the topic. Therefore – always provide the examiner with ammunition by having a go at all the relevant questions.

Final Thoughts

Exam technique often requires you to do things, which do not come naturally in the heat of exam conditions. Producing plans before answering the question, avoiding the problem until you have fully set out the principles first, carefully devising a timetable at the start to indicate where you should be for the rest of the time – none of these come easily at the time they are most needed. You should therefore develop these approaches over a period of time and practice them in mock conditions or even when simply producing an answer to a coursework question. If you practise these recommended approaches, your standard of presentation will inevitably improve and with it your confidence and your chances of success.

Appendix Two

Legal Case Studies – How to Approach Their Analysis

There may be a number of organisations against whom potential legal claims may be available. The following series of questions will help you formulate a suitable response:

Questions to ask (for each 'target' organisation):

Is there a contract with them?

If there is a contract:

1.   What type of contract is it? (Sale of goods or services).

2.   Was the contract broken? – if so, how (breach of express terms or implied terms or both)?

3.   If it was broken, what remedies are available (repudiation &/or damages)?

4.   Are there any complications with the claim for damages (e.g. restrictions on their awarding)?

If there is no explicit contract*:

1.   Is there an implied (collateral contract) involved?

2.   Are you a third party with rights (under the 1999 Act)?

3.   Can you bring a tort action for negligence?

4.   Is there a consumer who can bring a claim under the Consumer Protection Act 1987?

        [* See next section for further detail on this theme].

Appendix Three

Example of Examination Technique – Approach to Questions on Third Party Liability

Section A case studies will sometimes focus on the issue of third party liability. For example, the scenario could involve work being carried out on building new premises or renovating existing ones. The owner of the property engages a main contractor to carry out the work. Specialist work (electrical fittings, plumbing etc) may then be delegated to sub-contractors by the main contractor. Problems arise and the potential claims of the owner of the property have to be examined. This requires candidates to demonstrate an understanding of the doctrine of privity of contract and the need sometimes to rely on alternative claims (non-contractual) against sub-contractors who have performed incompetent work.

The doctrine of privity states that only the parties to a contract have the right to sue for its breach. Third parties (organisations who were not parties to the contract but who may be affected by its performance) have no such ability even though they could suffer harm as a result of its defective performance – as with the property owner in the above scenario if a sub-contractor performs incompetent work.

To answer the relevant tasks accompanying the case study, it can be extremely useful to ask a number of questions. They relate to each of the contractors identified in the scenario. Assuming you are the claimant organisation:

1.   Did you have a contract with the organisation?

Contractual claims are always easier to win. Liability is strict – simply failing to perform obligations which were promised is enough. There is no need to prove fault – that the contractor was in some way to blame for the breach. Clearly, the most likely target here is the main contractor with whom you negotiated a contract. The terms of this contract should clearly make the main contractor responsible for any faulty performance of sub-contractors. This should be in the form of warranties and indemnities obtained form the main contractor. It is also possible you made a contract with a consultant surveyor or architect – check the facts of the scenario here.

2.   If a contract does exist, what type of contract is it?

You need to ask this question in order to know which law governs your rights. If it is a sale of goods contract, you can refer to the Sale of Goods Act 1979, in particular, sections 12 –15 and the implied rights of a buyer relating to the goods (satisfactory quality, fitness for purpose etc.). If it is a contract for work and materials (which is clearly more likely in building or renovation scenarios) or professional services, you should refer to the Supply of Goods and Services Act 1982 (Part One for the quality of materials supplied; Part Two for the competence of the work done).

3.   If there is no explicit contract, can you discover an implied (collateral) contract?

This requires you to check the facts of the case study to see if any assurances were given during the negotiations by a business which caused you to insist on the purchase of their specific goods or materials by your contractors. Even if the scenario does not seem to include this possibility it is good technique to ask the question, explain briefly what is meant by a collateral contract and refer to a case in support – Shanklin Pier Ltd v Detel Products Ltd. is a useful example.

4.   If there is no explicit or implied contract, were you identified as a third party with rights?

This requires you to show an awareness of changes brought about by the Contracts (Rights of Third Parties) Act 1999, which came into force on 11th May 2000 and constitutes a major inroad to the doctrine of privity.

5.   If none of the above apply, is there a non-contractual claim which gives you rights?

The two most likely claims here will be:

(a)   The tort of negligence.
(b)   A statutory claim under the Consumer Protection Act 1987 (Part One).

This requires you to set out the essential ingredients for success. In negligence, you should identify the three requirements (duty of care, breach of duty, consequent damage). Spend some time explaining each one and be careful to consider the issue of claimable damage. Remember that although personal injury and damage to property is claimable in negligence, it is not normally possible to claim for purely economic loss (unless a nominated sub-contractor is involved). Therefore, lost orders and profits will not be recoverable in such claims.

Under Part One of the Consumer Protection Act 1987 you need to establish whether a consumer has sustained damage. If this is the case, you should outline the main provisions of the Act. These include the requirements for a successful claim and the parties who can be made liable, the meaning of 'dangerous' product, the meaning of 'damage' and the main defences available.

A useful additional point would be to ask if a collateral warranty had been obtained from the sub-contractor at the outset – a guarantee given in exchange for a payment (possible nominal) which entitles you to bring a direct contractual claim against the sub-contractor.

Appendix Four

Landmark Cases

This is a list of essential cases that you must have included in your revision for the CIPS examination in 'Legal Aspects'. It is not therefore a list representing all the cases you should know. Just how many more you include will depend on your available time and your need to feel well-placed on the eve of the examination.

Section A

Letters of Intent	BSC v Cleveland Bridge & Engineering Co.
Invitation to Treat	Pharmaceutical Society of G.B. v Boots Cash Chemists
Counter Offer	Hyde v Wrench (& unconditional acceptance)
Communication of Acceptance	Felthouse v Bindley
Implied Acceptance	Brogden v Metropolitan Rly. Co.
Battle of the Forms	Butler Machine Tool Co. v Ex Cell O Ltd.
Tenders	Blackpool & Fylde Aero Club v Blackpool Corporation
	Camelot Group Plc v National Lottery Commission
Consideration (& duress)	Atlas v Kafco Williams & Co v Roffey Bros
Mistake	Scott v Coulson (or Couturier v Hastie)
Liquidated Damages	Dunlop Pneumatic Tyre Co. v New Garage Ltd.
Unliquidated Damages	Hadley v Baxendale

Misrepresentation	Hedley Byrne & Co. v Heller & Partners
	Leaf v International Galleries
Exclusion (reasonableness)	George Mitchell v Finney Lock Seeds Ltd.
	Watford Electronics Ltd. v Sanderson CFL Ltd.
Frustration	Taylor v Caldwell
Time of the Essence	Charles Rickards v Oppenheim
Instalment Deliveries (right to cancel all of contract)	Maple Flock Ltd. v Universal Furniture Products Ltd.
Privity of Contract	Dunlop v Selfridge
Collateral Contracts	Shanklin Pier Ltd. v Detel Products Ltd.
Negligence	Donoghue v Stevenson
	Hedley Byrne & Co. v Heller & Partners
	Simaan General Contracting Ltd. v Pilkington Glass Ltd.
	Junior Books Ltd v Veitchi Co. Ltd.

Section B

Competition Law

Article 81 infringement	Consten Grundig v Commission
Definition of dominant position	United Brands v Commission
Intra State effects on trade	Hugin v Commission
Article 82 infringement	Tetra Pak v Commission

IPR

Passing Off	Bollinger v Costa Brava Wine Co.
Passing Off	Erven Warninck v Townend
Confidential Information	Saltman Engineering v Campbell

Confidential Information   Seager v Copydex Ltd.

Confidential Information   Faccenda Chicken Co. v Fowler

Design Right   British Leyland v Armstrong Patents Ltd.

International Trade

CIF   Manbre Co. Ltd. v Corn Products Ltd.

TUPE   Berriman v Delabole Slate Ltd.

Appendix Five

Legal Aspects - Revision List

For those readers studying for the Legal Aspects paper of the Professional Stage of the CIPS Graduate Diploma, or other law exams, the following list of questions will be useful as a revision aid. It is recommended that you study a particular legal topic and then look for the relevant questions in the list below and work through questions progressively in discrete sections.

Formation of Contract

1.   What is a contract (basic definition)?

2.   What are the legal differences between deeds and simple contracts?

3.   What are the essentials of a simple contract? (basic headings)

4.   What is the difference between void and voidable contracts (and what gives rise to each type of defective agreement)?

5.   Is a letter of intent legally binding?

6.   What happened in British Steel Corporation v Cleveland Bridge & Engineering Co. Ltd.[14] and what was the outcome?

7.   What is meant by *quantum meruit* and when can it be useful to a contractor?

8.   What is an offer? (definition)

9.   What is an invitation to treat (definition) and give some examples?

10.   What happened in Fisher v Bell (or Pharmaceutical Society of G.B. v Boots Cash Chemists) and what was the outcome?

11.   In what ways can an offer terminate?

12.   What is the only correct way in which to accept an offer?

13.   What happened in Hyde v Wrench and what was the outcome?

14.   What is the effect of agreeing 'subject to contract' and why does it have this consequence?

15.   What happened in Felthouse v Bindley and what was the outcome?

---

14. It is recommended that a card be created for each case, containing the name, facts and decision (Held...). If 3 vertical columns are used [NAME/FACTS/DECISION], you can easily test your memory for each case by blanking out one or two of the columns and checking what you can remember from the visible column(s).

16.   What happened in Brogden v Metropolitan Railway Co. and what was the outcome?

17.   What is the postal rule of acceptance and when does it not apply to acceptances sent by post?

18.   What is meant by the battle of the forms and why is it important to win it?

19.   How can you link the previous section on offer and acceptance to the battle of the forms?

20.   What happened in Butler Machine Tool Ltd. v Ex-Cell-O Corporation and what was the outcome?

21.   What happened in BRS v Arthur Crutchley Ltd. and what was the outcome?

22.   What is meant by consideration in a simple contract?

23.   What are the requirements for valid consideration?

24.   What happened in Stilk v Myrick and Hartley v Ponsonby and what were the outcomes?

25.   What happened in Atlas v Kafco and what was the outcome?

26.   What is meant by duress and economic duress?

27.   What happened in North Ocean Shipping Co. v Hyundai Construction (also known as 'The Atlantic Baron' case) and what was the outcome?

28.   What happened in Williams & Co. v Roffey Bros and what was the outcome?

29.   When are restraint of trade clauses permitted? (identify at least three cases in your response)

30.   Do mistakes normally invalidate contract and why?

31.   What examples can you give of operative (or fundamental) mistake and indicate any cases that may be given in support?

32.   What is meant by rectification

33.   What happened in Joscelyne v Nissen and what was the outcome?

34.   What is a misrepresentation? (a definition, broken down into its component parts)

35.   What remedies are available for fraudulent, negligent and wholly innocent misrepresentation? (include the legal sources for your response too)

36.   When is the remedy of rescission lost?

37.   What happened in Leaf v International Galleries and what was the outcome?

Content of Contract and Liability for Breach

38.   What is meant by 'express' terms and 'implied' terms?

39.   When does the common law imply terms into a contract? (Which cases

would you include in your response)

40. What is the difference between conditions and warranties and why is it necessary to know which is involved?

41. What is meant by the expression 'innominate term' and why was it developed as a new way of helping to classify terms in a contract?

42. What happened in the Hong Kong Fir Shipping case and what was the outcome?

43. What is the effect of 'acceptance' of the goods on the remedies of a buyer who wished to claim breach of contract?

44. When are goods deemed to be accepted according to the Sale of Goods Act 1979? (include reference to section numbers here)

45. What are liquidated damages? (definition)

46. What are their main advantages and disadvantage?

47. What is a penalty? (definition)

48. How can liquidated damages be distinguished from penalties? (identify the case that established the tests involved and the tests themselves)

49. What is meant by unliquidated damages?

50. What is the underlying purpose of an award of damages?

51. What are the rules in Hadley v Baxendale?

52. What happened in Victoria Laundry v Newman Industries and what was the outcome?

53. What happened in Parsons (Livestock) Ltd. v Uttley Ingham & Co. and what was the outcome - what principle of law was illustrated here?

54. What types of 'damage' can be claimed for in a breach of contract action?

55. What happened in Lambert v Lewis and what was the outcome? (what principle of law was illustrated here)

56. What happened in Anglia TV v Reed and what was the outcome? - what principle of law is being illustrated?

57. What is meant by mitigation of loss and which case can be used to illustrate it in operation?

58. What is meant by anticipatory breach?

59. What is meant by an exclusion of liability?

60. What two barriers to effectiveness of exclusion can you identify as being common law (judge-made) in origin?

61. What happened in Olley v Marlborough Court Hotel and what was the outcome?

62. What happened in Baldry v Marshall (or Andrews v Singer) and what was the outcome?

63. How is exclusion of liability for negligence regulated by section 2 of the Unfair Contract Terms Act 1977?

64. How is exclusion of liability for breach of contract regulated by section 3 of the Act?

65. How is exclusion of liability for breach of the implied terms found in sale of goods contracts regulated by section 6 of the Act?

66. What factors are identified in the Act as relevant in deciding whether an exclusion clause is fair and reasonable?

67. What happened in George Mitchell v Finney Lock Seeds Ltd. and what was the outcome? (alternative cases - RW Green v Cade Bros Farm, or St Albans City & District Council v ICL)

68. What is meant by frustration of contract? (definition of the doctrine and the effect it has on the contract)

69. What are the main examples of events that can frustrate contracts?

70. What happened in Taylor v Caldwell and what was the outcome?

71. What happened in Avery v Bowden and what was the outcome?

72. What happened in Chandler v Webster and what was the outcome?

73. What happened in Metropolitan Water Board v Dick, Kerr & Co. and what was the outcome?

74. In what way can Davis Contractors v Fareham UDC be contrasted with the Water Board case?

75. What are the consequences of the Law Reform (Frustrated Contracts) Act 1943 on contracts which have become frustrated?

76. What is a force majeure clause? (definition)

77. What are the main advantages to one or both parties of their inclusion in a contract?

78. What is the relationship between force majeure clauses and the Unfair Contract Terms Act 1977?

Sale of Goods and Services

79. The Sale of Goods Act 1979 is an example of laissez faire legislation.

80. What is meant by this statement?

81. What are the five implied conditions found in the Sale of Goods Act 1979 and which sections apply?

82. In what situation is it no longer possible (since1995) for a buyer to repudiate a contract for breach of the above implied conditions?

83. What examples can you give of how section 12 can be broken?

84. What examples can you give of how section 13 can be broken?

85. What is meant by 'satisfactory quality'? (definition, including additional features added in 1995)

86. In what types of contract does the Supply of Goods & Services Act 1982 imply a number of terms?

87. What implied terms are attached by Part One of the Act?

88. What implied terms are attached by Part Two of the Act?

89. What happened in Charles Rickards v Oppenheim and what was the outcome? What principle of law is being illustrated?

90. Why is it necessary to know when there has been a transfer of property (ownership) from seller to buyer?

91. When does property in goods transfer?

92. What is meant by Nemo Dat Quod Non Habet?

93. What are the exceptions to the doctrine, including the relevant sections and any supporting case law?

94. What are the rights of a buyer under the Sale of Goods Act 1979 where the wrong quantity is delivered? (including section number)

95. What are the rules governing the right of a buyer to cancel the remainder of a contract for delivery by instalment where one delivery is in breach of contract?

Non-Contractual Liability

96. What principle of law was established in Dunlop v Selfridge and what does this principle (or doctrine) mean?

97. What impact has the Contracts (Rights of Third Parties) Act 1999 had on this doctrine? What are its main provisions?

98. What is meant by a collateral warranty?

   What is meant by a collateral contract and how does Shanklin Pier v Detel Products Ltd. illustrate it in practice?

99. What area of law do negligence claims form an example? (together with defamation, nuisance, deceit etc)

100. When is a duty of care owed in the law of negligence:

101. What happened in Donoghue v Stevenson and what was the outcome?

102. What are good examples of duty of care relationships in commercial/ financial activities?

103. What happened in Hedley Byrne & Co. v Heller & Partners and what was the outcome?

104. When is a duty of care broken by a defendant & what factors are used to help determine the decision?

105. Why are negligence claims difficult to win in court and how does the doctrine known as res ipsa loquitor help the claimant sometimes?

106. What is meant by the 'but for' test when deciding damages in negligence actions?

107. What types of 'damage' are claimable in negligence actions and what types are not?

108. What happened in Simaan General Contracting Co. v Pilkington Glass and what was the outcome? (or Spartan Steel & Alloys Ltd. v Martin & Co)

109. How did the case of Junior Books Ltd v Veitchi Co Ltd. affect this position?

110. Why was the Consumer Protection Act 1987 passed?

111. What is the basic difference between this statutory claim and one brought in negligence?

112. Who can be made liable under the Act?

113. When is a product 'defective'?

114. What 'damage' is recoverable under the Act?

115. What is meant by the 'developmental risks' defence?

116. How long is it possible to bring a legal action under the 1987 Act?

Agency

117. What is meant by actual and apparent authority in the law of agency?

118. Which is the more important when deciding whether a principal is bound by the actions of an agent?

119. What is meant by ratification?

120. What is the doctrine of the undisclosed principal?

Assignment

121. What is meant by contractual assignment? What can and cannot be assigned in a contract?

122. What is meant by novation?

Bailment

123. Define bailment. Identify four examples of bailee situations

124. What legal responsibilities are placed on a bailee in relation to the goods in question?

Tenders

125. What are the legal stages involved in a tender procedure?
126. What are the implied (collateral) duties that attach to tendering procedures?
127. What happened in Blackpool & Fylde Aero Club v Blackpool Borough Council and what was the outcome?
128. What happened in Camelot Group plc v National Lottery Commission and what was the outcome?
129. What is the purpose of the EC Procurement Directives?
130. Which organisations are governed by their requirements?
131. Which types of contract are regulated and when do the rules become relevant?
132. What are the basic requirements that must be satisfied?
133. What can happen if the Directives (&/or UK Regulations) are not observed correctly?

TUPE & Outsourcing

134. What is the purpose of the Acquired Rights Directive 2001 and, consequently, the Transfer of Undertakings (Protection of Employment) Regulations 2006 (TUPE)?
135. What are the basic legal consequences of TUPE?
136. In what situations does TUPE become relevant
137. Does TUPE apply to contracting out/contracting in arrangements?
138. What is meant by 'ETO' reasons linked to a dismissal?
139. What are the information and consultation requirements where TUPE applies to a transaction? What remedies are available for infringement?

Redundancy

140. What is 'redundancy'? (definitions)
141. What is the difference between redundancy and severance?
142. What are the 3 requirements for a successful redundancy claim?
143. Does an employee have to accept an offer of alternative work to that which he has been doing?

144. Re selection for redundancy, what cannot be used as criteria for selection without it being unfair dismissal?

145. What factors can be taken into account in making the selection decision?

146. What basic rules need to be observed to satisfy procedural fairness where redundancies are being carried out?

147. What consultation requirements exist where collective redundancy is involved?

148. What options exist as an alternative to redundancy?

Competition Law

149. Why was the Competition Act 1998 passed?

150. What is the basic distinction between Article 81 & Article 82 of the European Treaty (as to when they apply)?

151. Re Article 81, what is meant by an 'undertaking'?

152. Re Art 81, what is meant by an 'agreement'?

153. What are the main examples of anti competitive practice identified in Article 81?

154. What are 'horizontal' and 'vertical' agreements and how does this distinction affect the approach of the European Commission?

155. What are the requirements regarding impact on trade for Article 81 to be infringed?

156. What happened in Consten Grundig v Commission and what was the outcome?

157. What are the requirements for an exemption to be obtained under Article 81?

158. How is the relevant market analysed for purposes of Article 81?

159. What is the difference between a block exemption & an individual exemption?

160. What is meant by a 'comfort letter'?

161. What is meant by a 'dominant position' for purposes of Article 82? (definition + reference to precedent case)

162. What are the main examples of anti competitive practice identified in Article 82?

163. Can you explain the facts and outcomes of the following cases - United Brands v Commission; Hugin v Commission; Tetra Pak v Commission?

164. What are the enforcement powers of the European Commission regarding Articles 81 & 82?

165. How does the Enterprise Act 2002 attempt to strengthen the operation of the Competition Act 1998?

166. How does the Enterprise Act 2002 (which has replaced the Fair Trading Act 1973) deal with the issue of monopolies and mergers in the UK? (Include definitions of 'monopoly' and 'merger')

167. How does the Merger Regulation (Regulation 4064/89) deal with the issue of control of mergers in the European Union?

168. What are the similarities and differences between Articles 81 & 82 of the European Treaty and Chapters One and Two of the Competition Act 1998?

169. What is the role and modus operandi of the following competition law agencies - the European Commission; the Office of Fair Trading; the Competition Commission; the Department of Business, Enterprise & Regulatory Reform?

International Trade

170. Why were INCOTERMS established and when do they attach to a contract of sale?

171. What are the responsibilities of the seller and buyer in a CIF contract? When does ownership and risk pass?

172. What are the responsibilities of the seller and buyer in a FOB contract? When does ownership and risk pass?

173. What is meant by FOB with additional services?

174. What differences exist between FOB contracts and FAS contracts?

175. What are the responsibilities of the seller and buyer in an ex works (EXW) contract? When does ownership and risk pass?

176. What is meant by DDP and who is responsible for what?

177. What is a bill of lading? (definition)

178. What 3 characteristics does a bill of lading possess?

179. What different forms of bill are used in practice?

180. What is a charterparty?

181. What is the purpose of the Hague-Visby rules. What are the rules and which Act contains them?

182. What are the shipping documents? Could you summarise their differing functions?

183. What is a letter of credit and how does it work in practice?

184. What are the different types of letter of credit?

International Sale of Goods

185. What is the purpose of the Uniform Laws on International Sales Act 1967?

186. What rules apply governing formation of the contract and its contents?

Arbitration

187. What is meant by arbitration and how does it differ from mediation?

188. What are the advantages and disadvantages of arbitration over litigation?

189. Is it possible to appeal against an arbitration award?

190. What is meant by a Scott Avery clause?

191. How did the Arbitration Act 1996 change the procedural rules relating to arbitration?

192. What additional benefits and disadvantages apply when arbitration is used in international disputes?

Intellectual Property Rights (especially confidentiality, passing off and contractual provisions)

193. What are the 3 requirements for a successful confidentiality claim?

194. What is meant by 'confidential information'?

195. What tests are used to decide where there is a duty not to confide?

196. What happened in Saltman Engineering v Campbell and what was the outcome?

197. What are the two possible bases of claim on which confidentiality actions can be brought?

198. What happened in Seager v Copydex Ltd. (or Coco v Clark Engineers Ltd.) and what was the outcome?

199. In what circumstances can an employer restrict an employee's use of information during and after he is employed by him?

200. What happened in Faccenda Chicken Co. Ltd. v Fowler and what was the outcome?

201. What is meant by the economic tort of 'passing off'? (definitions)

202. What is meant by 'get up'?

203. What happened in Hoffman La Roche v DDSA and what was the outcome?

204. What happened in Maxim v Dye and what was the outcome?

205. What is meant by 'common field of activity'?

206. What happened in Wombles Ltd. v Wombles Skips and what was the outcome?

207. What happened in Lego v Lemelstrich and what was the outcome?

208. What type of damage is recoverable under passing off actions?

209. What happened in Harrods Ltd v R. Harrod Ltd and what was the outcome?

210. What happened in Bollinger v Costa Brava Wine Co (and Erven Warninck v Townend) and what were the outcomes?

211. What are the key issues relating to IPR that must be dealt with in a contract?

212. What provisions should be included in a contract to encourage respect for confidentiality of information and other IPR?

213. How could a newly established business protect its business activities by the use of intellectual property rights? (assume the business is in manufacturing, and a range of products and processes are involved).

Freedom of Information Act 2000

214. What are the two main legal requirements which the Act imposes on public authorities under section 1 and section 19?

215. Which two exemptions are of particular importance to public authorities when requests are made in relation to their procurement activities?

Appendix Six

Recent Procurement Law Cases

These cases are not essential for revision purposes for candidates preparing for the CIPS Level Six examination in Legal Aspects of Purchasing and Supply. They are included to add an extra dimension to the book and show how the courts have interpreted procurement law principles in the last few years. Most of the cases were decided between 2006-2009. As such, this appendix can be seen as useful for those readers wishing to update their awareness of developments in procurement case law.

---

1. Photolibrary Group Ltd v Burda (2008)

[Simple Contracts – Ease of Formation]

Photolibrary Group Ltd (PGL) supplied photo transparencies to Burda (B) - a publisher of gardening magazines. Transparencies were sent to B's office in London with a delivery note (including PGL's standard terms).
One term imposed a fee varying between £450 - £750 per item lost whilst in the possession of the customer. PGL sent a parcel containing 1856 transparencies which were subsequently lost by B. PGL claimed £1,085,100 relying on above clause. B argued no contract had been agreed.
Held: The delivery note amounted to an offer which had been accepted by B when it accepted receipt of the goods. A contract existed, entitling PGL to rely on the fees claimed.

Haden Young Ltd v Laing O'Rourke Ltd (2008)

[Contract Formation – Complexity with more high value contracts]

This case involved a design and build contract between a client and Laing O'Rourke Ltd (L). A subcontract was sought by L with Haden Young (HY). L sent a draft letter of intent and proposed form of sub-contract to HY at end of 2003.

Several further draft sub-contracts were later sent. HY started on-site work and completed the required work by August 2005. A majority of key terms in the sub-contract had been agreed (including payment terms). However, one key term (limit on design liability), had not been agreed. No contract document had ever been signed. A dispute arose and legal arguments centred on whether a contract existed and on what basis was remuneration to be based. HY argued there was no contract and *quantum meruit* should be used to govern payment. L argued HY had accepted a sub-contract by implication – starting and carrying out work. On this basis, the payment clause should apply.

Held: No contract had been entered into because of the failure to agree on a term of fundamental importance – the limit on design liability.*

Stress was placed on correspondence indicating the parties intended to proceed on the basis that there would be no contract unless and until a formal agreement was signed.

The courts will demand stricter formality in terms of contract formation where the contract is more complex and for contracts of high value. With more routine arrangements, the position is more flexible and the courts may be more inclined to find contracts based on work having been carried out.

Confetti Records v Warner Music (UK) Ltd (2003)

[Contract Formation – Subject to Contract/Later Actions]

Warner Music Ltd wanted a music track to be recorded. It sent an initial contract document (deal memo) by fax to Confetti Records. It was clearly headed 'subject to contract'. Warner Music subsequently sent a music track with accompanying invoice to Confetti Records. (It was argued in court that this amounted to a fresh offer based on the terms referred to in the deal memo). The claimant proceeded to start recording the album (which was argued to be implied acceptance - by conduct).

Held: These later actions removed the effect of the 'subject to contract' provision and a binding contract had already been created

Rhodia v Huntsman International (2007)

[Reasonable endeavours]

R owned a chemical plant which it decided to sell to HI. Steam and electricity to the plant was supplied by NPL via a power plant sited at the location. There was a long-term contract between R and NPL for this arrangement to continue for several years. HI agreed that it would use 'reasonable endeavours' to obtain a novation (transfer) of the power contract so that HI will replace R as party to this contract. HI also agreed to provide security or guarantees to NPL if these were required. Upon completion of the sale of the chemical plant by Rhodia to HI in 2001, HI agreed to take over R's obligations under the energy contract while negotiations with NPL for the novation of the contract were under way. When NPL were approached to see if it would agree to HI taking over the power contract, it indicated it would probably require financial guarantees form HI before doing so. Negotiations were not taken further by HI and the novation was not completed.

In 2004, HI gave notice to R that it no longer intended to perform its obligations under the energy supply contract and later that year it announced it intended to close the plant. NPL made a claim (almost £15m) against R for remaining sums due under the power supply contract. R sought to claim an indemnity from HI for any sums it was found liable to pay to NPL. R argued that HI had failed to use 'reasonable endeavours' to complete the novation or the power supply contract (which would have made HI responsible for NPL's claims), including failure to provide a guarantee.

Held: R's claim was successful and HI had failed to use reasonable endeavours. HI could not rely on NPL's initial refusal to enter into the novation given that it was not an absolute refusal – there was still further potential to reach agreement (with provision of guarantees etc.).

RYANAIR v SR TECHNICS (2007)

[Implied terms; best endeavours, suitable remedy]

(Commercial agreements cannot cater for every eventuality and the Court can introduce terms to ensure that parties honour their intended obligations).

The defendant, SRT, provided maintenance services for Ryanair's aircraft at Stansted. In 2002, it successfully persuaded Ryanair to agree to the maintenance work being transferred to Dublin where SRT could undertake it much more profitably. As part of the incentives offered to Ryanair to move, SRT offered to grant it a 15 year licence of hangar space in Dublin, subject to their landlord consenting to a licence for this period. The landlord, the Dublin Airport Authority, could not unreasonably refuse consent to the grant to SRT of such a licence.

The formal contract documentation was not entered into until 3 years after the move in 2005. It confirmed that, subject to landlord's consent, SRT was to grant Ryanair a 15 year licence of the hangar space. Ryanair had already taken occupation of hangar space. In 2006, the landlord proposed to offer SRT 5 million euros in return for a surrender of their Lease of the hangar so it could be let to Aer Lingus.

In January 2007, SRT served notice on Ryanair requiring it to vacate by 30 September 2007. This was the first time that Ryanair was informed that the landlord had refused to consent to the 15 year licence. SRT claimed they had sought a 15 year licence but the landlord had refused to grant consent for this. It claimed that it had no obligation to take any further steps and, in the absence of the specified consent, Ryanair had to vacate. Ryanair claimed that the agreement had to be construed on the basis that, if the landlord refused a 15 year licence, SRT still had to use best endeavours to obtain as long a licence as they could. Furthermore, they sought to rely on assurances they claimed were given to this effect by SRT in writing before the agreement was signed.

Held: The Court was very critical of SRT. It had failed to disclose a considerable amount of relevant documentation and had kept Ryanair in the dark about their dealings with the landlord. It did not consider that SRT had ever properly pursued the obtaining of consent to a 15 year licence or sought a shorter licence which the landlord would have been prepared to agree to.

The Court examined the whole course of dealings between the parties in detail in order to determine the origin and aim of the agreement It held that SRT knew it was essential for Ryanair to have hangar space for their aircraft and that the parties clearly contemplated that the landlord might only be willing to consent to a licence of less than 15 years.

The Court found that it would flout business common sense if SRT could escape any liability to provide space just because the landlord would not agree to a 15 year period. It held that there was an implied term that SRT would use its best endeavours to obtain whatever length of licence up to 15 years that it could and, on expiry of a shorter licence, would then seek to renew it.

The Court also held that, even though the agreement sought to exclude any reliance on any matters not contained within the agreement itself, SRT was bound by the representations it had made before the agreement was entered into to obtain a shorter licence if necessary.

Having been found liable, SRT argued that damages would be an adequate remedy for Ryanair. However, the Court noted how important it was for Ryanair to have hangar space so they could maintain their aircraft. It therefore granted an injunction preventing SRT from evicting Ryanair and requiring it to use best endeavours to obtain the landlord's consent for a 15 year licence or, if the landlord could reasonably refuse consent for this, for such length of time as could reasonably be obtained.

Connelly v Bellway Homes Ltd (2007)

[Mistake; Misrepresentation]

Negotiations for the purchase of land contained an indexation formula. The seller would share in any increase in value between the exchange of contracts and planning approval. The seller's surveyor relied on the buyer's surveyor's superior knowledge of the area to arrive at a suitable figure. The buyer's surveyor deliberately over-estimated the base value of land, expecting the other side to negotiate. However, his estimate was accepted. Subsequently there was no uplift in value gained by the seller. Two arguments were raised by the seller:

1. Fundamental mistake, entitling rectification of the contract
2. Fraudulent misrepresentation

Held: The base value could not be rectified because, although C had made a bad bargain in agreeing it, that was the figure the parties had intended should apply. It also ruled the base value suggested by B was at such variance from what would have been a genuine estimate that dishonesty could be inferred, and B not only knew that it was not genuine but intended C to believe it was. As C relied on B's misrepresentation it could recover damages for deceit.

N.B. While a degree of exaggeration about the value of goods (or land) is an accepted element of the process, representations which are too wide of the mark run the risk of going beyond what is reasonable and of raising inferences of dishonesty.

Opel and Renault (Car Manufacturers) v Mitras Automotive (UK) Ltd (2007)

[Economic Duress]

The defendant supplied a component part to the claimants. Opel and Renault decided to redesign their vans and gave 6 month's notice of termination to the defendant. Mitras demanded an increase in price for the rest of the contract as recompense for the loss of contract and threatened suspension of deliveries if its demand was not met. With a stock level of only 24 hours, the claimants felt they had no choice but to agree (otherwise, large financial losses would have resulted). After completion of the contract, Opel and Renault claimed for the return of the additional monies, arguing economic duress.
Held: The claim was valid. £500,000 was recoverable.

Balmoral v Borealis (2007)

[Sale of Goods – Section 14(3) Fitness for Purpose]

Balmoral (suppliers of storage tanks to its customers) were hit by several complaints that the tanks had serious defects. It identified the problem as defective polymer supplied to it by Borealis and argued that Borealis was in breach of contract (goods not fit for purpose).
Judge indicated 5 requirements for successful claim:

1.   The sales must be in the course of a business.
2.   The purpose for which the goods were being purchased had to have been made known to the supplier.
3.   The buyer must be seen to be relying on the skill and judgement of the supplier that the goods will be fit for that purpose.
4.   The goods actually are not reasonably fit for that purpose because of a defect for which the supplier is responsible.
5.   This unfitness was the cause of the loss.

Judge concluded that the first three requirements were satisfied for a breach of Section 14(3) of the Sale of Goods Act 1979 (fitness for purpose). However, he also found that the failure of the plastic was significantly affected by how the tanks were assembled by the purchaser and that there had been inadequate testing on how best to adapt the manufacturing process to accommodate the new plastic material Therefore, it was not possible to make the supplier responsible for the failure - it had not caused the problem.

Whitecap Leisure v John Rundle (2007)

[Acceptance of Goods – Loss of right to terminate]

The case involved a contract for the supply of a cable tow system for water skiers. Problems with the system led to an agreement that the supplier would rectify problems (and maintain system) if the claimant agreed not to pursue any claim based on the initial supply of the system. Problems persisted and the claimant argued it had the right to reject the goods based on breach of contract (fitness for purpose, satisfactory quality).
Held: The claimant's initial compromise in allowing the arrangement to be continued through the second agreement amounted to acceptance of the goods and there was no right to terminate. The breach had to be treated now as a breach of a warranty only.

Alfred McAlpine Capital Projects Ltd v Tilebox Ltd (2005)

[Liquidated Damages/Penalties]

A contract for the refurbishment of a building had been agreed between Tilebox and a client. Payment was subject to 'erosion' if there was a delay in completion. The defendant (Tilebox) engaged the claimant as contractor to do the actual work (Tilebox was effectively acting as project managers overseeing the work). This contract (between Tilebox and McAlpine) included a liquidated damages clause of £45k per week of delay. This figure had been based on the defendant's back to back liability to the client for delay. The claimant challenged the clause as being a penalty and void. One argument was that the erosion provision would be exhausted after 40 weeks and the defendant therefore would be able to recover an excessive amount. **Held:** The liquidated damages clause was valid. There must be a substantial discrepancy between likely losses and the level of damages claimed for it to be seen as a penalty clause. The parties would not have anticipated such a long delay.

Volkwagen Financial Services (UK) Ltd v George Ramage (Cambridge) (2007)

[Liquidated Damages/Penalties]

Ramage (R) agreed to hire a car for 36 months. Early termination required him to pay the balance of monthly instalments still outstanding at the time (less the amount already paid and less rebate of 4% on rentals still owing). After 14 months, R fell into arrears. Volkswagen Financial Services (V) treated this as repudiation of the contract and terminated the agreement. V recovered the car one month later and claimed liquidated damages under the above provision. R argued it amounted to a penalty and was void.
Held: The district judge (this was a county court case) decided not to overturn a clause freely entered into by two business entities. On appeal, the circuit judge decided it was a penalty – chiefly because no account had been made of the value of the car when it was repossessed – the clause was too rigid to be a genuine pre-estimate of loss in the circumstances.

Top Layers Interiors Ltd v Azure Maritime (2006)

[Right to terminate/ foreseeability of loss]

This claim was based on late (and faulty) completion of furnishing work on a yacht.

Azure argued that time had been made 'of the essence' and, by being late, the boat had not been available for a yacht charter show that was crucial to having a successful season. The damages sought amounted to £2m for alleged loss of charter revenue.

Held: The contract had not expressly made time for completion 'of the essence' and previous correspondence could not imply such importance. No clear date for completion of the work had been given. Therefore there had been no breach of contract.

N.B. As there had been no mention of the charter show in the negotiations, the claim could have been defeated on grounds that the loss was not reasonably foreseeable to the other party

Interfoto Picture Library v Stiletto Visual Programs (1988)

[Reasonable notification of terms/Onerous terms]

A contract had been made for the loan of 47 photo transparencies. The printed terms included a 'holding fee' of £5 per day per transparency if the goods were not returned within 14 days. They were returned four weeks late. A bill for £3750 was submitted.

Held: Such an onerous term cannot be effective without being brought fairly and reasonably to the attention of the other party. The court felt empowered to substitute a reasonable fine of £3-50 per transparency per week (an unusual action by the court here).

Hotel Services Ltd v Hilton International (UK) Ltd (2000)

[Exclusion of liability – interpretation of wording – indirect loss]

A contract had been agreed for the supply of minibars to some of the hotels within the Hilton Hotel group. Some of the minibars were faulty and were leaking gas in the bedrooms. Hilton argued breach of contract (goods not fit for purpose, not of satisfactory quality) and claimed damages for (amongst other things) loss of profits from the minibars not being in the bedrooms. Hotel Services defence was that the contract contained an exclusion clause - they would not be liable 'for indirect or consequential loss…'.

Held: Costs and loss of profits were direct loss, not indirect or consequential loss. The exclusion clause therefore did not relate to the type of loss claimed. Damages were claimable.

Cover Version Ltd v DHL Logistics (UK) Ltd (2007)

[Incorporation of standard terms; Fairness of limitation clause]

Clothing importers (CV) claimed DHL was in breach of a contract to provide freight handling and distribution services. CV alleged DHL failed to deliver garments to its customers on time and delivered the wrong goods and sizes. DHL argued the claim was bound to fail as the contract incorporated its standard terms and conditions, which provided various defences. In particular the standard terms included provisions that meant the claim was time barred.

It was argued the terms excluded claims for most losses (i.e. the loss of business claims) and that DHL could limit its liability for any remaining claims. CV argued that DHL's terms did not form part of the contract and were therefore not binding on it. The High Court judge first considered whether the standard terms had been incorporated into the contract. The issue was complex because, although DHL made several references in correspondence to the existence of standard terms, CV alleged these terms had never been provided to it.
Held: The standard terms did form part of the contract and that in business dealings, it is unnecessary that conditions contained in a standard document should have been read by the other party or that it actually knew of its effect. It is enough that the other party had notice of the conditions and that enough was done to make the other party aware of any onerous or unusual terms. The judge went on to consider the effect of the inclusion of the standard terms into the contract.

CV argued the various clauses on which DHL relied should not be upheld on the basis that they were unreasonable and in breach of the UCTA 1977. Having considered the provisions and found them similar to those in general use in the freight forwarding industry, the judge was not persuaded that they could be considered unreasonable. He held that the claims were subject to the nine month time bar provisions, that the claims for consequential loss were excluded and that DHL was entitled to limit its liability for any remaining claims.

Ofir Scheps v Fine Art LogisticsLtd (2007)

[Incorporation of contractual terms]

The claimant was a fine art collector who had bought a sculpture by a then unknown artist for £17,200. The defendants were a specialist art storage and transport company that were instructed to store the sculpture until renovation could be carried out on it. When the time came, the defendants were unable to find the sculpture in any of its storage units. The claimant started legal proceedings, seeking either the return of the sculpture or damages for its loss. By the time the case came to court, the value of work by that artist had increased significantly and damages were sought of £600,000. The defendant argued its liability was limited under standard terms and conditions and the claimant was entitled to only £587-13.

The issue was whether the defendant's standard terms formed part of its agreement with the claimant. At the time that the sculpture was placed in storage, no mention was made of the standard terms and no copy was given to the claimant. However, the defendants argued that its terms were incorporated into that contract as usual practice in the trade, and that the claimant was aware of this as a result of previous experience.

The judge accepted it was usual for standard terms to include a limit of liability. A more difficult issue was whether the claimant could be said to have had sufficient experience of the business of transport and storage of works of art for him to be aware of this. While the claimant admitted he was aware that transport companies had terms and conditions, he argued he had no real knowledge of particular terms and was not familiar with the extent to which they limited liability.
Held: The standard terms were not incorporated into the contract. Given that the claimant was not provided with a copy of the terms, his knowledge of their probable existence was not enough to allow the defendant to rely on them. The claimant was awarded damages for the full market value of the sculpture, which was assessed at £351,000.

N.B. The decision illustrates that, even when dealing with an experienced party, it is dangerous to assume that the inclusion of standard terms can be taken as read. It is always advisable to make sure standard terms and conditions are given in writing (preferably with a copy provided) and that specific attention is drawn to any particularly onerous terms, such as those limiting liability.

Balmoral v Borealis (2007)

[Exclusion of liability – fairness of clause – Unfair Contract Terms Act 1977]

Balmoral (suppliers of storage tanks to its customers) were hit by several complaints that the tanks had serious defects. Balmoral identified the problem as defective polymer supplied to it by Borealis – and argued it was in breach of contract (goods not fit for purpose). Borealis' terms included:
'B does not assume any responsibility for products being suitable for any particular purpose unless B in writing has approved such suitability'.

B's terms also limited its liability to an exchange or refund, excluding liability for any direct, indirect or consequential loss caused by any defect in the goods.

Held: the above clauses effectively deprived Balmoral of any remedy, despite the foreseeability of substantial losses if it was in breach of contract with its customers. The limitations were therefore unfair under the Unfair Contract Terms Act 1977 and void.

Regus (UK) Ltd v Epcot Solutions Ltd (2007)

[Exclusion of liability – fairness of clause – Unfair Contract Terms Act 1977]

A contract had been entered into for the lease of an office near Heathrow. The contract arrangement included a number of office services. A claim was made by a tenant (Regus) for breach of contract – defective air conditioning in building. The defendant (Epcot) relied on a two-part disclaimer of liability in its contract terms and conditions:

1.   Exclusion of liability for any loss of business, loss of profits and consequential loss.
2.   Limitation of liability of £50,000 for all other losses, damages, expenses and claims.

These exclusions were challenged as not reasonable under the Unfair Contract Terms Act 1977.

Held: the High Court decided the exclusion was too wide – it effectively amounted to a total exclusion of any remedy. Therefore, it was unreasonable and void under UCTA 1977.

On appeal, the Court of Appeal (reversing the decision) held:
*   the exclusion did not prevent recovery in all circumstances e.g. still possible to claim for fraud or malicious damage.
*   given the nature of the business pursued by Regus, it was not unreasonable for it to restrict damages for loss of profits and consequential losses.
*   there was no inequality of bargaining power.
*   Regus had advised its customers to protect themselves with insurance for business losses.

Lion Apparel Systems v Firebuy (2007)

[EU Rules – Infringement Claim]

Firebuy invited tenders for the supply of personal protective equipment for firefighters (through an OJOU notice). The contract was awarded to Bristol Uniforms. Lion came 3rd of 4 bidders. Lion challenged the award, identifying several alleged flaws in procedure, including the scoring mechanism and a general complaint of favouritism. At this stage, the court was looking to see if, at first evidence, there was enough evidence to warrant a full hearing.
Held: Lion's case was too weak. Unless there is a manifest error (a glaring fault), it is not for the court to substitute its own decision for that of the contracting authority. The court will not be inclined to favour the sort of 'scatter-gun' approach used by Lion in this case.

Lianakis v Dimos Alexandroupolis (2008)

[EU Rules – Infringement Claim]

A Greek town council invited tenders for a town project, using restrictive procedure. The Contract notice indicated award criteria to be as follows (in order of priority):

1.   Experience.
2.   Staffing levels and equipment.
3.   Ability to perform contract within set timescale.

During the evaluation of tenders, the Council applied weightings to the above criteria and added sub-criteria. The process was later challenged as infringing the EU rules.

Held (by the European Court):
•   There was a lack of transparency by adding weightings and sub-criteria after receipt of tenders.
•   The addition of sub-criteria would only be possible if the original criteria were not altered and no new elements introduced (otherwise, could be discriminatory because submitted tenders might have been redrafted in the light of the additional information).
•   The award criteria were inappropriate in the first place – these should have been used at the pre-questionnaire (shortlisting) stage.

(If open procedure was used, can combine and judge simultaneously on suitability and award of contract)

Letting International Ltd v Newham London BC (2008)

[EU Rules – Frameworks - Infringement Claim]

Newham had advertised its intention to enter into framework contracts for the procurement, maintenance and management of housing leased from the private sector. After unsuccessfully tendering for the contract, Letting International argued that Newham had failed to administer a fair and transparent tender process in accordance with the EU public procurement principles.

Held: The court, following Lianakis (see previous), agreed and stated that contracting authorities must make bidders aware before bids are submitted of the criteria, weightings and methodology that will be applied to judge the bids and that these cannot subsequently be modified or expanded. Although the tender documentation issued by Newham had set out three weighted contract award criteria, Newham failed to disclose further subcriteria that were used to evaluate the tenders and the way in which those sub-criteria were weighted relative to each other.

Also, one of the published award criterion ("compliance with specification") suggested that bidders would score full marks for that criterion if they could demonstrate total compliance with the specification but Newham's undisclosed evaluation methodology only allowed full marks to be awarded for bids which exceeded the specification.

(This case supports the Lianakis decision and emphasises that sub-criteria and their weightings (if applicable) must be disclosed in good time to inform the preparation of bids. This case is important because for the first time a UK court has clearly referred to an obligation to disclose evaluation methodology. Best practice for contracting authorities will always be to take a safe approach and disclose their evaluation methodologies to bidders).

Henry Bros (Magherafelt) Ltd v Dept. of Education for Northern Ireland (2008)

[EU Rules – Frameworks - Infringement Claim]

(This ruling by the High Court in Belfast highlights the obligations on contracting authority to ensure an objective and fair evaluation of cost and the potential for framework agreements to be set aside where procurement rules are breached).

Construction firm Henry Brothers had been excluded from a £650 million Schools Modernisation Programme to be undertaken in the context of a four-year framework shared by eight separate contractors. Henry Brothers argued that the system devised by the Department to assess the most economically advantageous tenders was flawed insofar as the Department's financial assessment of tenders was by reference to fee percentages only, i.e. tenderers were not required to submit costs samples. They further claimed that the Department was wrong to assume that costs would be the same across the entire construction industry.

Held: The Court agreed that to rely solely on fee percentages was fundamentally flawed and held that an objective assessment of economic advantage necessitated some indication of price and/or cost. Accordingly, the Court held that the procedure adopted was contrary to the UK Public Contracts Regulations 2006.

The parties returned to Court to resolve the issue of remedies. The Department argued that the Court's jurisdiction was limited to an award of damages on the basis that under the UK Public Contracts Regulations, once a contract has been concluded, damages are the only available remedy. However, this argument was rejected by the Court on the grounds that a framework agreement did not constitute a public contract for the purposes of the Regulations. Accordingly, the Court ordered that the framework agreement should be set aside. It is likely that the parties will return to Court in 2009 in regard to remedies available to the plaintiff for specific contracts already entered into by the Department under the framework agreement.

Asemfo v Tragsa (2007)

[EU Rules – Infringement Claim]

Tragsa was created as a public sector organisation to carry out certain agricultural and forestry work on behalf of the Spanish government. Asemfo argued that the work in question should have been subject to competitive tender and the EU rules had been broken. The European Court applied the Teckal principle* and asked:

1.   Did the Government exercise a similar level of authority over Tragsa as it had over its own departments?
2.   Was the essential part of Tragsa's activities carried out on behalf of the authorities that own it?

Held: because the Government owned 99% and regional authorities the other 1%, and because 90% of its essential activities were carried out for these bodies, it did not have to engage in competitive tendering – it was as if the work was being carried out by the Government itself.

* an earlier ruling of the European Court.

Aquatron v Strathclyde Fire Board (2007)

[EU Rules – Infringement Claim]

Strathclyde invited tenders for servicing and maintenance of breathing apparatus and other equipment. The OJEU notice stated that MEAT (most economically advantageous tender) would be the award criterion, and listed 6 specific evaluation criteria. Aquatron (one of three tenderers) complained on following bases:

- The eventual list of criteria for tender evaluation contained three items, only one of which formed part of the six originally specified in the Notice.
- Already, Aquatron had been excluded on the basis that it had failed to supply certain details and comply with other requirements, none of which had been expressly requested in the OJEU Notice.

Held: The Board had infringed the rules by not complying with the Regulations and making decisions during the evaluation process not based on the published criteria. There was no finding of bad faith – it was the result of changes in personnel and inexperienced personnel becoming responsible for the decision. On the facts, the decisive criterion was price. Since Aquatron's tender price was lower than the successful tenderer's, had the evaluation been conducted in line with the Regulations, then Aquatron would have been awarded the contract It was entitled to recover the full loss of profits - £122,149.

Taylor v Connex South Eastern Ltd (1999)

[Transfer of Undertakings – how long after transfer can changes be introduced?]

Mr Taylor was a chartered accountant, employed as an administrator by the SouthEastern Train Company, a sub division of British Rail. It was privatised and sold to Connex South Eastern Ltd in 1996. In 1998 he was given, according to ongoing changes throughout the company, a new contract, which contained clauses that were to his detriment (he lost some holiday and redundancy entitlement). He complained, but the company insisted he accept the terms or have three weeks' notice.

The Employment Appeal Tribunal held that under Regulation 7 of the Transfer of Undertakings (Protection of Employment) Regulations, Mr. Taylor was actually dismissed in connection with the transfer of the railway from public to private hands. This was so despite the fact that privatisation took place 2 years beforehand.

John Connor Press Associates v Information Commissioner (2006)

[Freedom of Information Act 2000 – damage to commercial interests exemption]

A request was made by John Connor Press Associates to the National Maritime Museum in relation to payments made to an artist for work commissioned by the museum. The Commissioner held that:

1.   The museum was involved in active negotiations with another artist and the premature release of the details of the financial arrangements between the museum and the artist would prejudice the museum's bargaining position in these negotiations.

2.   The commercial interests exemption (s.43(2)) applied.

3.   That the public interest in withholding the information at the time outweighed the public interest in disclosing it.

The decision was appealed to the Information Tribunal. The Tribunal considered the ambit of "likely to prejudice" in s.43(2) and held that there had to be a real and significant risk involved and not some hypothetical or remote possibility. Applying that test, the Tribunal found that the threshold of "likely to prejudice" had not been met on the basis that:

1.   A considerable amount of information had been disclosed by the museum which would have been of use to those with whom the museum was engaged in negotiations.

2.   Some details of the contract with had already been disclosed.

3.   The works of art of the two artists were so different that they could not be used as comparables for purposes of a negotiation.

Scottish and Newcastle International v Othon Ghalanos (2006)

[Jurisdiction of English courts to decide dispute involving a CF contract]

S and N sold a consignment of cider to the defendants who were drinks distributors. The contract of sale was governed by English law and was on CFR Limassol terms. S and N was claiming to recover the price due under the contract and started proceedings in England on the basis that this was the jurisdiction in which the goods had been delivered (where the cider was loaded on board the carrying vessel). OG argued that the contract was in effect an ex-ship contract for delivery in Limassol and that it was therefore the courts of Cyprus (OG's place of business) that should have jurisdiction.

The Court had to consider the position under the European Judgments Regulation 2001 (No44). As the parties had not agreed on jurisdiction, under those regulations proceedings could be brought either in the place of business (domicile) of the defendant or, under contracts for sale of goods, in the state where the goods were delivered or ought to have been delivered.

Held: The Court of Appeal ruled in favour of the English courts having jurisdiction. It held that the contract terms 'CandF Limassol' meant the possession of the goods would be transferred to OG at the port of shipment (in this case, Liverpool). On the facts of this case, there was no question of the goods being bought afloat, nor was there any question of title being retained until payment or transfer of documents. In any event, the court doubted whether the transfer of documents or title would be a suitable point at which to determine the jurisdiction under which claims should be decided. It considered the place of shipment to be far more suitable.

N.B. In CF and CIF contracts, the place of delivery is the port of shipment

Inntrepreneur Pub Co v East Crown Ltd (2000)

[Entire agreement clause – effect on earlier 'collateral contract']

This case involved a 'beer tie' agreement in the lease of pub. The tenant started to buy beer from another source. Inntrepreneur subsequently claimed breach of contract. The defendant claimed there was a collateral agreement releasing him from the tie (an earlier assurance which he had relied upon). The claimant pointed to the presence of an entire agreement clause in contract .
Held: Any possible collateral contract could not survive this clause.

Rice v Great Yarmouth BC (2000)

[Termination Clause – Interpretation]

A four year contract for provision of ground maintenance and leisure management services had been agreed between the claimant and the defendant. It included the following clause:

'If the contractor commits a breach of any of its obligations under the contract the council may…terminate the contractor's employment by notice in writing having immediate effect'.

The contractor (7 months later) failed to cut and mark out a cricket pitch. The Council gave notice of termination.

Held: A common sense interpretation should be placed on the wording of the clause (breach could occur in multiple different ways, some serious, some not). Breach in this case was not serious enough to allow for termination. The Council was therefore in breach and liable to pay damages to the contractor.

Somerfield Stores v Skanska Rashleigh Weatherfoil (2006)

[Interpretation of terms; limits to judges' discretion and creativity]

The case centred on problems that arose in a contract between the two firms relating to maintenance work carried out at various Somerfield stores. The appointment of Skanska as maintenance contractor was made following a tendering process in which Sommerfield's request for tender was accompanied by a draft Facilities Management Agreement (FMA). Having chosen Skanska, Sommerfield entered into discussions concerning the scope and terms of the ultimate FMA, which, when finalised, would govern the parties for three years. However, as Sommerfield were anxious that Skanska should start providing services immediately, they wrote to Skanska 'subject to contract' requesting them to start work even though negotiations for the final FMA were continuing.

A clause in the letter stated that Skanska should provide these initial services 'under the terms of the contract'. When problems arose concerning the early work provided by Skanska, Sommerfield tried to rely on the strict terms of the FMA. The dispute covered a number of issues but a key point was whether the temporary agreement included all, or only part, of the FMA.
Held: in the High Court, the judge ruled that the terms governing the initial work that Skanska incorporated only those parts of the FMA that were necessary to define the work that Skanska had to do. The full agreement (including some of the terms on which Sommerfield was hoping to rely) was not enforced.

On appeal, the CA disagreed.
Held: The Court of Appeal ruled that the natural meaning of the works 'you will provide the services under the terms of the contract' was such that the parties were prepared to be bound by the terms of the FMA in full for a short period while negotiations for the longer term contract continued.

N.B. The CA is sending a signal that courts do not have a licence to re-write a contract merely because its terms appeared unexpected, unreasonable or commercially unwise. The courts should be reluctant to change the meaning of a contract just because it may not seem to make common business sense or to reflect what the parties must have thought or intended.

When finalising agreements, particularly where these incorporate standard terms, it is essential to make sure these are fully understood and are appropriate to the circumstances. Any temptation to rush through a contract for commercial reasons should be weighed against the risk of that contract being enforced strictly by the courts, who may be reluctant or unable to intervene to correct a poor bargain.

Ruttle Plant Hire Ltd v DEFRA (2009)

[Statutory right to interest on late payment]

Ruttle (R) performed some work for Defra under a contract, the terms of which had not been precisely defined and did not make provision for the payment of interest on late payments. R submitted invoices for the work performed at various intervals. The amounts calculated as due in one of the invoices were based on incorrect rates. The Department failed to pay this disputed invoice (even though, in the meantime, R had submitted a final account of all amounts due and had used the correct rates this time). Later, R claimed interest on the overdue amount based on the Late Payment of Commercial Debts (Interest) Act 1998. Under this Act, this amounted to 8% above bank base rate ('unless the demands of justice require otherwise').

Held: On the facts of this case, it was not in the interests of justice to permit the 8% figure. A more suitable interest rate was held to be 2% above bank base rate.

Transfield Shipping v Mercator Shipping (2008)

[Claimable loss – effect of trade custom]

A cargo ship was chartered out by a shipping company (Mercator) to a client – Transfield Shipping. The ship was due to be returned by 2nd May 2004. There was a delay and the vessel was not returned until the 9th May. This caused serious financial losses to Mercator who had let the vessel out to another client from the 7th May. Because the market price of ship hire had dramatically fallen in the interim, this second hiring of the ship had to be renegotiated at a significantly lower price. Instead of an original figure of £22,000 per day, the rate became £17,700 per day.

At arbitration, the arbitrator awarded £913,000 to Mercator i.e. the lost profits between the original and revised charter price over the new charter period. This was on the application of the general principle of law that 'reasonably foreseeable' losses are recoverable as a result of a breach of contract.

Transfield appealed to the House of Lords.
Held: Transfield should only be required to pay £106,000 i.e. the profits lost over the nine days' delay in returning the vessel. The decision took into account normal shipping industry custom which is only to award damages for the period of delay. This decision therefore has to be seen to be of limited significance as applicable to where there is a well-known understanding within a trade or business activity as to the extent of liability for breach of contract.

Index

Acceptance 2, 3, 5, 7-11, 15-19, 71, 93, 202, 206, 220, 249, 252, 273, 278, 279, 290, 294

Acceptance and Rejection 80

Acquired Rights Directive 219, 227, 283

Advertisement 8, 11

Agency 117, 282

alternative dispute resolution 209, 210, 216

anticipatory breach 53, 70, 71, 279

Arbitration Act 209, 213, 214

Assignment 117, 119, 121

Auctions 11, 226

Bailment 117, 120, 121

Basis of Contract clauses 71

Battle of the Forms 15-19

Bids - see Tenders

Bills of Lading 192, 196, 203

Bill of Exchange 202

Block Exemptions – see EU

Breach of Contract 21-26, 34, 40, 43, 47, 50-58, 60-63, 70, 71, 75, 79, 82, 95, 98, 101, 104, 105, 107, 111, 176, 232, 236, 248, 257, 279, 280, 294, 296, 298, 299

Breach of Duty of Care 110, 115, 270

Buyers' Rights 73-85

Buyer in Possession, Sale by 96, 98, 99

Carriage of Goods by Sea Act (1992) 196

Cartels – see EU Price Fixing

Catalogues 8

Caveat Emptor 29, 31, 35

Centre for Dispute Resolution 210

Certificate of origin 202

Charterparties 197

Circulars 8

Coercion 23, 27

Comfort – see Letters of

Collateral contracts 101, 103

Commercial Agents (Council Directive) Regulations 1993 117, 118

Compensation 43, 47-51, 61, 112, 119, 163, 197, 219, 230-232, 235, 237, 250, 257
Competition Act (1980) 137, 143
Competition Act (1998) 123, 124, 135, 137, 139, 145, 146, 147, 149, 150, 151
Competition Law 123-151, 274
Condition 40-42
Confidentiality, Doctrine of 27
Confidential Information (see also Intellectual Property Rights) 142, 153, 174
Consequent Damage (see also Negligence) 105, 110, 112
Consideration and Duress 21-28
Consumer Protection Act (CPA) 101, 103, 112, 116, 270, 271, 282
Contracts (Applicable Law) Act (1990) 207
Contracts (Rights of Third Parties) Act (1999) Act (1999) 270
Contractual Assignment 119
Contractual Rights and Obligations 117
Contractual Terms – see Terms
Contract - Definition 1
Contract Formation 1-5
Contra proferentem 55, 57, 63
Copyright 153, 155, 171, 172, 175, 179, 180-189
Copyright, Designs and Patents Act (CDPA) (1988) 182-184, 186, 187, 189
Cost, Insurance, Freight (CIF) 191, 192, 203
Counter Offer – see Offer
Criminal liability 101, 115

Damages 23, 33, 34, 35, 38, 40-45, 47-54, 58-60, 67, 70, 76, 79, 81, 102, 103,
        111, 120, 144, 145, 150, 189, 192, 197, 221, 225, 243, 257, 263, 267, 279,
        282, 292, 293, 295, 296, 298, 299, 302
Data Protection Act (DPA) 241, 244
Deeds 1, 5
Defective Contracts – see Void
Delivery 15, 16, 37, 43, 51, 53, 66, 73, 76, 79, 82-85, 88, 90, 98
Delivery Duty Paid (DDP) 195
Demurrage and Lay Days 197
Description (Section 13) 76
Design & Design Rights (see also CPDA) 153, 155, 178-183, 184, 186, 188, 189
Discharge of Contract 65
Dispute Resolution 209, 210, 217
Documentation – see Forms, Battle of the Forms
Duress – see Consideration and Duress
Duty of Care 105-109, 115

Employee Rights (see also TUPE) 153, 163
Employment Rights Act 230, 231, 239

Enterprise Act (2002) 123, 124, 137, 145-151, 285
Estoppel 67, 96
European Union (EU) Article 81 123-132, 138, 139, 144, 151, 274, 284
European Union (EU) Article 82 123, 125, 131-135, 139, 151, 274, 284
European Union (EU) Article 85 128
European Union (EU) Block Exemptions 131, 139
European Union (EU) Competition Commission (CC) 137, 142, 144-147, 149, 150, 151, 285
European Union (EU) Horizontal & Vertical Agreements 127, 128, 138
European Union (EU) Market analysis 123, 130, 138
European Union (EU) Monopolies & Mergers Commission (MMC) 146, 149
European Union (EU) Notice of Agreements of Minor Importance 128
European Union (EU) Price Fixing/Cartels 136, 138, 143, 145
European Union (EU) Public Procurement 222, 225
European Union (EU) Treaty of Amsterdam 134
European Union (EU) Treaty of Nice 124
Ex-Works 191, 194
Exclusion Clauses 55-64
Express Terms 38, 39

Factors Act (1889) 96, 97
Fair Trading Act 1973 124, 137, 140, 145-147, 149
Fit for purpose 52, 58, 77-79, 81, 82, 85, 189, 270, 294, 296, 298
Force Majeure 62, 63, 69
Forms 15-19
Fraud – see Misrepresentation
Freedom of Information Act (FoIA) 241, 244
Free Alongside Ship (FAS) 194
Free on Board (FOB) 193, 194
Frustration of Contract 62, 63, 67, 71, 263, 280

General Product Safety Regulations (1994) 115
Goodwill 26, 154, 168, 169, 170, 173
Gross Domestic Product (GDP) 124

Hague-Visby Rules 197, 198, 203
Hague Conventions 206
Hamburg Rules 197, 198
Hire Purchase Act 99
Housing Grants, Construction and Regeneration Act 1996 (HGCR) 212

Illegality – see Subsequent
Implied Terms and Conditions 38, 44, 73, 80-84, 291

Impossibility – see Subsequent
Incoterms 191, 201, 203
Innocent Party/Parties 3, 32, 33, 43, 66, 95
Innominate terms 42, 43
Instalment Delivery – see Delivery
Insurance cover and Insurance Law 60, 61, 157, 253, 258
Insurance Types 254-258
Intellectual Property Rights (IPR) 153-189, 286
Intent – see Letters of
International Chamber of Commerce (ICC) 191
International Sale of Goods 205, 206, 286
International Trade 191, 275, 285
Invitation to Treat 7, 11, 16, 221, 239, 273

Laissez faire 55, 63, 73, 74, 85, 87, 280
Landmark cases 15, 21, 262
Lapse of time 9, 11, 33
Law – see Competition Law
Law of Confidence – see Intellectual Property Rights
Law of Property Act (1925) 119
Law Reform (Frustrated Contracts) Act (1943) 70, 280
Lay Days – see Demurrage
Legal Aspects CIPS Professional Stage 273, 277, 289
Letters of Credit 199, 200
Letters of Intent 3, 273
Liability – see Non-Contractual Liability
Litigation 215

Marine Insurance Act (1906) 247
Market analysis – see EU
Market Rule, The 47, 54
Mercantile Agent, Sale by 96, 97, 99
Merchantable Quality – see Quality
Merger Regulations – see EU
Misrepresentation 3, 21, 27, 29, 30-35, 38, 55, 58, 60, 63, 96, 97, 169, 170, 173,
    247, 250-252, 278, 293
Misrepresentation Act (1967) 33, 38
Mistake 3, 29, 35, 68, 97, 250, 261, 278, 293
Mitigation of Loss 47, 53
Monopolies (see also EU Monopolies & Mergers Commission) 123, 146, 149

Negligence 33, 34, 52, 55, 56, 58, 61, 63, 87, 101, 104-107, 109, 111, 112, 115,
    121, 143, 248, 257, 263, 267, 270, 271, 280-282

Nemo Dat Doctrine 95, 99, 281
Nice, Treaty of – see EU
Non-Contractual Liability 101-116
Non Est Factum 30, 31, 35
Novation 120, 282, 291

Offer & Acceptance 5, 7, 15, 16, 206, 278
Office of Fair Trading (OFT) 125, 138, 139, 145, 148, 285
Officious Bystander Test 39
Outsourcing 219, 22-231, 234, 239
Ownership/Ownership Transfer 88-93

Partnership Agreement 1
Passing Off 153, 168-173, 189, 286, 287
Patents Act (1977) 156, 157, 159-162, 179, 182-184, 189
Patents and Patent Office 150, 153, 155, 156-163, 179, 181-184, 189, 275
Penalties/Penalty Clauses 47, 54
Postal Rule, The 11
Price Fixing – see EU
Price Lists 8
Privity of Contract, Doctrine of 101, 102, 115, 269
Promissory – see Warranties
Property Ownership 92
Property Transfer 87-93
Public Interest, The 24, 25, 147, 242, 304
Puffs – see Traders
Punitive Damages 50

Quality, Wrong, and Of Satisfactory 74, 77-85
Quantum meruit 4, 65, 69, 277, 290

Ratification 118, 134, 282
Reasonableness, Test of 26, 55, 61, 63, 64, 81, 85, 177, 198, 220, 233, 236, 237, 274
Redundancy 227, 231-237, 238, 239, 283, 284, 303
Refunds 82
Registered Designs Act (1949) 179, 180
Rejection – see Acceptance
Remedies (see also Dispute Resolution) 29, 32, 34, 35, 37, 42, 47, 146, 153, 156, 179, 189, 237
Repudiation 70, 267, 295
Resale Prices Act (1976) 137
Rescission 33, 278

Restraint of Trade 2, 23, 27, 177, 278
Restrictive Trade Practices Act (1976/1977) 137, 143
Res ipsa loquitur 109
Retention of Title Clauses (RoT) 90
Risk 53, 61, 70, 75, 87, 93, 109, 116, 157, 173, 188, 191, 193, 195, 197, 202, 205,
    247, 248, 249, 250, 252-254, 258, 285, 293, 304, 307
Romalpa Clause 120
Rome Convention 205, 207

Sale and Supply of Goods Act (1994) 79
Sale of a Business 23, 26
Sale of Goods (see also International) 73-83
Sale of Goods Act (SOGA) (1979) 29, 41-44, 61, 66, 73, 74, 79-81, 83, 85, 87, 90,
    95, 270, 280, 281, 294
Sample 78-85
Satisfactory – see Quality
Seller in Possession, Sale by 96, 98, 99
Simple Contracts 1, 2, 5, 21, 249, 277
Solus Agreements 23, 26
Statutory Protection – see Buyers' Rights
Subject to Contract 9, 10, 277, 290, 306
Subrogation 256, 259
Subsequent Illegality 68
Subsequent Physical Impossibility 71
Supply of Goods and Services Act (SGSA) (1982) 83, 84, 270
Supply of Services 73, 83

Tenders/Tendering & Outsourcing 8, 219, 221, 227, 228, 234, 239, 273, 283
Termination 7, 8, 15, 43, 305
Terms, Contractual 29, 32, 37-45, 153, 174, 187, 210, 297
Third Parties – see Contracts (ROTP) Act (1999)
The European Union (EU) Merger Regulation (Regulation 4064/89) 136, 148
Traders' Puff 29-32
Trade Marks 153-156, 164-166, 173, 189
Trade Marks Act (1994) 163, 164
Transfer of Title 87, 92, 93, 95, 99, 131, 196, 227, 235, 237, 238, 283
Transfer of Undertakings (Protection of Employment) (TUPE) 227, 235, 237, 283,
    303
Treaty of Amsterdam 134

Uberrimae fidei 247, 251-253, 258
Undisclosed Principle, Doctrine of 117
Unenforceable Contracts 1

Unfair Contract Terms Act (UCTA) (1977) 55, 58, 63, 74, 81, 82, 102, 280, 298, 299
Unfair Dismissal – see Employment Rights
Unfair Terms in Consumer Contracts Regulations (1999) 56
Uniform Laws on International Sales Act (1967) 205
UN Convention on Contracts 206

Vagueness 4
Vienna Convention 206, 207
Vitiation 29-35
Void contracts 2, 3, 5, 277

Warranties 41, 42, 45, 57, 75, 247, 251, 254, 255
Wrong Quantity – see Delivery